ABORTION

AN ETERNAL SOCIAL AND MORAL ISSUE

Mei Ling Rein

INFORMATION PLUS REFERENCE SERIES
Formerly published by Information Plus, Wylie, Texas

Detroit
New York
San Francisco
London
Boston
Woodbridge, CT

ABORTION: AN ETERNAL MORAL AND SOCIAL ISSUE
was produced for the Gale Group by Information Plus, Wylie, Texas

Information Plus Staff:

Mei Ling Rein, Author

Jacquelyn Quiram, Designer

Editorial: Abbey Begun, Cornelia Blair, Nancy R. Jacobs, Barbara Klier, Virginia Peterson, Mark A. Siegel

The Gale Group Staff:

Editorial: Rita Runchock, Managing Editor; John F. McCoy, Editor

Graphic Services: Randy Bassett, Image Database Supervisor; Robert Duncan, Senior Imaging Specialist

Product Design: Michelle DiMercurio, Senior Art Director; Michael Logusz, Graphic Artist

Production: NeKita McKee, Buyer; Dorothy Maki, Manufacturing Manager

ABORTION — AN ETERNAL SOCIAL AND MORAL ISSUE

CHAPTER I

ABORTION — AN ETERNAL SOCIAL AND MORAL ISSUE

Abortions have been performed since the beginning of recorded history. There have always been women who, for a variety of reasons, were determined to terminate their pregnancies. Today, the abortion issue has developed into a conflict about whether the unborn are entitled to the same rights as the born, and whether a woman's right to control her life and body includes the right to end an unwanted pregnancy. Although abortion has been debated for centuries, the motivations to condemn or support it have varied with the political and social situations of the debate.

ANCIENT TIMES

Abortion is mentioned in the ancient Assyrian Code of the twelfth century B.C.E. (before the Common Era). Provision 53 explicitly ordered that any woman who aborted herself should be impaled on stakes without the dignity of burial. If the abortion killed the woman, her body was to be similarly impaled, again without burial. Likewise, ancient Jewish law strictly forbade abortion as a method of avoiding childbirth, although it allowed the sacrifice of the fetus to save the life of the mother.

In ancient Greece and Rome, abortion was commonly used to limit family size. It was as socially acceptable as the practice of disposing of deformed and weak infants through exposure (abandonment of babies outdoors with the intent that they die). Parents who did not want to incur the expense of raising a female infant categorized her as "weak" and resorted to exposure.

Both Plato (c. 428-347 B.C.E.) and Aristotle (384-322 B.C.E.) approved of abortion as a means of population control. They also advocated exposure in the belief that it would genetically ensure the best possible offspring. Plato wrote in his *Republic* that any woman over 40 years old (an age when the rate of birth defects rises sharply) should be compelled to abort a pregnancy.

Scholars who credit Hippocrates (c. 460-370 B.C.E.) with the Hippocratic Oath claim that he opposed abortion. (The Hippocratic Oath, modified for modern use as a medical code of ethics, in its early form prohibited abortion.) Others claim that this prohibition was a reflection of the Pythagorean teaching opposing abortion and that physicians in the ancient times generally did not follow this oath.

The consequences of adultery or prostitution were very compelling reasons for a woman or her family to end her pregnancy. In the ancient Roman household, the father was judge and jury when it came to the ethical life of the family. He alone had the authority to order or forbid an abortion. The Romans were not concerned with the life of the child but with the health of the mother. Since some women were getting poisoned due to the improper mixing of abortion-inducing drugs, the fathers usually opted for infanticide (killing of an infant after birth).

CHRISTIAN POSITION ON ABORTION

Christianity generally consists of the Roman Catholic Church, the Eastern Orthodox churches, and the Protestant churches. While Roman Catholicism and Eastern Orthodoxy have existed since the earliest days of the Christian era, Protestantism dates back to the sixteenth-century Reformation.

Eastern Orthodoxy and Roman Catholicism consider an artificially procured abortion as a grave sin. Because Protestantism consists of various denominations and sects, many of which have differing teachings, Protestantism, as a whole, does not have a specific position on abortion.

Abortion in the Christian Era

The first works of the Christian Church hardly mentioned abortion. The earliest known Christian document that declared abortion a sin was the *Didache* (Teachings of the Lord through the Apostles; c. 100 C.E.). *Didache* 2:2 stated, "… You shall not kill the embryo by abortion and shall not cause the newborn to perish.…" Although the early church leaders agreed that abortion was a sin (requiring penance) if it was performed to hide the consequences of fornication and adultery, the debate as to whether or not abortion was murder had just begun.

Roman Catholic Position on Abortion

During the first six centuries of the history of the Roman Catholic Church, theologians, such as St. Augustine (354-430 C.E.), theorized and debated about the starting point of human life. (See also Chapter X.)

Originally, church theologians taught that *hominization* (point at which a fetus acquires a soul and becomes a human being) occurred at 40 days after conception for males and 80 days for females. This was also referred to as the "ensoulment" of the fetus. From the twelfth through the sixteenth centuries, the various popes imposed excommunication (exclusion from church membership), depending upon their personal beliefs about the moment of ensoulment.

In 1701, the acceptance of the doctrine of the Immaculate Conception of Mary (that Mary was without original sin at conception) paved the way for the present position of the Catholic Church on abortion. On December 8, 1854, Pope Pius IX pronounced the Immaculate Conception of Mary a Catholic dogma, thus upholding the idea of hominization upon conception and revoking any concept of ensoulment at a later time.

This decision was reaffirmed in 1917 with the issuance of the *Code of Canon Law*. Canon 2350, Paragraph I, explicitly stated, "Persons who procure abortion, not excepting the mother, incur, if the effect follows, an automatic excommunication reserved to the Ordinary (non-clergy), and if they be clerics, they are moreover deposed." Recent popes have firmly upheld this canon. Pope Pius XII, deeply concerned about abortion, wrote in his *Allocution to Midwives* (1951),

> Every human being, even the child in the mother's womb, receives its right to life directly from God, not from its parents, nor from any human society or authority, no science, no "indication" whether medical, eugenic (selective breeding), social, economic, or moral that can show or give a valid juridical title for a deliberate and direct disposing of an innocent human life — which is to say, a disposition that aims at its destruction either as an end in itself or as the means of attaining another end that is perhaps in no way illicit in itself.

In 1968, in the encyclical letter *Humanae Vitae*, Pope Paul VI stated,

> We must once again declare that the direct interruption of the generative process already begun and, above all, directly willed and procured abortion, even if for therapeutic (medically necessary) reasons, are to be absolutely excluded as licit (legal) means of regulating birth.

The Second Vatican Council (1962-1965), the largest Roman Catholic Church gathering in Christian history, declared abortion a "supreme dishonor to the Creator." The Council further observed that "from the moment of its conception, life must be guarded with the greatest care, while abortion and infanticide are unspeakable crimes." In 1995, Pope John Paul II repeated his firm stand against contraception, abortion, and euthanasia (mercy killing) in his encyclical letter, *Evangelium Vitae* (Gospel of Life), charging modern society with promoting a "culture of death." (See Chapter X for more on the *Evangelium Vitae* and the position of the Catholic Church on abortion.)

In November 1998, the Catholic Conference of Bishops of the United States, in *Living the Gospel of Life: A Challenge to American Catholics*, stated,

> Direct abortion is never a morally tolerable option. It is always a grave act of violence against a woman and her unborn child. This is even so when the woman does not see the truth because of the pressures she may be subjected to, often by the child's father, her parents or friends.

ISLAMIC POSITION ON ABORTION

Islam has over a billion adherents worldwide who follow the words of Muhammad (c. 570-632 C.E.). The Quran (Koran), which Muslims believe to contain God's revelations to Muhammad, describes the development of the fetus.

> O Mankind! If ye are in doubt concerning the Resurrection, then lo! We have created you from dust, then from a drop of seed, then from a clot, then from a little lump of flesh shapely and shapeless, that We may make (it) clear for you. And We cause what We will to remain in the wombs for an appointed time, and afterward We bring you forth as infants…. [Quran 22:5, as translated by Mohammed Marmaduke Pickthall, *The Meaning of the Glorious Quran*, The Islamic Computing Centre, London, UK, undated]

The Quran teaches that fetal development is divided into three stages, each 40 days long. At the end of these stages, the soul enters the fetus. Muslims, who belong to various groups, differ in their beliefs as to when abortion is allowed. Some sects believe it is permissible to have an abortion before ensoulment, while others argue that God forbids the killing of both the born and unborn, even those who have not received a soul. They claim the Quran specifically teaches, "They are losers who besottedly have slain their children without knowledge, and have forbidden that which Allah bestowed upon them…." (See Pickthall above.) However, the followers of Islam generally agree that abortion is permissible to save the mother's life, even after the first three months of pregnancy.

JEWISH POSITION ON ABORTION

Like Islam, Judaism has no one position on abortion. In the United States, most Jews belong to one of three groups — Orthodox, Conservative, or Reform Judaism. Reform and Conservative Jews generally believe that abortion is the choice of the woman. Jewish law does not recognize a fetus, or even an infant under 30 days old, as having legal rights. The laws of mourning do not apply to an expelled fetus or a child who does not survive to his thirtieth day. The biblical text that is the basis for this states,

> If a man strikes and wounds a pregnant woman so that her fruit be expelled, but no harm befall her, then shall he be fined as her husband shall assess, and the matter placed before the judges. But if harm befall her, then thou shalt give life for life (Exodus 21:22).

The Mishnah is the code of Jewish law that forms the basis of the Talmud, the most definitive statement of Jewish law. The Mishnah, which dates back to the second century B.C.E., states,

> If a woman is having difficulty in giving birth, it is permitted to cut up the child inside her womb and take it out limb by limb because her life takes precedence. However, if the greater part of the child has come

out, it must not be touched, because one life must not be taken to save another.

Maimonides (1135-1204), a rabbi, a doctor, and one of the greatest Jewish philosophers, wrote that abortion was permitted if it would ease a mother's illness, even if the illness was not life-threatening. Other scholars, however, have differed, saying abortion was permitted only to save the mother's life. During the Holocaust, Jewish women who became pregnant were encouraged by their rabbis to abort when the Germans declared that all pregnant Jewish women would be killed.

Orthodox Judaism takes a restrictive position on abortion. A fetus is an organic part of the mother and, as such, does not have legal status. Nonetheless, termination of a pregnancy is strongly condemned on moral grounds. Although a mother's life takes precedence over the unborn, the fetus, particularly after the fortieth day of conception, has a right to life that cannot be denied. Cases of rape or fetal deformity do not give a mother permission to terminate a pregnancy unless they are a threat to her mental health. An example is if the mother becomes suicidal as a result of the pregnancy.

Rabbi Moshe Feinstein protested the liberal abortion law in Israel to then-Prime Minister Menahem Begin. Feinstein wrote, "We hereby state with absolute finality, that a law which says you can abort a child prior to its birth is tantamount to murder and according to Halakhah [the laws of the Talmud], it amounts to the taking of a Jewish life for which the penalty is very grave."

THE ENGLISH TRADITION

American legal tradition has developed from the English tradition. Until England broke away from the Roman Catholic Church in the fifteenth century, it had observed the Church's laws. Henry de Bracton (c. 1210-1268), the Father of English Common Law, was the first to mention abortion in English law. (The English Common Law was a body of laws based on judicial precedents, or court decisions and opinions, rather than on written laws.) Greatly influenced by the Church law and religious theologians, Bracton wrote, "If there is anyone who has struck a pregnant woman or has given poison to her, whereby he has caused an abortion, if the fetus be already formed or animated and especially if animated, he commits a homicide."

Four hundred years later, when Sir Edward Coke wrote *The Institutes of the Laws of England* (1634), the law had changed. "If a woman be *quick* with a childe," Coke wrote, "and by a potion or otherwise killeth it in her womb or if a man beat her, whereby the child dieth in her body and she is delivered of a dead child, this is a great misprision (misdemeanor) and no murder; but if the child be born alive and dieth of poison, battery, or other cause, this is murder." *Quickening* refers to the fetus's first movement in the womb felt by the mother, occurring about the sixteenth to eighteenth week of pregnancy.

A century later, Sir William Blackstone, in his *Commentaries on the Laws of England* (1765), upheld Coke's interpretation of a serious misdemeanor if the child was in the womb and of murder if it was born. Despite the observations of Coke and Blackstone, abortion was not a criminal offense in England from 1327 to 1803.

English Statutes

In England, the first actual written statute against abortion was the Miscarriage of Women Act of 1803 (also known as Lord Ellenborough's Act), which punished the administration of drugs to induce abortion. Punishment for abortion before quickening included exile, whipping, or imprisonment. Abortion performed after quickening was punishable by death. However, after the abolition of the death penalty in 1837, abortion before and after quickening was considered a felony.

The last major English abortion law of the nineteenth century, the Offenses Against the Person Act, was passed in 1861. It stated,

Every woman, being with child, who, with intent to procure her own miscarriage, shall unlawfully administer to herself any poison or other noxious thing, or shall unlawfully use any instrument or other means whatsoever with the like intent, and whosoever, with intent to procure the miscarriage of any woman, … shall be guilty of felony, and being convicted thereof shall be liable … to be kept in penal servitude for life….

In addition, any person who assisted another in obtaining an abortion was guilty of a misdemeanor and could receive a three-year prison sentence.

In 1929, Parliament enacted the Infant Life (Preservation) Act, supplementing the Offenses Against the Person Act. The Infant Life Act stated that an abortion, particularly of a viable (potentially capable of surviving outside the womb) fetus, was unlawful except when it could be proved to have been done in good faith to save the mother's life. This act had actually been a part of the English Common Law, but had never before been codified (compiled into a complete system of written law). The passage of the Infant Life Act was the first time that written English law considered the fetus expendable; however, the law did not offer specific explanations for such restrictions as a viable fetus, the physician's good faith, and the necessity for the procedure.

In 1939, a health exception was added to the Offenses Against the Person Act of 1861. A fourteen-year-old girl who was raped and became pregnant went to a London physician, Dr. Aleck Bourne, for an abortion. The doctor performed the abortion for free and then reported it to the authorities. In *Rex v. Bourne,* Justice MacNaghten noted that the threat to life also involved health and that childbirth might have threatened the young girl's mental health. He instructed the jury to vote for the physician's acquittal if the jurors found he believed the abortion would preserve the girl's mental health. The jury acquitted. More than a legal

precedent, the case became a rallying cry for advocates of liberalized abortion laws.

In 1948, an English court ruled that the attending physician could decide on the necessity of an abortion. In 1958, a court determined that mental health was justification for abortion. In the spring of 1968, following a long and bitter struggle, the Abortion Act of 1967 went into effect. This law permitted abortion if it had been determined by two doctors that the pregnancy threatened the mental and physical health of the mother or the potential child would suffer physical or mental deformities that would seriously handicap it.

THE AMERICAN EXPERIENCE

In colonial America, midwives, not doctors, helped mothers deliver their children. In most cases midwives were regulated and forbidden to perform abortions. For example, in 1716, New York City laws licensing midwives required them to swear, among other things, not to "give any Counsel or Administer any Herb, Medicine or Potion, or any other thing to any Woman being with Child whereby She Should Destroy or Miscarry or that she goeth withal before her time."

These common laws, enacted to prevent women from dying from the poisons used to terminate pregnancies, remained in effect until the American Revolution. In post-Revolutionary America, abortion before quickening was legal.

The First Laws

The first abortion laws in the United States were based on English Common Law, as described by Coke and Blackstone (see above). In 1821, Connecticut passed the first abortion law. Although it was patterned after the British 1803 Miscarriage of Women Act, the Connecticut statute just addressed post-quickening abortion, which constituted a felony.

In 1828, New York passed a statute with two provisions. The first provision imposed a second-degree manslaughter penalty for a post-quickening abortion and considered as a misdemeanor a pre-quickening abortion. The second provision contained an exception clause permitting "therapeutic" abortion if "necessary to preserve the life of such a mother or shall have been advised by two physicians to be necessary for such a purpose." This New York law served as a model for many statutes prohibiting abortion.

Nonetheless, despite these state statutes regulating abortion, the sale of abortifacients (abortion-inducing drugs) continued during the first half of the nineteenth century. The newspapers regularly advertised "Monthly Pills," and new methods to relieve "obstructions of the womb." (See Figure 1.1.)

In 1871, the *New York Times* called abortion the "Evil of the Age." A newspaper article stated, "The enormous amount of medical malpractice [a euphemism for abortion] that exists and flourishes, almost unchecked, in the city of New York, is a theme for most serious consideration. Thousands of human beings are thus murdered before they have seen the light of this world."

The American Medical Association

The American Medical Association (AMA), founded in 1847, campaigned vigorously against abortion. Women did not regularly turn to doctors for questions on childbirth and "women problems." Doctors realized women went to quacks, friends, pharmacists, and midwives for abortions. While some AMA members were honestly concerned about the dangers of "quack" abortions on women, others feared the loss of business. The association further condemned as unprofessional those medical providers who performed abortions, thus ignoring their Hippocratic Oath — "I will give no deadly medicine to anyone if asked, nor suggest any such counsel."

The simplest solution to this difficult situation was to make abortion illegal. The medical profession saw this as an opportunity to drive quacks out of the field and bolster their own professional image. In addition, medical science had recently recognized that life existed in the fetus before "quickening," and many doctors were morally offended by the act of aborting a live fetus. Ironically, when the AMA turned to organized religions for support, it was denied. It was not until after the Civil War that organized religions got involved with the anti-abortion movement.

The AMA was not motivated to criminalize abortion for moral or professional reasons alone. Physicians were swept up by the growing nativist, anti-immigrant sentiments of the time. There were concerns that, because of the uncontrolled use of abortion, the proportion of "good Anglo-Saxon stock" was diminishing in the face of increasing immigration, which was predominantly Catholic at the time. (See the Comstock Law below.)

Anti-Abortion Laws

Due to the intense lobbying by the AMA, the period from 1860 to 1880 produced the most important proliferation of anti-abortion legislation in American history. States and territories enacted

---

FIGURE 1.1

MEDICAL

ADVICE TO MARRIED LADIES.—MADAME RESTELL, Professor of Midwifery, can be consulted as usual at 162 Chambers Street. Her infallible French, Monthly Pills, No. 1 (price $1), or No. 2, which are four degrees stronger than No. 1, and can never fail, are safe and healthy; price $5. Also sold at 127½ Liberty street, or sent by mail.

ALL DISEASES, FROM WHATEVER CAUSE PRO-duced, are safely and successfully treated, by Madame DESPARD. But one interview is necessary. N.B.—Board and elegant Rooms for ladies during confinement, with medical attendance. Residence 101 Sixth Avenue, opposite Eighth Street. Relief-warranted in 24 hours.

CHARLES LUTZE, M.D., 614½ BROADWAY, WISHES the ladies to distinctly understand that he is the only safe and reliable physician in this city for removing all obstructions and irregularities in females. His monthly regulating medicines warranted safe and sure. Price $5. Elegant accommodations for ladies during confinement.

DR. GRINDLE, FEMALE PHYSICIAN AND ACCON-cheur, No. 6 Amity place, between Bleecker and Amity streets, makes it his special practice to treat all female complaints, from whatever cause produced. Is sure to give relief to the most anxious patient in twenty-four hours time. Elegant rooms for ladies requiring nursing.

DR. SELDEN, 233 BLEECKER STREET, RELIEVES obstructions of the womb at one interview, by a new method, without pain and without medicine.

Source: *New York Herald*, 1865

more than 40 anti-abortion statutes. Of these, 13 outlawed abortion for the first time, and 21 revised old anti-abortion laws by making them more stringent. In 1873, the United States Congress passed the Comstock Law (named after its chief supporter, Anthony Comstock). Primarily intended to ban the dissemination of pornography and birth control devices, this legislation also prohibited the use of abortion devices.

Today, birth control measures are often perceived as freeing women, but in the late nineteenth century, contraceptives were often seen as freeing men to pursue adulterous relationships. The contemporary belief that birth control, like masturbation, sapped bodily strength and led to physical decay, also influenced the passage of the law.

In 1934, Congress held hearings to amend the Comstock Law to allow doctors to provide birth control information and prescribe contraceptive devices. The physicians' bill to amend the Comstock Law did not stand a chance in committee hearings. The debate concerning the proposed amendment in 1934 was no different from that concerning the current Medicaid funding of abortions (see Chapters II and III). Allowing doctors to provide birth control information, according to the Comstock Law supporters, was tantamount to the government supporting population control. The Comstock Law remained in effect for almost four more decades. On January 8, 1971, President Richard Nixon signed a law overturning the 98-year-old federal anti-contraception law. The law was sponsored by then-Representative George Bush of Texas.

Abortion continued despite the new laws that banned it. In the early twentieth century, as many as 1 in 3 pregnancies was terminated (abortion was the only form of birth control available to women). Women of means generally found doctors who lent their own interpretations to the allowable exceptions for "therapeutic," or medically necessary, abortions. Poor women, however, usually had to resort to self-induced or illegal abortions, accounting for innumerable mutilations and deaths.

Legal requirements made it almost impossible to convict an abortionist. The state had to prove that there had been a pregnancy, that there had been a live, unborn child at the time of the abortion, and that the death of that child was caused by the abortion. The pregnancy itself could not be proven until quickening, and the presence of a living child up until the time of the abortion could only be vouched for by the mother or others who had felt the baby move. Finally, there was rarely a corpse or witness to provide evidence. Thus, in New York state there were nine abortion convictions from 1895 to 1904, a decade when a least 90,000 abortions were performed.

CHANGING ATTITUDES

Over time, advances in medicine enabled most women to carry their pregnancies to term uneventfully. Doctors became hard-pressed to diagnose life-threatening complications in order to prescribe "therapeutic" abortions. Suddenly, they found their abortion decisions being second-guessed by a new development in the medical establishment — the review board.

In 1959, the American Law Institute proposed a revised Model Penal Code, which not only gave physicians guidelines to work with, but also helped counterbalance the restricting power of the review boards. The Model Penal Code proposed that physicians be permitted to terminate a pregnancy

• If they believed it threatened the life of the mother or would critically impair the mother's physical or mental condition.

• If the child would be born with a grave physical or mental defect.

• If the pregnancy resulted from rape or incest.

The need for abortion had to be approved by two physicians. The inclusion of the mother's mental condition became a factor for doctors because the definition of health was then beginning to include mental health.

By the 1960s, all 50 states and the District of Columbia allowed "therapeutic" abortions to save the life of the mother. Colorado and New Mexico also permitted abortions to prevent serious irreparable harm to the mother, while Alabama, Oregon, Massachusetts, and the District of Columbia allowed abortions simply to protect the health of the mother.

Thalidomide and Rubella

No sooner were these laws adopted than their restrictions were tested by events that occurred in the early 1960s. In 1962, Sherri Finkbine of Arizona found out that the drug thalidomide she had taken during pregnancy might have deformed the child she was carrying. European women who used the drug to treat morning sickness were reported to be delivering severely deformed babies. Finkbine decided, upon her physician's advice, to have a legal abortion.

After Finkbine publicized her dilemma to warn others of the effects of thalidomide, the hospital refused the legal abortion for fear of criminal liability. An appeal to the Arizona State Supreme Court was unsuccessful and, in frustration, the Finkbines flew to Sweden, where the abortion was performed. The Swedish doctor confirmed that the embryo was deformed.

During the early 1960s, a rubella (German measles) epidemic swept the United States. Many women who had contracted the measles during early pregnancy, fearing potential birth defects, obtained legal abortions. Many others could not, either due to legal restrictions or lack of funds. Consequently, they either delivered their children at the heightened risk of disabilities or had illegal abortions. During that period, an estimated 15,000 infants were born with birth defects.

The AMA became alarmed that the abortion laws it had helped pass were now slipping out of its control. In 1967, it called for the liberalization of abortion laws and, in 1970, urged that abortion be limited only by the "sound clinical judgment" of a physician. (See Chapter III for the AMA's position on strict abortion laws in response to the Supreme Court's *Rust v. Sullivan* decision.)

WOMEN SPEAK OUT

The thalidomide and rubella episodes stimulated interest in the abortion issue and created empathy for the mothers-to-be who had found themselves in these difficult situations. Furthermore, the 1960s were a period of change, a time when many people questioned accepted beliefs. Americans were discussing human sexuality more openly, making it easier to talk about abortion.

At the same time, the civil rights movement was sparking debates over individual freedom, an area that many people believed included abortion. By the end of the decade, the women's movement had emerged as one of the major results of the civil rights movement. Many women saw abortion as an issue related directly to their freedom and independence as women. They suspected male legislators denied abortions to females to keep them in the home, subjugated and weighed down by the responsibilities of motherhood.

As the women's movement gained power, many women began to tell their stories of abortions outside the United States or by back-alley abortionists. They realized that they were not alone in these experiences. Many sought to put a stop to the deaths and mutilations brought on by unqualified abortionists.

The Laws Begin to Change

Increased interest in the abortion problem caused many states to reform their laws, using the Model Penal Code (see above) as a guide. In 1967, Colorado, California, and North Carolina became the first states to liberalize their statutes. By 1973, 13 states had passed similar legislation.

In 1970, Alaska, Hawaii, New York, and Washington chose the radical alternative of legalizing all abortions performed by a doctor — up to a le-

9

gally determined time in the pregnancy. Alaska, Hawaii, and Washington also established state residency requirements and shorter time periods during which women could have abortion on demand. By one vote, New York passed the most liberal law of the four states. It permitted abortion for any reason up to 24 weeks and after that, only to save the mother's life.

In 1972, the American Bar Association approved the Uniform Abortion Act as a model for all state statutes. It was based on the New York law. That same year, the President's Commission on Population Growth and the American Future, headed by John D. Rockefeller III, released its final report, recommending "the liberalization of state abortion laws along the lines of the New York statute."

Meanwhile, as legislatures continued to re-examine their state abortion laws, state and federal courts were beginning to declare state abortion laws unconstitutional because they were vague and interfered with a woman's right to privacy. Many thousands of women traveled to states where abortion had become legal in order to obtain an abortion. The New York State Department of Health reported that, between July 1, 1970, and December 31, 1972, over 300,000 women traveled to New York to get abortions. Many states watched to see what would happen in New York, Alaska, Hawaii, and Washington, and everyone awaited the legal clarification that inevitably would have to come from the U.S. Supreme Court. It came on January 22, 1973, in the historic *Roe v. Wade* decision (see Chapter II).

CHAPTER II

SUPREME COURT DECISIONS*

[F]reedom to differ is not limited to things that do not matter much. That would be a mere shadow of freedom. The test of its substance is the right to differ as to the things that touch the heart of the existing order. —Justice Harry Blackmun in *Rust v. Sullivan*, 1991

On January 22, 1973, after considering for a year and hearing the abortion issue debated twice, the Supreme Court finally came to the landmark decision, *Roe v. Wade*, that would profoundly affect the lives of the nation's women and men. Depending on one's viewpoint, the Supreme Court handed down either one of its most terrible judgments, sanctioning the murder of innocent life, or one of its most enlightened judgments, recognizing a woman's right to control her own body.

Now, nearly three decades and many dozens of court decisions later, the essential holding of *Roe* (that abortion is a constitutional liberty) has not been overturned. However, several court decisions have permitted increasing restrictions and preconditions on a woman's right to an abortion. This chapter will examine the major steps in the Supreme Court's interpretation of *Roe* from 1973 to the present. The cases are presented by issue, but a chronology and a brief explanation of the major cases can be found in Table 2.1.

ROE V. WADE

In 1969, Texas abortion law, dating back to 1857, permitted abortion only when the mother's life was endangered. A pregnant, single woman, "Jane Roe," challenged the constitutionality of the law. In *Roe v. Wade* (410 U.S. 113, 1973), the Supreme Court, in a 7-2 decision, found that a law that prohibited abortion, except to save the life of the mother, without regard for the state of the pregnancy, violated the "due process" clause of the Fourteenth Amendment. The Fourteenth Amendment, said the High Court, protects the right to privacy against state action, including a woman's right to terminate her pregnancy. The Supreme Court based this right to privacy on a 1942 case, *Skinner v. Oklahoma* (316 U.S. 535), which struck down a state law that called for sterilizing persons convicted two or more times of "felonies involving moral turpitude" (immoral acts).

In *Roe*, however, the Court noted that, while the right to abortion is guaranteed, the state has legitimate interests in protecting the health of the pregnant woman and the potentiality of human life. Each of these interests increases and becomes more "compelling" at various stages of pregnancy as the scheduled delivery date approaches.

The Court divided a normal pregnancy into three-month stages (trimesters).

- First Trimester — During approximately the first three months, the decision to abort must be left up to the woman and her physician.

- Second Trimester — After the first trimester of pregnancy, the state may regulate the abortion procedure in ways necessary to promote the mother's health.

---

* See Chapter VI for judicial rulings on clinic violence and disruption.

TABLE 2.1

CHRONOLOGY OF MAJOR ABORTION CASES

Roe v. Wade — 1973, 410 U.S. 113
Found abortion legal and established the trimester approach of unrestricted abortion in the first trimester, reasonably regulated abortion in relation to the woman's health in the second trimester, and permitted states to prohibit abortion, except when necessary to preserve the woman's life or health, in the third trimester.

Doe v. Bolton — 1973, 410 U.S. 179
Held unconstitutional Georgia's statute requiring performance of abortions in hospitals, approval by hospital abortion committee, confirmation by two consulting physicians, and restriction to state residents.

Planned Parenthood of Central Missouri v. Danforth — 1976, 428 U.S. 52
Ruled that a state may not require the written permission of a spouse or the consent of a parent, in the case of a minor, for an abortion. Further ruled that the state could not prohibit the use of saline injection abortions and found the provision requiring the physician to preserve the life of the fetus "unconstitutionally overbroad."

Maher v. Roe — 1977, 432 U.S. 464; ***Beal v. Doe*** — 432 U.S. 438; ***Poelker v. Doe*** — 432 U.S. 519
Ruled that, while the state could not ban abortion, it was under no legal obligation to fund nontherapeutic abortions or provide the public facilities for such abortions.

Colautti v. Franklin — 1979, 439 U.S. 379
Overturned a Pennsylvania law that required physicians to try and save the fetus even if the fetus was less than six months old and not yet viable.

Bellotti v. Baird — 1979, 443 U.S. 622
Found that a statute requiring a minor to get her parents' consent or to obtain judicial approval following parental notification unconstitutionally burdened the minor's right to abortion.

Harris v. McRae — 1980, 448 U.S. 297
Found that the Hyde Amendment did not impinge on a woman's freedom to terminate a pregnancy but, rather, encouraged alternatives deemed to be in the public interest. In addition, the Hyde Amendment was found not to violate the separation of church and state.

H. L. v. Matheson — 1981, 450 U.S. 398
Upheld a Utah statute requiring a physician to notify a minor's parents of their daughter's intention to get an abortion.

Planned Parenthood of Kansas City, MO v. Ashcroft — 1983, 462 U.S. 476
Found unconstitutional that all abortions after 12 weeks be performed in a hospital, but upheld provisions requiring pathology reports for every abortion, the presence of a second physician for abortions performed after viability, and parental consent or judicial bypass for minors.

City of Akron v. Akron Center for Reproductive Health, Inc. — 1983, 462 U.S. 416
Held unconstitutional the following requirements: that all abortions after the first trimester be performed in a hospital, parental consent or judicial order be required for all minors under 15 years of age, specific information designed to dissuade a woman from abortion be presented, a 24-hour waiting period be observed, and methods for the disposal of fetal tissue be established.

Thornburgh v. American College of Obstetricians and Gynecologists — 1986, 476 U.S. 747
Ruled that the information required under "informed consent," public reports, and disclosure of detailed information about abortions performed were not reasonably related to protecting a woman's health.

Webster v. Reproductive Health Services — 1989, 492 U.S. 490
Upheld the Missouri law stating that "the life of each human being begins at conception." Also ruled that the state had the right to require physicians to perform viability tests on any fetus believed to be 20 or more weeks old, to forbid the use of public employees and facilities to perform abortions not necessary to save a woman's life, and to prohibit the use of public funds, employees, or facilities to counsel a woman to have an abortion not necessary to save her life.

(continued)

TABLE 2.1 (Continued)
CHRONOLOGY OF MAJOR ABORTION CASES

Hodgson v. Minnesota — 1990, 497 U.S. 417
Upheld a law requiring minors to notify both parents of an abortion decision because there was a provision for judicial bypass within the law.

Rust v. Sullivan — 1991, 500 U.S. 173
Prohibited clinics that used Title X funds from counseling regarding abortion or giving abortion referrals.

Planned Parenthood of Southeastern Pennsylvania v. Casey — 1992, 505 U.S. 833
Stopping just short of overturning *Roe v. Wade*, this ruling dropped the trimester framework and adopted an "undue burden" standard. Specifically, it upheld informed consent, a 24-hour waiting period, parental consent, and reporting and record-keeping requirements. It rejected a requirement for spousal consent.

SEE CHAPTER VI FOR DISCUSSION OF THE FOLLOWING CASES.

Bray v. Alexandria Women's Health Clinic — 1993, 506 U.S. 263
Found that the anti-abortion protests outside of clinics could not be interpreted as a violation of the Civil Rights Act. Women seeking abortions were not a class of persons qualifying for protection under the act and the protesters' behavior did not show class-based discriminatory ill-will against women.

National Organization for Women v. Scheidler — 1994, 114 S. Ct. 798
Ruled that the Racketeer-Influenced and Corrupt Organizations Act did not have to include an economic motive and could be used to prosecute the protest activities of anti-abortion groups and any other groups that seek to prevent the operation of legitimate businesses.

Madsen v. Women's Health Center — 1994, 114 S. Ct. 2516
Upheld an injunction forbidding anti-abortion protesters from a 36-foot fixed buffer zone in front of an abortion clinic. Upheld noise restrictions, preventing the use of bullhorns and shouting. The Court did not uphold the injunction preventing protesters from approaching patients and staff workers in a 300-foot buffer zone around clinics and staff residences or the prohibition against non-threatening posters and signs in the 36-foot buffer zone.

Schenck v. Pro-Choice Network — 1997, 117 S. Ct. 855
Upheld an injunction forbidding anti-abortion protesters from a 15-foot fixed buffer zone in front of an abortion clinic. Also upheld the provision of "cease and desist," whereby two protesters at a time could perform "sidewalk counseling." However, the protesters had to stop counseling and leave the buffer zone upon request. The Court did not uphold the injunction preventing protesters from coming within a 15-foot floating buffer zone of people entering or leaving an abortion clinic.

Source: Data from various sources, compiled by Information Plus

• Third Trimester — After the fetus is "viable" (potentially capable of surviving outside the womb), the state, to protect the potential life of the fetus, may regulate and even forbid abortion, except where necessary to preserve the life or health of the mother.

DOE V. BOLTON

At the same time, the Supreme Court also overturned the Georgia law, one of the "reform" abortion statutes (see Chapter I). In *Doe v. Bolton* (410 U.S. 179, 1973), the High Court, while reiterating their *Roe* ruling that states may not prevent abortion by making it a crime, observed that states may not make abortions hard to obtain by imposing complicated procedural conditions. The Court found unconstitutional the state requirements that all abortions take place in hospitals accredited by the Joint Committee on Accreditation of Hospitals, that abortions be approved by a hospital abortion committee, and that two consulting physicians confirm the judgment of the performing physician.

GOVERNMENT SUPPORT (OR NONSUPPORT) OF ABORTION

Public Funding of Nontherapeutic Abortions

On June 20, 1977, the Supreme Court ruled on three cases concerning women too poor to afford an abortion. In *Maher, Commissioner of Social Services of Connecticut v. Roe* (432 U.S. 464), the Court held that the Equal Protection Clause of the Fourteenth Amendment does not require a state participating in Medicaid to pay for needy women's expenses arising out of nontherapeutic (not medically necessary) abortions simply because it pays childbirth expenses. The Court observed that a state may choose to favor childbirth over abortion and is under no obligation to show why it chooses to do so.

In *Beal, Secretary, Department of Public Welfare of Pennsylvania v. Doe* (432 U.S. 438, 1977), the Supreme Court found that nothing in Title XIX of the Social Security Act (Medicaid) requires any state to fund every medical procedure. However, a state may fund nontherapeutic abortions should it choose to do so. Finally, In *John H. Poelker v. Jane Doe* (432 U.S. 519, 1977), the Court upheld a directive forbidding nontherapeutic abortions in city hospitals. In these three cases, the Supreme Court found that, while the state cannot ban abortions, it is under no legal obligation to fund nontherapeutic abortions or provide the public facilities for such abortions.

The Hyde Amendment — Constitutional or Not?

Maher, Beal, and Poelker (see above), however, did not address the issue of whether federal law, such as the Hyde Amendment (September 1976), or state laws with similar provisions, was constitutional. (The Hyde Amendment was designed to limit federal funding of abortion through the Medicaid program; see Chapter III for more on this federal law.) Since most federal funding for abortion was done through the Medicaid program, cutting federal monies most directly affected the poor. Not surprisingly, the issue of the constitutionality of the Hyde Amendment soon made its way into the nation's courts.

In June 1980, in a 5-4 majority decision, the Supreme Court, in *Harris v. McRae* (448 U.S. 297), held that the Hyde Amendment is constitutional. The Court ruled that the funding restrictions of the Hyde Amendment do not infringe on a woman's right to terminate her pregnancy as held in *Roe*. The Court observed,

> It simply does not follow that a woman's freedom of choice carries with it a constitutional entitlement to the financial resources to avail herself of the full range of protected choices. Although government may not place obstacles in the path of a woman's exercise of her freedom of choice, it need not remove those not of its own creation, and indigency (being poor) falls in the latter category.... Abortion is inherently different from other medical procedures, because no other procedure involves the purposeful termination of a potential life.

Public Funding of Therapeutic Abortions

In *Harris v. McRae* (see above), the High Court further ruled that a state that participates in the Medicaid program is not required to fund therapeutic abortions if federal reimbursement has been withdrawn under the Hyde Amendment. On that same day, the Supreme Court, in three related cases — *Williams v. Zbaraz, Miller v. Zbaraz,* and *United States v. Zbaraz* (448 U.S. 358) — held that an Illinois law, with similar funding restrictions as the Hyde Amendment, did not violate the Equal Protection Clause of the Fourteenth Amendment.

Federally Funded Clinics Cannot Counsel About Abortion Option

In May 1991, the Supreme Court, in *Rust v. Sullivan* (500 U.S. 173), approved the right of the

U.S. Department of Health and Human Services (HHS; Louis Sullivan was then the secretary of the department) to control through funding what was said at family planning clinics. While the Hyde Amendment prevented government-funded clinics from providing abortions, in *Rust*, the Court upheld the HHS's Title X regulation that "none of the funds appropriated under this title shall be used in programs where abortion is a method of family planning." (See Chapter III for more on Title X.)

The Court decided that providing information was included in this prohibition and that First Amendment (free speech) and Fifth Amendment (prevents government from taking away personal liberty) rights were not infringed upon by this prohibition. Chief Justice Rehnquist stated,

> Nothing in them [Title X regulations] requires a doctor to represent as his own any opinion that he does not in fact hold.... The program does not provide post-conception medical care, and therefore a doctor's silence with regard to abortion cannot reasonably be thought to mislead a client into thinking that the doctor does not consider abortion an appropriate option for her....

Justice Blackmun, in his dissenting opinion, saw the case very differently. He stated,

> Whatever may be the Government's power to condition the receipt of its largess (generosity) upon the relinquishment of constitutional rights, it surely does not extend to a condition that suppresses the recipient's cherished freedom of speech based solely upon the content or viewpoint of that speech.

> The Regulations are also clearly viewpoint based. While suppressing speech favorable to abortion with one hand, the Secretary compels anti-abortion speech with the other. [The clinics are required to give prenatal advice; see Chapter III.]

STATE RESTRICTIONS ON ABORTION

Abortion laws have been generally marked by the continual adding of restrictions on the ability to get an abortion. Over the years, many states have passed statutes stretching the limits of the law, mainly in the areas of informed consent, waiting periods, spousal or parental consent, parental notice, and place of abortions, as well as fetal viability and the disposal of the fetus.

Informed Consent and Spousal/Parental Consent

Planned Parenthood of Central Missouri v. Danforth, Attorney General of Missouri (428 U.S. 52, 1976) was the first case to go before the Supreme Court to challenge *Roe* and *Bolton*. Two Missouri-licensed physicians challenged several restrictions of the Missouri Code, which required the following:

- A woman must sign a written consent to the abortion and certify that "her consent is informed and freely given and is not the result of coercion."

- A woman must get a written consent from her husband for the abortion.

- The attending physician must exercise professional care to preserve the fetus' life and health, failing which he or she would be held guilty of manslaughter and liable for damages.

- An unmarried woman under 18 must get the written consent of a parent or person in *loco parentis* (in the place of a parent) to permit abortion.

The Supreme Court, in *Planned Parenthood v. Danforth*, ruled that during the first 12 weeks of pregnancy, an abortion was a matter of interest only to the woman and her physician. The state cannot "delegate to a spouse a veto power that the State itself is absolutely and totally prohibited from exercising during the first trimester of pregnancy," as ruled in *Roe v. Wade*. Similarly, the Court struck down the parental consent requirement. The majority also ruled that the state could not prohibit the use of saline amniocentesis or any other proven safe abortion method. Finally, the Court found the provision requiring the physician to preserve the life and health of the fetus "unconstitutionally overbroad," especially since it covered the first three months of pregnancy when the fetus is not viable (potentially capable of surviving outside the womb).

Parental Consent

"Mary Moe" was a minor residing at home with her parents and wanted to have an abortion without telling her parents. Moe was considered to be mature and fully competent to make the decision to have an abortion. However, the case soon included consideration of those minors who were not mature and fully competent to give such a consent.

In an 8-1 ruling on Mary Moe's case, the Supreme Court, in *Bellotti v. Baird* (443 U.S. 622, 1979), observed, "A child, merely on account of his minority, is not beyond the protection of the Constitution." The Court declared the Massachusetts statute unconstitutional on two grounds.

First, it permits judicial authorization for an abortion to be withheld from a minor who is found by the superior court to be mature and fully competent to make this decision independently. Second, it requires parental consultation or notification in every instance, whether or not in the pregnant minor's best interests, without affording her an opportunity to receive an independent judicial determination that she is mature enough to consent or that an abortion would be in her best interests.

Parental Notification

Two years later, in 1981, the Supreme Court ruled again on whether a minor (this time, in Utah) fully dependent on her parents, had to inform her parents of her decision to have an abortion (notification, not consent). Referring to *Bellotti*, the Court, in *H. L. v. Matheson* (450 U.S. 398), noted,

A statute setting out a mere requirement of parental notice does not violate the constitutional rights of an immature, dependent minor.... [Abortion] is a grave decision, and a girl of tender years, under emotional stress, may be ill-equipped to make it without mature advice and emotional support.

Informing Both Parents

In 1981, Minnesota passed a law requiring a minor to inform both parents 48 hours before having an abortion of her decision, even if the parents were no longer married and one parent had little or nothing to do with the minor's upbringing (Subdivision 2 of Minn. Stat. 144.343). Subdivision 2 was mandatory except in cases of parental abuse or neglect. The law, however, also created a judicial bypass procedure. Subdivision 6 allowed a minor who did not want to inform either parent to go to court, be supplied with counsel, and be judged whether she was mature enough to make the decision alone or if an abortion was in her best interests.

The Supreme Court, in *Hodgson v. Minnesota* (497 U.S. 417, 1990) ruled that "the constitutional objection to the two-parent notice requirement is removed by the judicial bypass option provided in Subdivision 6 of the Minnesota statute." The decision, however, was divided, with some of the justices agreeing with parts of the decision and not others.

Justice Stevens, although the author of the majority opinion, disagreed with the key finding of the Court. He felt that judicial bypass was being misused because it was designed to handle exceptions to a "reasonable general rule, and thereby preserve the constitutionality of that rule," and not as a justification to permit an unconstitutional rule to stand.

Justice Marshall, agreeing with Stevens, wrote in his dissent,

> The bypass procedure cannot save those requirements because the bypass itself is unconstitutional both on its face and as applied. At the very least, this scheme substantially burdens a woman's right to privacy without advancing a compelling state interest. More significantly, in some instances it usurps a young woman's control over her own body by giving either a parent or a court the power effectively to veto her decision to have an abortion.

Place Restriction, Fetal Development and Viability Discussion, and Fetal Disposal

In 1978, the city of Akron, Ohio, enacted an ordinance titled "Regulations of Abortions," which determined how abortions should be performed in the city. Among the restrictions on abortions were the following:

- All abortions performed after the first trimester of pregnancy had to be done in a hospital.

- The attending physician must inform the patient of the status of her pregnancy, the development of the fetus, the date of possible fetal viability, the physical and emotional complications that may result from an abortion, the availability of agencies to provide her with assistance and information with regard to birth control, adoption, and childbirth, as well as the particular risks associated with her pregnancy and the abortion method to be used.

- Physicians performing abortions must ensure that fetal remains were disposed of in a "humane and sanitary manner."

Violation of any provision constituted a criminal misdemeanor. Many anti-abortion groups considered the Akron ordinances model legislation to be followed by other communities wishing to regulate abortion within their jurisdictions.

After mixed rulings in the federal district court and in the federal court of appeals, the case was argued before the Supreme Court. In 1983, in *City of Akron v. Akron Center for Reproductive Health, Inc.* (462 U.S. 416), the Supreme Court, in a 6-3 decision, upheld its earlier ruling in *Roe v. Wade.*

Noting the significant medical improvements in abortion procedures and the concurrent sharp drop in the number of deaths resulting from late-term abortions, the High Court ruled that it was not necessary to have all second-trimester abortions performed in a hospital.

The High Court also ruled that the provision regarding what information the physician must give the woman before abortion was unconstitutional.

> [The ordinance provision that] begins with the dubious statement that "abortion is a major surgical procedure" and proceeds to describe numerous possible physical and psychological complications of abortion is a "parade of horribles" intended to suggest that abortion is a particularly dangerous procedure.... By insisting upon recitation of a lengthy and inflexible list of information, Akron unreasonably has placed "obstacles in the path of the doctor upon whom [the woman is] entitled to rely for advice in connection with her decision."

Finally, the Supreme Court invalidated the provision requiring a "humane and sanitary" disposal of the fetal remains because it violated the Due Process Clause of the Fourteenth Amendment. Although Akron claimed the purpose of this provision was to prevent the disposal of aborted fetuses in garbage piles, the city was not clear that this alone was the main reason for the provision. The High Court agreed with the appellate court that the provision suggested a possible regulation on "some sort of 'decent burial' of an embryo at the earliest stages of formation." The High Court concluded that this unclear provision is "fatal" where a physician could be criminally held liable for disposing of the fetal remains.

Dissenting from the majority, Justice O'Connor observed that the trimester concept established in *Roe v. Wade* had now become virtually unworkable and should be thrown out because the High Court was now extending the rules that applied in the first trimester well into the second trimester.

Just as improvements in medical technology inevitably will move *forward* the point at which the State may regulate for reasons of maternal health, different technological improvements will move backward the point of viability at which the State may proscribe (prohibit) abortions except when necessary to preserve the life and health of the mother.

The *Roe* framework, then, is clearly on a collision course with itself. As the medical risks of various abortion procedures decrease, the point at which the State may regulate for reasons of maternal health is moved further forward to actual childbirth. As medical science becomes better able to provide for the separate existence of the fetus, the point of viability is moved further back toward conception.

In conclusion, O'Connor indicated that potential life exists at any time during the pregnancy. Since the difference between potential life and capable life has never been clearly defined, she stated, "the State's interest in protecting potential human life exists throughout the pregnancy." Although this appeared to be a call for a reversal of *Roe v. Wade*, Justice O'Connor later turned out to be not as anxious to overturn *Roe* as this dissent would seem to indicate.

THE FETUS AND MAJOR CHANGES IN INTERPRETATION

Saving a "Viable Fetus"

In January 1979, almost six years after the landmark *Roe* decision, the issue of the legal identity of the fetus first reached the Supreme Court. In *Colautti v. Franklin* (439 U.S. 379), the plaintiff challenged the provisions of the Pennsylvania law giving the state the power to protect an unborn child beginning in the sixth month of pregnancy.

This abortion law required physicians performing abortions to save the fetus if they had grounds to believe that the fetus "may be viable." The Supreme Court held that the provisions of the law were "void for vagueness" because the meanings of "viable" and "may be viable" were unclear. These provisions further interfered with the physicians' proper exercise of judgment. The Court also found the law unconstitutional because it could impose criminal liability on physicians if they were thought to have failed to take proper action.

Life Begins at Conception

Two landmark cases, *Webster* and *Casey* (see below), represented a major departure by the Supreme Court from its original reasoning in *Roe v. Wade*. In 1986, Missouri passed a law amending a number of laws concerning unborn children and abortion. The new law

- Declared that life begins at conception.

- Required physicians to perform tests to determine the viability of fetuses after 20 weeks of gestational age.

- Forbade the use of public employees and facilities for abortions not necessary to save the mother's life.

- Prohibited the use of public funds, employees, or facilities for the purpose of counseling a woman to have an abortion not necessary to save her life.

The Supreme Court 1989 decision, *Webster v. Reproductive Health Services* (492 U.S. 490), marked a turning point. In its first case in which a majority of the justices generally opposed abortion, the High Court upheld the Missouri law, indicating a willingness to adopt a more lenient attitude towards reviewing state limitations on abortions.

Writing for the 5-4 majority, Chief Justice Rehnquist (joined by Justices White and Kennedy) found nothing wrong with the preamble of the Missouri law, which stated that "the life of each human being begins at conception." The Court observed that *Roe v. Wade* "implies no limitation on the authority of a State to make a value judgment favoring childbirth over abortion.... The preamble can be read simply to express that sort of value judgment." The Court chose not to rule on the constitutionality of the law's preamble because they considered it to be merely an "abstract proposition."

Relying on *Maher*, *Poelker*, and *McRae* (see above), the Court ruled that "a government's decision to favor childbirth over abortion through the allocation of public funds does not violate *Roe v. Wade*." In addition, "Missouri's decision to use public facilities and employees to encourage childbirth over abortion places no governmental obstacle in the path of a woman who chooses to terminate her pregnancy, but leaves her with the same choices as if the State had decided not to operate any hospitals at all."

Perhaps the most controversial aspect of the Missouri law was the requirement that a physician determine the viability of the fetus if she or he thought the fetus might be 20 or more weeks old. There was no debate over whether a fetus is viable at 20 weeks — it is not. The earliest that a fetus is viable is at 23 1/2 to 24 weeks of gestational life. However, there could be a four-week error in estimating gestational age. The Court ruled the testing for fetal viability constitutional because it furthered Missouri's interest in protecting potential human life.

Chief Justice Rehnquist thought the "rigid" trimester system outlined in *Roe* was no longer useful, if it ever was. Rehnquist felt the *Roe* framework — consisting of such specific elements as trimesters and viability — is not consistent with the concept of a Constitution that supposedly deals with general principles.

Although they came very close, the majority did not overturn *Roe v. Wade*. While respecting the preamble of the Missouri law, the Chief Justice concluded that although the state's interest had been moved back well into the second trimester of pregnancy, *Webster* did not revisit the *Roe* rulings.

Justice Scalia, however, believed *Roe* should have been overturned in this case since most of the justices thought the *Roe* decision was wrong. "It thus appears," Scalia stated, "that the mansion of constitutionalized abortion law, constructed overnight in *Roe v. Wade*, must be disassembled door-jamb by door-jamb, and never entirely brought down, no matter how wrong it may be."

Justice Blackmun (who wrote the *Roe* decision) was equally angry, but for the opposite reason. In a dissent joined by Justices Brennan and Marshall, Blackmun observed that the "fundamental constitutional rights of women to decide whether to terminate a pregnancy, survive but are not secure." Although *Roe* still remains, the *Webster* ruling would return to the states the right to control whether a woman has to carry a fetus to term or not.

Justice Blackmun saw little sense in the plurality opinion that the concepts of trimester and viability did not appear in the U.S. Constitution or that *Roe* has led to a "web of legal rules." So have dozens of other issues. Justice Blackmun concluded,

> The plurality does so either oblivious or insensitive to the fact that millions of women, and their families, have ordered their lives around the right to reproductive choice, and that this right has become vital to the full participation of women in the economic and political walks of American life. The plurality would clear the way once again for government to force upon women the physical labor and specific and direct medical and psychological harms that may accompany carrying a fetus to term. The plurality would clear the way again for the State to conscript (to force into service for the government) a woman's body and to force upon her a "distressful life and fu-

ture." For today, the women of this Nation still retain the liberty to control their destinies. But the signs are evident and very ominous, and a chill wind blows.

ROE V. WADE IS NOT OVERTURNED

From the "Trimester Framework" to "Undue Burden"

Pennsylvania has had a long history of trying to pass restrictive abortion statutes going back to the Abortion Control Act of 1974. In 1989, having seen how, in *Webster*, a more conservative Supreme Court seemed ready to overturn decisions made by an earlier, more liberal court, the Pennsylvania legislature passed an amended 1974 abortion law.

Before the 1989 Abortion Control Act took effect, five abortion clinics and one physician (representing himself and a group of physicians who provided abortion services) sued the state of Pennsylvania, represented by Governor Robert Casey. For many, the Supreme Court decision in *Planned Parenthood of Southeastern Pennsylvania v. Casey* (505 U.S. 833, June 29, 1992) represented either the overturning of 20 years of reproductive freedom or the end of the ruthless killing of the unborn. When the decision was finally made public, neither side was happy.

Casey was a 5-4 split decision, with the plurality opinion written by Justices O'Connor, Kennedy, and Souter and joined in part by Justices Stevens and Blackmun. The justices reaffirmed the essential holding in *Roe v. Wade* — "a recognition of the right of the woman to choose to have an abortion before [fetal] viability and to obtain it without undue interference from the State." After viability, however, the State may prohibit abortion, but only if it provides exceptions for pregnancies that may endanger the woman's life or health. Most importantly, the Court rejected the trimester framework, which had strictly limited the state from regulating abortion during early pregnancy, and replaced it with the "undue burden" standard (see below).

The justices upheld Pennsylvania's proposed restrictions — a 24-hour waiting period, informed consent, parental consent, and reporting and record-keeping requirements — except for the spousal-consent requirement.

Chief Justice Rehnquist and Justices Thomas, White, and Scalia agreed with the provisions upheld by the plurality decision but felt the decision did not go far enough. They proposed that requiring spousal consent was a rational attempt to encourage communication between spouses and should be upheld. Furthermore, they felt that a woman's liberty to abort her unborn child is not a right protected by the Constitution and *Roe* had been a mistake from the beginning.

On the other hand, Justice Stevens wrote an opinion supporting *Roe* and rejecting the 24-hour waiting period and the "biased" (the information was required to be specifically pro-life) informed-consent provision, while Justice Blackmun rejected all the provisions of the Pennsylvania law and reaffirmed the constitutionality of *Roe*.

The Basis for Maintaining Roe

While conceding that people differ in their beliefs about the morality of terminating a pregnancy, even during its earliest stage, the justices explained that it upheld *Roe's* essential holding because their duty is to "to define the liberty of all," not to impose their own moral standards.

> ... These matters, involving the most intimate and personal choices a person may make in a lifetime, choices central to personal dignity and autonomy, are central to the liberty protected by the Fourteenth Amendment. At the heart of liberty is the right to define one's own concept of existence, of meaning, of the universe, and of the mystery of human life. Beliefs about these matters could not define the attributes of personhood were they formed under compulsion of the State.

... Though abortion is conduct, it does not follow that the State is entitled to proscribe it in all instances. That is because the liberty of the woman is at stake in a sense unique to the human condition, and so, unique to the law. The mother who carries a child to full term is subject to anxieties, to physical constraints, to pain that only she must bear. That these sacrifices have from the beginning of the human race been endured by woman with a pride that ennobles her in the eyes of others and gives to the infant a bond of love cannot alone be grounds for the State to insist she make the sacrifice. Her suffering is too intimate and personal for the State to insist, without more, upon its own vision of the woman's role, however dominant that vision has been in the course of our history and our culture. The destiny of the woman must be shaped to a large extent on her own conception of her spiritual imperatives and her place in society.

The High Court also upheld the right to abortion because of their obligation to follow precedent. Under the rule of *stare decisis* (literally, to stand by things decided), requiring courts to reach consistent conclusions in cases that raise the same factual and legal issues, a majority of the Court could not justify overthrowing the findings of *Roe*.

Undue Burden

The Supreme Court, however, rejected *Roe's* trimester framework as too rigid in its prohibition of regulations that sought to protect the fetus before viability. The Court found that the "undue burden" standard was better suited to reconcile the woman's constitutional right and the state's interest in potential life. The Court added that it did not consider the trimester framework to be part of the essential holding of *Roe*.

Under the "undue burden" standard, states may put restrictions on the abortion process (throughout the whole pregnancy) as long as they do not have "the purpose or effect of placing a substantial obstacle in the path of a woman seeking an abortion of a nonviable fetus." The Court added that just because a particular law makes a certain right difficult to exercise does not necessarily mean the law is infringing on that right.

What is at stake is the woman's right to make the ultimate decision, not a right to be insulated from all others in doing so. Regulations which do no more than create a structural mechanism by which the State, or the parent or guardian of a minor, may express profound respect for the life of the unborn are permitted, if they are not a substantial obstacle to the woman's exercise of the right to choose.... Unless it has that effect on her right of choice, a state measure designed to persuade her to choose childbirth over abortion will be upheld if reasonably related to that goal.

Despite the justices' emphasis on the importance of *stare decisis*, the *Casey* decision, although reaffirming the right to abortion, was in many ways closer to *Webster* than to *Roe*. The decision explicitly overruled both *Akron* and *Thornburgh* (See Table 2.1), permitting regulations that the Court had found unacceptable less than 10 years earlier.

The Supreme Court opinion theoretically approved the possibility of overturning the Pennsylvania regulations if it could be proven that restrictions did impose an undue burden. However, the burden of proof had now shifted onto the women and physicians who would challenge the laws and had to prove the restrictions were an "undue burden."

CHAPTER III

ABORTION IS A MAJOR POLITICAL ISSUE

On January 22, 1973, the Supreme Court legalized abortion, setting the stage for this politically sensitive issue to become a continuing topic of debate on the floor of Congress. The *Roe v. Wade* decision (see Chapter II) proved a catalyst for the fledgling right-to-life movement. Pro-lifers consider the *Roe* decision to be government-sanctioned mass killing of the unborn. Following the landmark decision, anti-abortion activists tried to get constitutional amendments passed to overturn *Roe*, but failed to do so. A constitutional amendment requires two-thirds approval of each House of Congress and ratification by three-quarters of the states' legislatures. Anti-abortion groups have since attempted to limit *Roe* both by influencing the appointment of lower court and Supreme Court judges and by restricting the rights to abortion conferred by *Roe*.

THE HYDE AMENDMENT

Medicaid was established in 1965 to pay for medical care for the nation's needy through a federal-state cost-sharing arrangement. During the (Richard) Nixon Administration (1969-1974), the Department of Health, Education, and Welfare (HEW, now the Department of Health and Human Services or HHS) reimbursed states for abortions for poor women. Following the *Roe v. Wade* decision, the HEW considered abortion a medical procedure funded by Medicaid.

In 1974, abortion opponents attached a rider to the annual HEW appropriations bill. The rider forbade or restricted the use of federal funding for abortion. (A rider is a provision added to a piece of legislation that has no direct bearing on the subject of the bill.)

In 1974 and 1975, the House of Representatives overwhelmingly defeated the anti-abortion rider. The Senate, however, approved an amendment prohibiting the funding of Medicaid abortions, except when necessary to save the life of the mother, but this amendment was later dropped in conference committee.

After the Supreme Court ruling in *Roe*, the number of abortions increased rapidly until, by 1976, according to the Centers for Disease Control and Prevention (CDC), almost one million abortions were being performed annually. An estimated 300,000 of these were federally funded. Abortion foes were angered by what they considered a mass slaughter being partially financed with tax dollars, and they responded by lobbying their senators and representatives.

In 1976, then-freshman Congressman Henry Hyde (R-IL) introduced an abortion rider to the HEW-Labor appropriations bill (a bill authorizing money to run the departments). Reflecting changing political attitudes in Congress, this anti-abortion amendment passed. In fact, the 1976 rider, since known as the Hyde Amendment, has become the subject of an annual battle in Congress over abortion.

Representative Hyde originally proposed that no federal funding be used for abortion. Following considerable debate, Congress settled on a compromise, stating that "none of the funds contained [in the appropriations bill] shall be used to perform abortions except where the life of the mother would be endangered if the fetus were carried to term." The Departments of Labor and Health, Education, and Welfare Appropriation Act (PL 94-439), which included the abortion provision, became law in September 1976 but, due to legal challenges, did not go into effect until almost a year later in August 1977.

Almost immediately, the Hyde Amendment was challenged in the courts. The U.S. Supreme Court heard and ruled on public funding cases involving funding limitations both for therapeutic (medically necessary) and nontherapeutic (elective, or not medically necessary) abortions (see Chapter II).

Heated Debate

Over the years, the language of the Hyde Amendments has occasionally changed. The conflict had typically involved the House demanding strict control over the use of federal monies for abortion and the generally more liberal Senate trying to modify House demands. In 1977, the House passed an amendment calling for Hyde's original proposal that no federal funds be used for any abortion, even one necessary to save the life of the mother. However, the final compromise, the result of lengthy debate and political maneuvering, prohibited the use of federal funds to pay for abortions except

- For victims of rape or incest if the occurrence was reported promptly to the proper authorities.

- If justified to save the mother's life.

- In instances where two doctors determined that "severe and long-lasting physical health damage to the mother" may result.

During the early years of the (Jimmy) Carter Administration (1977-1981), the "prompt" reporting of rape or incest to the proper authorities required by the Hyde Amendment was defined as

60 days. This time limit was changed in the 1980 version of the Hyde Amendment, which required that the rape be reported within 72 hours. The rape and incest clause of the Hyde amendment is rarely put to practice. Although exact statistics are unavailable, apparently fewer than 100 women annually receive Medicaid-funded abortions on the basis of incest or rape.

In any case, these exceptions were soon eliminated for needy women. Starting with the 97th Congress (1981-1982), federal funds were available for abortions for Medicaid recipients only if the life of the woman would be endangered if the pregnancy were carried to term.

Abortion Supporters Are Still Disappointed

In 1993, pro-choice supporters thought that they could overturn the Hyde Amendment. The Congress had new members who favored abortion rights, and President Bill Clinton, unlike Presidents Reagan and Bush, would support them. Nonetheless, abortion rights supporters were disappointed when Congress kept the Hyde Amendment, only changing it back to the pre-1980 regulation permitting abortion funding to save the mother's life and in cases of rape or incest.

The 1993 Departments of Labor, Health and Human Services, and Education, and Related Agencies Appropriations Act (PL 103-112) stated, "None of the funds appropriated under this Act shall be expended for any abortion except when it is made known to the Federal entity or official to which funds are appropriated under this Act that such procedure is necessary to save the life of the mother or that the pregnancy is the result of an act of rape or incest." Some states with laws that excluded funding abortion in cases of rape or incest strongly objected to the federal directive. Because the states partially funded Medicaid, they objected to being required to pay for abortions they felt were immoral.

As of December 1999, 28 states and the District of Columbia allowed the funding of abortion under Medicaid in cases of life endangerment, rape, and incest. Two states (Mississippi and South Dakota), in violation of federal law, provided Medicaid funding for abortion only if a woman's life was in danger. Five states (Idaho, Illinois, Iowa, Virginia, and Wisconsin) paid for abortion in cases of rape, incest, and life endangerment, and also under limited health circumstances. On the other hand, 15 states funded abortion in all or most circumstances. (See Table 3.1.)

Abortion Funding and Managed Care

For the first time since *Roe*, the 1996 congressional elections resulted in a pro-life majority in the Senate. Both Houses now consisted of a majority of pro-life legislators. Pro-life lawmakers pointed out that, because states are increasingly contracting with managed care to provide Medicaid recipients with health services, the Hyde

TABLE 3.1

PUBLIC FUNDING FOR ABORTION

State	Life Endangerment Only [1]	Life, Rape, and Incest Only	Life, Rape, Incest, and Some Health Circumstances	All or Most Circumstances
Alabama		X		
Alaska				X[3]
Arizona		X		
Arkansas		X[2]		
California				X[3]
Colorado		X[2]		
Connecticut				X[3]
Delaware		X[6]		
District of Columbia		X		
Florida		X		
Georgia		X		
Hawaii				X
Idaho			X[3,6]	
Illinois			X[2,4]	
Indiana		X[6]		
Iowa			X[5,6]	
Kansas		X		
Kentucky		X[2]		
Louisiana		X[2,6]		
Maine		X		
Maryland				X[5,6]
Massachusetts				X[3,6]
Michigan		X[2]		
Minnesota				X[3]
Mississippi	X			
Missouri		X[2]		
Montana				X[3,6]

(continued)

24

TABLE 3.1 (Continued)

PUBLIC FUNDING FOR ABORTION

State	Life Endangerment Only [1]	Life, Rape, and Incest Only	Life, Rape, Incest, and Some Health Circumstances	All or Most Circumstances
Nebraska		$\bar{X}^2$		
Nevada		X		
New Hampshire		X		
New Jersey				X^3
New Mexico				X^3
New York				X
North Carolina		X		
North Dakota		X^2		
Ohio		X^6		
Oklahoma		$X^{2,6}$		
Oregon				X^3
Pennsylvania		X^6		
Rhode Island		X		
South Carolina		X^6		
South Dakota	X			
Tennessee				
Texas		X		
Utah		$X^{2,6}$		
Vermont				X^3
Virginia			$X^{5,6}$	
Washington				X
West Virginia				X^3
Wisconsin			X^6	
Wyoming		X^6		
TOTAL	2	28	5	15

1. Such state policies violate federal law prohibiting participating states from excluding abortion from the Medicaid program in cases of life endangerment, rape, and incest.
2. A court has ruled that this state must comply with federal law prohibiting the exclusion of abortion from Medicaid in cases of rape or incest as well as life endangerment.
3. A court has ruled that the state constitution prohibits the state from restricting funding for abortion while providing funds for costs associated with childbirth or other medically necessary services.
4. A court has ruled that the state constitution prohibits the enforcement of a state law restricting funding to the extent it bars funding for an abortion necessary to preserve the woman's health.
5. This statute provides funding for some cases of fetal anomaly.
6. This state requires that cases of rape and incest be reported to a law enforcement or social service agency in some circumstances in order for the woman to be eligible for a publicly funded abortion.

Source: *Who Decides? A State-by-State Review of Abortion and Reproduction Rights*, The National Abortion and Reproductive Rights Action League Foundation, Washington, DC, 2000

Amendment had to be revised. (That was the twentieth year that the Hyde Amendment continued to be revised.) Representative Hyde sought to forbid health plans from offering abortion coverage when they contracted with states under Medicaid. He claimed that in cases where states used their own funds to pay for abortions beyond the federally mandated cases of rape, incest, and life endangerment, purchasing a health plan using a "commingling" of federal and state monies presented the possibility of indirect federal abortion subsidy.

Hyde's proposed change met with great opposition from pro-choice Democrats. They protested that the new law would negatively affect privately insured women whose insurance companies contracted with the states. It would also affect Medicaid recipients in those states where abortions were subsidized. In the end, the revised version passed with the provision that federal funds would not be used to purchase managed care packages that included coverage of abortion. States that covered abortion with their own funds would be able to continue doing so under a separate program. In November 1997, President Clinton signed the FY (Fiscal Year) 1998 Departments of Labor, Health and Human Services, and Education, and Related Agencies Appropriations Act (PL 105-78) with the abortion provision.

Abortion May Be Funded Under the State Children's Health Insurance Program (CHIP)

In August 1997, the Balanced Budget Act (PL 105-33) amended the Social Security Act (PL 89-97) by adding Title XXI (State Children's Health Insurance Program, or CHIP) in order to allocate funds to states to provide child health assistance to uninsured, low-income children who are not Medicaid-eligible. Under CHIP, state funds may be used for abortion only to save the life of the mother or if the pregnancy resulted from rape or incest.

Abortion Services for Military Personnel

Before 1970, the armed forces of the United States did not have any official policy regarding the provision of abortion. Individual commanders had unwritten policies, which lower-rank personnel followed. Military medical facilities followed the laws in the states where they were located, and it was up to individual physicians whether or not to offer abortion services.

In 1970, the Department of Defense (DOD) issued an order that "military hospitals perform abortion when it is medically necessary or when the mental health of the mother is threatened." Military physicians, however, were not required to perform abortions. After the 1973 Supreme Court decision on *Roe*, the DOD funded abortions for women eligible for military health care. To perform an abortion, two physicians had to satisfy the above stipulation of "medical necessity" or "risk to mental health." In addition, the funding had to fall within the state regulations concerning abortions.

During the rest of the 1970s, varying abortion language was added to the DOD appropriations acts, with the exceptions ranging from saving the mother's life, rape, and incest, to severe, long-lasting physical damage to the mother. Women whose condition did not satisfy the law paid for their abortions at the military medical facilities.

By 1981, the DOD's abortion regulation was similar to that for civilians — abortion was allowed only to save the life of the mother (see above). In 1988, the DOD began banning all abortions at military medical facilities overseas, even those privately funded. Supporters lauded this action because they claimed it prohibited abortion on demand. Opponents argued that American women denied abortions in U.S. hospitals would be forced to seek abortion services elsewhere where it may not be safe.

In 1993, following his inauguration, President Clinton issued a memorandum, "permit[ting] abortion services to be provided [at U.S. military facilities], if paid for entirely with non-DOD funds...." However, in 1996, the National Defense Authorization Act (PL 104-106) again banned the performance of abortions in U.S. military medical facilities, except in cases of endangerment to the mother's life, rape, or incest.

At subsequent sessions of Congress, proposed amendments to PL 104-106, allowing privately paid abortions, were defeated. During the 1999 consideration of the FY 2000 National Defense Authorization Act (PL 106-65), Congress again left the law unchanged.

Public-Funded Abortions

Terry Sollom, Rachel Benson Gold, and Rebekah Saul, in "Public Funding for Contraceptive, Sterilization and Abortion Services in 1994," *Family Planning Perspectives*, vol. 28, no. 4, July/ August 1996), reported that, in 1994 (latest data available), state and federal governments spent $90 million for 203,200 abortions performed in the United States. The federal government paid for less than 1 percent ($464,000) of this amount. Almost all of the abortions (202,715) were performed in the states that funded all or most therapeutic abortions for needy women.

The Hyde Amendment
in the 105th Congress (1997-98)

During the 105th Congress, most of the abortion-funding restrictions debated for the 1999 appropriations bills of the different federal agencies became part of the Omnibus Appropriations Act of FY 1999 (PL 105-277). The provisions included

- Under Departments of Labor and Health and Human Services appropriations, the ban on abortion funding except in cases of life endangerment, rape, and incest was expanded to include trust funds to make it clear that the ban included younger women receiving Medicare benefits due to disabilities.

- Under Treasury and Postal Service appropriations, the ban on the use of the Federal Em-

ployee Health Benefit Plans for abortion except in cases of life endangerment, rape, or incest continued.

- The prohibition on paying for abortions for women in prisons was retained.

- The District of Columbia was not allowed to use federal or local monies for abortions except in cases of life endangerment, rape, or incest.

TITLE X REGULATIONS

In 1970, with broad bipartisan support, Congress enacted Title X of the Public Health Service Act (Family Planning Program, PL 91-572), which provides federal assistance to family planning clinics for contraception, infertility, and basic gynecologic services, mainly to low-income women and many adolescents (see below). Services are also available to men; about 2 percent of Title X clients are adult and adolescent males (see below). The law specifically prohibits abortion as a method of family planning and forbids the use of any program monies to perform or advocate abortion.

Guidelines instituted under the (Jimmy) Carter Administration (1977-1981) indicated that federally funded clinics could not advise a pregnant woman to have an abortion or pay for one should she choose an abortion. However, they "are to"* inform her in a "nondirective" manner that her options included keeping the baby, giving the child up for adoption, or terminating the pregnancy by having an abortion. Should the woman want an abortion, the federally funded agency had to provide her with a list of abortion clinics that operated without federal funding.

Male Involvement in Family Planning

Since 1996, the Title X program has provided additional funds for an adolescent male initiative that employs male high school students as interns

---

* In September 1986, the Reagan Administration (1981-1989) changed the wording in the guidelines from "are to" (mandatory requirement) to "may" (subject to individual judgment).

in the clinics. The students receive training in clinic operation and peer education, assistance in identifying possible careers in health and health-related occupations, and use of services in a family planning setting. In 1997, the program also awarded research grants to organizations that included social and educational services to males, enabling these organizations to evaluate the addition of reproductive health and family planning services to their existing program.

Confidential Family Planning Services for Adolescents

Of the five million persons receiving reproductive health and family planning services each year, about one-third are less than 20 years of age. Although the law requires Title X clinics to encourage parental participation in teenage reproductive health decisions, they have to respect a teenager's wish not to involve his or her parents. Courts have recognized the importance of confidential services for teenagers. In *Planned Parenthood Association of Utah v. Matheson*, 582 F. Supp. 1001, 1009 [D. Utah 1983]), a U.S. District Court prohibited a "blanket parental notification requirement" for minors seeking contraceptives. The court observed that adolescents who seek contraceptives are usually already sexually active. Therefore, these same adolescents would continue engaging in sexual activity even if they could not obtain contraceptives, thereby exposing themselves to "the health risks of early pregnancy and venereal diseases."

"Physically and Financially Separate"

Besides providing monies to over 4,000 family planning clinics run by state and local governments, Title X also provides grants to private nonprofit groups having family planning services. In 1988, the Department of Health and Human Services (HHS), acting on President Ronald Reagan's recommendation, reaffirmed that Congress intended Title X funds "to be used only to support preventive family planning services." To receive Title X funding, clinics had to be organized so that they "are physically and financially separate" from prohibited abortion activities.

Since several private nonprofit organizations that provided family planning counseling also performed abortions (most notably the Planned Parenthood Federation of America), the proposed regulations would have required complete separation of the family planning clinic from the abortion facility. For example, there would have to be separate entrances and exits, separate office space and equipment, separate waiting and examination rooms, separate financial and medical records, and even separate personnel files.

The two facilities could not share receptionists or telephones and would have to have different names and even different stationery. To have put such a regulation into practice might well have been too expensive for many clinics, forcing them to limit themselves to either family planning counseling or abortion, or to shut down altogether. The Reagan proposal further included prohibiting Title X clinics from "engaging in activities that encourage, promote, or advocate abortion as a method of family planning." Forbidden activities included lobbying Congress to enact pro-abortion laws, distributing literature promoting abortion as a method of family planning, and even the paying of dues to any group that advocated abortion as a means of family planning.

The "Gag Rule"

The Reagan Administration further prohibited counselors at federally funded clinics from discussing abortion as an alternative in an unintended pregnancy and from referring pregnant women to an abortion provider. If the woman requested such information, she was to be told that she was in a clinic that provided prenatal care only. This prohibition against discussing abortion in Title X clinics became known as the "gag rule."

The Supreme Court Supports the Gag Rule

About 36 state health departments and 78 national organizations opposed the gag rule because it violated the clinics' First Amendment right to free speech and infringed on doctor-patient relationship. In May 1991, in *Rust v. Sullivan* (500

U.S. 173), the Supreme Court, voting 5-4, upheld the gag rule, observing that it was a permissible exercise of executive power (see Chapter II). For abortion supporters, this decision symbolized the extent to which the High Court and the Executive branch of government were willing to reinterpret previous rulings in order to make them conform to interpretations that limited abortion. Many abortion opponents were also unhappy with the gag rule, fearing that it set a dangerous precedent for government censorship of material it might find politically objectionable.

Medical Response

The American Medical Association attacked the ruling, not only because it interfered with the doctor-patient relationship, but because it exposed doctors to the risk of medical malpractice lawsuits for not informing a woman with a high-risk pregnancy of all her options. Pregnancy can be a risk to the health of a woman with diabetes, cancer, AIDS, hypertension, renal (kidney) disease, sickle cell anemia, or malnutrition. Some of these diseases particularly affect Black women who, because of their greater rates of poverty, are more likely than White women to use federally funded clinics for health care.

Some federally funded clinics, including Planned Parenthood, chose, at the risk of having to close down, to turn down federal support rather than comply with the gag rule. The deputy assistant secretary of the HHS, William Archer, responded that if clinics would not comply, HHS would simply find other clinics to replace them. There were areas of the country, however, where there were no other existing health care providers ready to step in, leaving women who depended on subsidized health care with no source for prenatal care and contraceptive services.

Congress Votes and the President Vetoes

In Congress, those opposing *Rust v. Sullivan* fought to overturn the Title X gag rule regulation. In November 1991, when President George Bush received H.R. 2707, the appropriations bill for the Department of Health and Human Services, he vetoed it because of a section blocking the gag rule.

Supporters of the bill tried to get the two-thirds vote needed to overturn the presidential veto. In Congress, some legislators saw this as both a First Amendment issue and a women's issue. Olympia Snowe (R-ME) declared,

> A vote to sustain (support the gag rule) means that we feel women do not deserve the same doctor-patient relationship as men have. No male patient is affected by this gag rule; we are creating a situation for women only. A vote to sustain means that fundamentally you believe women are second-class citizens that deserve second-class treatment.

The abortion proponents failed to garner the two-thirds vote needed. In August 1992, a federal appeals court ruled that the HHS could move forward with implementation of the regulations whenever it pleased.

The Gag Rule Is Repealed

On January 22, 1993, the twentieth anniversary of *Roe v. Wade*, newly elected President Bill Clinton repealed the gag rule. He also signed four other abortion memoranda that

- Reversed the "Mexico City Policy" (below).

- Lifted the ban on privately funded abortions in military hospitals (see above).

- Lifted the ban on fetal tissue research (see Chapter VII).

- Ordered the Food and Drug Administration to review the scientific basis for the import ban on RU-486 (see Chapter IV).

Title X went back to Congress for final regulations and funding. In the end, Congress returned Title X to the regulations that were in effect before the gag rule was added in 1988.

Efforts to Revive the Gag Rule

In an effort to revive the gag rule, several pieces of legislation were introduced in the 106th Congress (1999-2000).

- In September 1999, Representative Joseph Pitts (R-PA) and Senator Rick Santorum (R-PA) introduced the Women and Children's Resources Act (H.R. 2901 and S. 1605, respectively) "to establish a program of formula grants to the States for programs to provide pregnant women with alternatives to abortion...." The bill would provide $85 million to the states for grants to pregnancy counseling centers that do not give abortion counseling or referrals. The bill would further prohibit funding contraceptive services under the program.

- In July 1999, Representatives Jim DeMitt (R-SC) and Tom Bliley (R-VA) and Senator John McCain (R-AZ) introduced the Adoption Awareness Act (H.R. 2511 and S. 1382, respectively) "to amend the Public Health Service Act to make grants to carry out certain activities toward promoting adoption counseling...." The legislation would limit the nondirective counseling at the Title X clinics to information about prenatal care and delivery, infant care, foster care, and adoption.

- In July 1999, Representatives Cliff Stearns (R-FL) and Sue Myrick (R-NC) introduced the Federal Adoption Services Act (H.R. 2485) to "amend Title X of the Public Health Service Act to permit family planning projects to offer adoption services." The bill proposes using the Title X funds to provide adoption services instead of contraceptive services.

Title X Funding Is Inadequate

Although the authorizing law (PL 91-572; see above) for the Title X family planning program expired in September 30, 1985, annual appropriations legislation has continued its funding. During the Reagan Administration (1981-1989), funding decreased. Despite the increasing appropriations under the Clinton Administration (1993-2001), Title X funding costs have not kept pace with inflation.

The Alan Guttmacher Institute, which supports abortion as an option, observed that, "taking inflation into account, the FY 1998 funding level of $203 million was still 61 percent lower than the $162 million appropriated in FY 1980...." (Cynthia Dailard, "Title X Family Planning Clinics Confront Escalating Costs, Increasing Needs," *The Guttmacher Report on Public Policy*, vol. 2, no. 2, April 1999). According to the National Abortion and Reproductive Rights Action League (NARAL), "if Title X funding had increased at the

TABLE 3.2					
Title X Appropriations FY1971-FY1999 ($ in thousands)					
FY	**Appropriation**	**FY**	**Appropriation**	**FY**	**Appropriation**
1971	6,000	1981	161,671	1991	144,311
1972	61,815	1982	124,176	1992	149,585
1973	100,615	1983	124,088	1993	173,418
1974	100,615	1984	140,000	1994	180,918
1975	100,615	1985	142,500	1995	193,349
1976	100,615	1986	136,372	1996	192,592
1977	113,000	1987	142,500	1997	198,452
1978	135,000	1988	139,663	1998	203,452
1979	135,000	1989	138,320	1999	215,000
1980	162,000	1990	139,135		

Source: Office of Population Affairs, U.S. Department of Health and Human Services, Washington, DC, 1999

rate of inflation from its FY 1980 funding ... it presently would be funded at approximately $500 million." For FY 1999, the Title X program received less than half that amount — $215 million. (See Table 3.2.) For FY 2000, the Clinton Administration requested an increase of $25 million over the current level.

"Defunding" Title X

Each year, anti-abortion lawmakers try to "defund," or eliminate federal monies from, the Title X program. Although the law prohibits Title X funds to be used for abortion, they argue that organizations, such the Planned Parenthood Federation of America, which provide abortion, should not receive Title X funds. They believe clinic clients might think abortion is a method of family planning. In addition, critics feel that instead of preventing teen pregnancy by providing adolescents with contraceptives, more efforts should be made in encouraging abstinence before marriage. (Title X clinics do offer adolescents abstinence counseling and education.)

WELFARE REFORM VERSUS ABORTION

In 1995, as Congress worked to overhaul the nation's welfare system, the legislators were split on issues concerning teen pregnancy and abortion. Some believed that discontinuing federal cash assistance to the needy would help discourage out-of-wedlock childbearing. These members regarded out-of-wedlock births, especially among adolescents, as "both a central cause of welfare dependency and a direct result of the 'culture' it create[d]." Others feared that limiting welfare benefits would lead poor women to choose abortion.

The National Conference of Catholic Bishops spoke publicly against the proposed welfare reform: "We grant the goodwill of those seeking to end the culture of teen parenting. But we cannot seek a good end by evil means. We must not penalize innocent children by cutting off their sup-

port.... And we cannot take action that will push more women toward abortion." Liberal pro-choice groups, such as the National Organization for Women, were surprised to be allied with traditional opponents, such as the National Right to Life Committee, in opposing the proposed discontinuance of federal cash aid to the poor.

In the end, the 60-year-old federal cash assistance program, the Aid to Families with Dependent Children (AFDC), was eliminated, and on August 22, 1996, President Clinton signed the new welfare reform law, the Personal Responsibility and Work Opportunity Reconciliation Act of 1996 (PL 104-193). The law created a single cash welfare block grant, the Temporary Assistance for Needy Families (TANF), leaving it to individual states to design their own programs.

The new welfare reform law outlined specific provisions on reducing out-of-wedlock and teen pregnancies. While it allowed states to spend a portion of their TANF funds on "prepregnancy family services," it prohibited funding of other medical services, such as abortions.

Although most out-of-wedlock births are to women not on welfare, Congress used the welfare reform law to stress the issue of illegitimacy. To encourage the states to develop effective solutions to reducing out-of wedlock births, PL 104-193 provided for a performance incentive called "Bonus to Reward Decrease in Illegitimacy Ratio." The federal government will award up to $100 million annually, in each of FY years 1999 through 2002, to a maximum of five states that reduce nonmarital births while decreasing their abortion rates below the 1995 levels.

In 1999, the Department of Health and Human Services awarded $20 million each to Alabama, California, Massachusetts, Michigan, and the District of Columbia. Table 3.3 shows the ranking of the states based on the decline in the percentage of nonmarital births.

TABLE 3.3
State Ranking

Percent of births to unmarried women, 1994-95 average and 1996-97 average, and percent change in the percent of births to unmarried women, 1994-95 to 1996-97, and rank order of States with respect to their change (in order of largest decline to largest increase) and rank order of territories (ranked separately from States)

State	Percent unmarried, 1996-97	Percent unmarried, 1994-95	Percent change in percent unmarried, 1994-95 to 1996-97	Rank order of States by largest decline in percent unmarried, 1994-95 to 1996-97		Percent change
				Rank	State	
United States 1/	32.394%	32.392%	0.003%		United States 1/	0.003%
Alabama	33.773%	34.470%	-2.022%	1	California	-5.665%
Alaska	30.815%	29.567%	4.220%	2	District of Columbia	-3.708%
Arizona	38.232%	38.289%	-0.148%	3	Michigan	-3.361%
Arkansas	34.061%	32.763%	3.962%	4	Alabama	-2.022%
California	30.422%	32.248%	-5.665%	5	Massachusetts	-1.493%
Colorado	25.045%	24.918%	0.511%	6	Illinois	-1.452%
Connecticut	32.035%	30.547%	4.872%	7	Virginia	-0.583%
Delaware	35.751%	34.821%	2.669%	8	Mississippi	-0.371%
District of Columbia	64.889%	67.388%	-3.708%	9	Georgia	-0.324%
Florida	35.980%	35.743%	0.662%	10	Pennsylvania	-0.211%
Georgia	35.222%	35.336%	-0.324%	11	Arizona	-0.148%
Hawaii	30.092%	28.760%	4.630%	12	Maryland	-0.102%
Idaho	21.009%	19.299%	8.862%		New Jersey	0.418%
Illinois	33.569%	34.064%	-1.452%		Colorado	0.511%
Indiana	32.457%	31.735%	2.272%		Florida	0.662%
Iowa	26.235%	25.008%	4.908%		Wyoming	0.888%
Kansas	27.213%	25.916%	5.004%		North Carolina	1.437%
Kentucky	29.612%	28.076%	5.471%		South Carolina	1.445%
Louisiana	43.688%	42.546%	2.684%		Tennessee	1.505%
Maine	29.221%	27.970%	4.469%		Oregon	1.593%
Maryland	33.489%	33.523%	-0.102%		Ohio	1.663%
Massachusetts	25.706%	26.095%	-1.493%		Wisconsin	1.838%
Michigan	33.510%	34.676%	-3.361%		New Mexico	2.270%
Minnesota	24.914%	23.932%	4.104%		Indiana	2.272%
Mississippi	45.228%	45.396%	-0.371%		Missouri	2.609%
Missouri	33.137%	32.294%	2.609%		Delaware	2.669%

(continued)

U.S. AID FOR FAMILY PLANNING OVERSEAS

In 1973, with little controversy, Congress passed the Foreign Assistance Act (PL 93-189), forbidding the use of American foreign aid funding "to pay for the performance of abortions as a method of family planning or to motivate or coerce any person to practice abortions."

In December 1984, the Reagan Administration cut U.S. funding to the International Planned Parenthood Federation because it included abortion among the options recommended for controlling family size. In July 1985, the administration indicated that the United States would provide monies to organizations that advocated only "natural" or noncontraceptive methods of family planning.

TABLE 3.3 (Continued)

State	Percent unmarried, 1996-97	Percent unmarried, 1994-95	Percent change in percent unmarried, 1994-95 to 1996-97	Rank order of States by largest decline in percent unmarried, 1994-95 to 1996-97		
				Rank	State	Percent change
Montana	28.311%	25.989%	8.934%		Louisiana	2.684%
Nebraska	25.289%	24.546%	3.028%		Nebraska	3.028%
Nevada	39.550%	36.727%	7.686%		West Virginia	3.199%
New Hampshire	23.598%	22.159%	6.493%		Washington	3.335%
New Jersey	27.988%	27.872%	0.418%		Arkansas	3.962%
New Mexico	42.821%	42.111%	2.270%		Minnesota	4.104%
New York	39.403%	37.748%	4.384%		Alaska	4.220%
North Carolina	32.100%	31.645%	1.437%		Utah	4.336%
North Dakota	25.587%	23.253%	10.036%		New York	4.384%
Ohio	33.520%	32.972%	1.663%		Maine	4.469%
Oklahoma	31.682%	30.143%	5.105%		Hawaii	4.630%
Oregon	29.257%	28.798%	1.593%		Vermont	4.655%
Pennsylvania	32.544%	32.612%	-0.211%		Connecticut	4.872%
Rhode Island	33.202%	31.636%	4.949%		Iowa	4.908%
South Carolina	37.677%	37.140%	1.445%		Rhode Island	4.949%
South Dakota	30.306%	27.862%	8.772%		Kansas	5.004%
Tennessee	33.750%	33.249%	1.505%		Texas	5.042%
Texas	30.565%	29.437%	5.042%		Oklahoma	5.105%
Utah	16.388%	15.707%	4.336%		Kentucky	5.471%
Vermont	26.260%	25.092%	4.655%		New Hampshire	6.493%
Virginia	29.065%	29.235%	-0.583%		Nevada	7.686%
Washington	27.223%	26.345%	3.335%		South Dakota	8.772%
West Virginia	31.338%	30.367%	3.199%		Idaho	8.862%
Wisconsin	27.771%	27.270%	1.838%		Montana	8.934%
Wyoming	27.176%	26.937%	0.888%		North Dakota	10.036%
Puerto Rico	44.975%	37.153%	21.055%		Virgin Islands	1.988%
Virgin Islands	65.987%	64.701%	1.988%		American Samoa	4.332%
Guam	48.926%	46.496%	5.226%		Guam	5.226%
American Samoa	34.351%	32.925%	4.332%		Puerto Rico	21.055%

1/ Excludes data for Puerto Rico, Virgin Islands, Guam, and American Samoa.

Data for California, Nevada, and New York are those for which adjusted birth data were provided because the States changed their methodology or procedures for reporting the mother's marital status. Calculations for all other States were done on the basis of data files provided by each State to the National Center for Health Statistics (NCHS), which has tabulated the entire national birth file by mother's place of residence; see attached text.

NOTE: Separate tables are available from NCHS for the adjusted birth data for California, Nevada, and New York City.

Prepared in the Division of Vital Statistics, NCHS, from published birth data and special tabulations provided by California, Nevada, and New York City.

Source: Centers for Disease Control and Prevention, U.S. Department of Health and Human Services, Washington, DC, 1999

The following year, the Reagan Administration withheld $10 million in aid to the United Nations Fund for Population Activities (UNFPA, now called the United Nations Population Fund), the United Nations agency dedicated to limiting the world's population increase. Specifically, the administration charged UNFPA with helping the government of the People's Republic of China (PRC) carry out forced abortions and sterilizations (see also Chapter VIII). The $10 million was roughly equal to the UNFPA's annual spending in the PRC. Funding for UNFPA has been debated in Congress every year since 1985.

The "Mexico City Policy"

At the United Nations' population conference in Mexico City (1984), President Ronald Reagan announced that the United States would no longer support private family planning groups overseas that, with their own funds, performed or promoted abortion. In June 1991, the Supreme Court upheld the policy by refusing to hear the case *Planned Parenthood Federation of America v. Agency for International Development* (cert. denied, 498 U.S. 933).

When the International Planned Parenthood Federation (IPPF) refused to implement the Reagan restriction on their affiliates in developing countries, the administration withdrew U.S. funds from the IPPF. The Reagan restriction, though never enacted into law, was enforced as an executive order for almost a decade. When President Clinton took office in 1993, he revoked the "Mexico City policy" and restored the U.S. contribution to the UNFPA.

Many Americans agreed. A 1992 poll commissioned for the Population Crisis Committee (a non-profit organization dedicated to providing international contraception and reproductive health care, later renamed Population Action International) found that 58 percent of Americans supported the use of U.S. funds for family planning in developing countries. About 65 percent said that family planning aid should not be denied to organizations that provided information about abortion, and 67 percent indicated that foreign aid should not be used to promote anti-abortion policies internationally.

"Global Gag Rule"

Since 1994, opponents of family planning have introduced abortion-related language to a number of foreign aid measures. These lawmakers, led by Representative Christopher Smith (R-NJ), have sought to restrict U.S. aid to family planning groups that provide legal abortion services or advocate abortion rights in their countries. Family planning advocates liken this effort to the "Mexico City policy" (see above), calling it the "Global Gag Rule" because it limits free speech and the provision of abortion services. They argue that, for over twenty-five years, a law (see Foreign Assistance Act above) has already been in place that prohibits using U.S. funds for abortion services overseas. Opponents claim that the United States indirectly subsidizes the provision of abortion services, because it enables family planning groups involved in abortion and who receive U.S. aid to have that extra money to engage in abortion-related activities.

The "Global Gag Rule" Is Included in Law

For the first time, the "Global Gag Rule" was written into law for a year in the omnibus appropriations bill for FY 2000. In exchange for the release by Congress of $926 million in dues owed the United Nations, President Clinton agreed to restrictions on the $385 million appropriated for international family planning. Private organizations that performed or promoted abortion could not receive U.S. funds, as was the case under the "Mexico City policy." As part of the compromise, the president could waive the restrictions which would result in a 3 percent cut ($12.5 million) to be used in children's health programs overseas. In addition, Congress set a $15 million cap in foreign aid to those groups that lobbied for changes in their countries' abortion laws.

PARTIAL-BIRTH ABORTION

In 1995, for the first time since the Supreme Court ruling in *Roe v. Wade* (410 U.S. 113, 1973) legalizing abortion, Congress passed a law criminalizing the performance of an abortion. The Partial-Birth Abortion Ban Act (H.R. 1122), authored by Representative Charles Canady (R-FL) and Senator Bob Smith (R-NH), would impose criminal and civil penalties on any physician performing a partial-birth abortion.

There is no actual medical procedure known as partial-birth abortion. The term, created by abortion opponents, describes a technique known as intact dilation and evacuation (D&E) or dilation and extraction (D&X). The procedure is sometimes performed in abortions after 20 weeks of pregnancy and involves the partial delivery of a fetus, legs first, through the birth canal, followed by drainage of its skull. Physicians who perform this late-term abortion claim that it is done only in cases of severe fetal abnormality or when continuation of the pregnancy seriously jeopardizes the woman's health.

The precise number of late-term abortions is unknown. According to the Centers for Disease Control and Prevention (CDC), 1.2 million abortions were performed in 1996, the last year for which figures are available. About 1.5 percent of these abortions were performed after 20 weeks of pregnancy (see Chapter IV, Table 4.1); however, not all such late-term abortions were done through D&E or D&X.

Stanley K. Henshaw, in "Abortion Incidence and Services in the United States, 1995-1996" (*Family Planning Perspectives*, vol. 30, no. 6, November/December 1998), reported that, in 1996, D&X accounted for about 0.03 to 0.05 percent of the nearly 1.37 million abortions counted by the Alan Guttmacher Institute (AGI). The AGI count is generally higher than that of the CDC because it directly surveys abortion providers (see Chapter IV).

Proponents of the bill describe the procedure as brutal and homicidal. "A living, breathing child," Senator Bob Smith claimed during a Senate debate, adding, "That little body, 90 percent through the birth canal. Three inches from the protection of the Constitution of the United States."

Opponents of the bill charge that anti-abortion legislators are intentionally trying to shock and horrify the public and open a debate on banning all abortions. Senator Barbara Boxer (R-CA), rebutting Senator Smith's arguments, asked her colleagues to think of the ban in terms of their own daughters. "Women will die," she said, "And they will be our babies that we raised. Our babies." Opponents further point out that the bill represents the regulation of a medical procedure and does not permit a physician the choice of the best care to preserve a woman's life or health, a direct conflict with the principles established in *Roe*. In April 1996, President Clinton vetoed H.R. 1122.

The National Abortion Federation (NAF), the professional association of abortion providers in the United States and Canada, initially estimated that about 450 late-term abortions are performed a year, or 0.03 percent of the yearly total. In September 1996, after the media reported that the numbers were far greater, the NAF attempted to obtain a revised estimate. Vicki Saporta, NAF's executive director, while appearing before the Joint Hearing of the House and Senate Committee on the Judiciary on March 11, 1997, reported,

Because of the absence of national statistics, because [NAF is] not aware of every doctor who performs intact D&E (some of whom may not elect to come forward for fear of harassment or even violence), and because of questions raised by physicians regarding what precisely qualifies as an intact D&E, ... an accurate estimate could not be obtained.

Saporta added that what NAF knew was that statistics collected by the Centers for Disease Control and Prevention and the Alan Guttmacher Institute show that 89 percent of all abortions are done during the first trimester, when intact D&E is not used.

Representative Charles Canady reintroduced the bill in January 1997. In February 1997, Ron Fitzsimmons, executive director of the National Coalition of Abortion Providers (NCAP) acknowledged that he had "lied through his teeth" in a 1995 television interview when he said that partial-birth abortions are performed rarely. He had also insisted at the interview that the procedure is performed only to save the mother's life or to abort severely malformed fetuses. Fitzsimmons admitted he had initially lied because he feared he would hurt the cause of abortion if the truth were told; now, he was convinced the abortion debate should be based on truth.

Fitzsimmons further revealed that in a great majority of cases, the procedure is performed on healthy women five months pregnant and with healthy fetuses. While the pro-choice movement dismissed Fitzsimmons' confession as his personal problem and not to be construed to represent the whole movement, pro-life leaders in Congress capitalized on the "weakened credibility" of their opponents by giving top priority to Canady's bill.

In May 1997, Senator Rick Santorum (R-PA) and the Senate's only physician, Bill Frist (R-TN), succeeded in obtaining the American Medical Association's (AMA) endorsement of the bill in exchange for some amendments to the proposed ban (see Chapter XV.) This was the second time the AMA had ever supported the criminalization of a medical procedure. (The first time was in 1996 when it asked Congress to outlaw female genital mutilation, or female circumcision.) Abortion rights advocates accused the AMA of playing politics in the hope of gaining certain concessions when the issues of Medicare, managed care, and malpractice laws came up for legislation in Congress.

For the second time, in October 1997, President Clinton vetoed the Partial-Birth Abortion Ban Act. The amended bill included an exemption to save the pregnant woman's life, but not an exemption for women whose health is seriously threatened by carrying their pregnancies to term.

On October 21, 1999, for the third time in three years, the Senate again passed the Partial-Birth Abortion Ban Act (S. 1692) by a vote of 63 to 34. The act amends the federal criminal code to prohibit any physician from knowingly performing a partial-birth abortion in or affecting interstate or foreign commerce, unless it is necessary to save the mother's life that is endangered by a physical disorder, illness, or injury. On October 25, 1999, the bill was received in the House of Representatives for consideration. (See Chapters XV and XVI for the arguments for and against the 1997 version of the bill.)

CHAPTER IV

ABORTION IN THE UNITED STATES
A STATISTICAL STUDY

WHO COLLECTS ABORTION DATA?

There are two major sources for abortion statistics. The Centers for Disease Control and Prevention (CDC) of the U.S. Department of Health and Human Services collects abortion statistics for the U.S. government. The Alan Guttmacher Institute (AGI), a private organization that studies reproductive health issues and strongly believes that abortion is an acceptable option, conducts periodic surveys of abortions performed not only in the United States but also all over the world (see Chapter VIII).

The CDC compiles abortion information collected by state health departments, hospitals, and other medical facilities. These data come from 52 reporting areas — the 50 states, the District of Columbia, and New York City. On the other hand, the Alan Guttmacher Institute directly contacts all known abortion providers for its periodic surveys. In addition, the Institute follows up its inquiries by letter and telephone. The AGI data, in the whole, are considered to be the most accurate available.

The total number of abortions reported to the CDC by the individual states is generally lower than that collected by the AGI. The CDC believes that the number of abortions performed in physicians' offices is probably underreported more often than those done in hospitals and other medical facilities. Since most abortions in physicians' offices are usually performed in the early stages of pregnancy, the CDC early-abortion counts are very likely less than the actual numbers.

HOW MANY ABORTIONS?

CDC Data

The latest CDC survey of legal induced abortions are compiled in "Abortion Surveillance — United States, 1996," *Morbidity and Mortality Weekly Report, CDC Surveillance Summaries,* vol. 48, no. SS-4, July 30, 1999. For 1996, 1.22 million abortions were reported, a 14.5 percent drop from the 1.43 million reported in 1990 (Table 4.1 and Figure 4.1).

The CDC began its abortion surveillance in 1969, two years after Colorado became the first state to liberalize its abortion statute. From 1970 through 1982, the reported number of abortions increased each year, with the largest percentage of increase occurring between 1970 and 1971. From 1976 through 1982, the annual increase slowed and then dropped slightly in 1983. From 1983 through 1990, the number of abortions increased again, with year-to-year fluctuations of 5 percent or less. The annual number of abortions has decreased since 1990 (the year in which the number of abortions was the highest reported by the CDC). (See Figure 4.1 and Table 4.2.)

The *abortion ratio* is the number of legal abortions for every 1,000 live births in a given year. In 1996, the abortion ratio was 314 per 1,000 live births, or about one abortion for every three babies born alive (Table 4.2).

The abortion ratio increased steadily from 1970 through 1980, and then leveled off for most of the

Characteristic	1972	1973	1976	1980	1985	1990	1992	1993	1994	1995	1996
Reported no. of legal abortions	586,760	615,831	988,267	1,297,606	1,328,570	1,429,577	1,359,145	1,330,414	1,267,415	1,210,883	1,221,585
					Percent distribution*						
Residence											
In-state	56.2	74.8	90.0	92.6	92.4	91.8	92.0	91.4	91.5	91.7	91.9
Out-of-state	43.8	25.2	10.0	7.4	7.6	8.2	8.0	8.6	8.5	8.3	8.1
Age (yrs)											
≤19	32.6	32.7	32.1	29.2	26.3	22.4	20.1	20.0	20.2	20.1	20.3
20–24	32.5	32.0	33.3	35.5	34.7	33.2	34.5	34.4	33.5	32.5	31.9
≥25	34.9	35.3	34.6	35.3	39.0	44.4	45.4	45.6	46.3	47.4	47.9
Race											
White	77.0	72.5	66.6	69.9	66.7	64.8	61.5	60.9	60.5	59.5	59.1
Black	23.0[†]	27.5[†]	33.4[†]	30.1[†]	29.8	31.8	33.9	34.9	34.7	35.0	35.2
Other[§]	—	—	—	—	3.5	3.4	4.6	4.2	4.8	5.5	5.7
Hispanic origin											
Hispanic	—	—	—	—	—	9.8	15.2	14.7	14.5	15.4	16.1
Non-Hispanic	—	—	—	—	—	90.2	84.8	85.3	85.5	84.6	83.9
Marital Status											
Married	29.7	27.4	24.6	23.1	19.3	21.7	20.8	20.4	19.9	19.7	19.6
Unmarried	70.3	72.6	75.4	76.9	80.7	78.3	79.2	79.6	80.1	80.3	80.4
No. of live births[¶]											
0	49.4	48.6	47.7	58.4	56.3	49.2	45.9	46.3	46.2	45.2	44.2
1	18.2	18.8	20.7	19.4	21.6	24.4	25.9	26.0	25.9	26.5	26.8
2	13.3	14.2	15.4	13.7	14.5	16.9	18.0	17.8	17.8	18.0	18.4
3	8.7	8.7	8.3	5.3	5.1	6.1	6.7	6.6	6.7	6.8	7.0
≥4	10.4	9.7	7.9	3.2	2.5	3.4	3.5	3.3	3.4	3.5	3.6
Type of procedure											
Curettage	88.6	88.4	92.8	95.5	97.5	98.8	98.9	99.0	99.1	98.9	98.8
Suction curettage	65.2	74.9	82.6	89.8	94.6	96.0	97.0	96.4	96.5	96.6	96.5
Sharp curettage	23.4	13.5	10.2	5.7	2.9	2.8	1.9	2.6	2.6	2.3	2.3
Intrauterine instillation	10.4	10.4	6.0	3.1	1.7	0.8	0.7	0.6	0.5	0.5	0.4
Other**	1.0	1.2	1.2	1.4	0.8	0.4	0.4	0.4	0.4	0.6	0.8
Weeks of gestation											
≤ 8	34.0	36.1	47.0	51.7	50.3	51.6	52.1	52.3	53.7	54.0	54.6
≤6	—	—	—	—	—	—	14.3[††]	14.7[§§]	15.7[¶¶]	15.7[¶¶]	16.4***
7	—	—	—	—	—	—	15.6[††]	16.2[§§]	16.5[¶¶]	17.1[¶¶]	17.4***
8	—	—	—	—	—	—	22.2[††]	21.6[§§]	21.6[¶¶]	21.2[¶¶]	20.9***
9–10	30.7	29.4	28.1	26.2	26.6	25.3	24.2	24.4	23.5	23.1	22.6
11–12	17.5	17.9	14.4	12.2	12.5	11.7	12.0	11.6	10.9	10.9	11.0
13–15	8.4	6.9	4.5	5.1	5.9	6.4	6.0	6.3	6.3	6.3	6.0
16–20	8.2	8.0	5.1	3.9	3.9	4.0	4.2	4.1	4.3	4.3	4.3
≥21	1.2	1.7	0.9	0.8	0.8	1.0	1.5	1.3	1.3	1.4	1.5

* Based on known values in data from all areas reporting a given characteristic with no more than 15% unknowns. The number of areas reporting a given characteristic varied. For 1996, the number of areas included for residence was 45; age, 45; race, 35; ethnicity, 23; marital status, 34; the number of live births, 39; type of procedure, 41; and weeks of gestation, 40.
[†] Reported as black and other races.
[§] Includes all other races.
[¶] For 1972–1976, data indicate number of living children.
** Includes hysterotomy and hysterectomy, medical (nonsurgical) procedures, and procedures reported as "other."
[††] Data are for 36 of 39 areas reporting weeks of gestation.
[§§] Data are for 38 of 41 areas reporting weeks of gestation.
[¶¶] Data are for 38 of 40 areas reporting weeks of gestation.
*** Data are for 37 of 40 areas reporting weeks of gestation.
—Not available.

NOTE: Among the charts selected from the "Abortion Surveillance — United States, 1996," prepared by the Centers for Disease Control and Prevention (CDC), there are small differences in some of the statistics. This is because not all states reported on the same data.

Source: "Abortion Surveillance — United States, 1996," *Morbidity and Mortality Weekly Report*, vol. 48, no SS-4, July 30, 1999

next decade. The CDC reported the highest ratio (364 per 1,000 live births) in 1984. Since 1987, the abortion ratio has declined steadily, increasing slightly from 311 in 1995. Nonetheless, despite this slight increase, the ratios for 1995 and 1996 were the lowest recorded since 1976. (See Figure 4.1 and Table 4.2.)

The *abortion rate* refers to the number of abortions performed per 1,000 women ages 15 to 44 years (prime child-bearing years). The abortion rate rose from 5 abortions per 1,000 women in 1970 to 25 per 1,000 in 1980. From 1981 through 1992, the rate remained stable at 23 to 24 abortions per 1,000 women. The abortion rate declined to 21 in 1994 and dropped another point to 20 in 1995 and 1996, the lowest rate recorded since 1975. (See Figure 4.1 and Table 4.2.)

The CDC suggests that the overall decreasing abortion rates may be due to several factors.

• Decreasing number of unplanned pregnancies.

• Reduced access to abortion services.

• Changes in contraceptive practices, including an increased use of contraception, particularly an increased use of condoms among young people.

- A shift in the age distribution of women of child-bearing age towards the older and less fertile ages.

Alan Guttmacher Institute Data

The Alan Guttmacher Institute (AGI) started collecting data on abortion in 1974, the year after the *Roe v. Wade* ruling (see Chapter II). Since the AGI directly surveys abortion providers, its abortion counts have been generally higher than those reported by the CDC. For 1996, the AGI counted 1.37 million abortions, about 11 percent more than those reported by the CDC. The abortion rate was 22.9 abortions per 1,000 women ages 15 to 44 (Figure 4.2), compared to the CDC's count of 20 abortions per 1,000 women of the same age group.

CHARACTERISTICS OF WOMEN SEEKING ABORTION

In 1996, about half (52.2 percent) of the women who had abortions were less than 25 years old. Most were White, unmarried, and in the first trimester (period of three months) of pregnancy. (See Table 4.1.)

Age

One-third (32.1 percent) of all abortions were obtained by women ages 20 to 24 years. One-

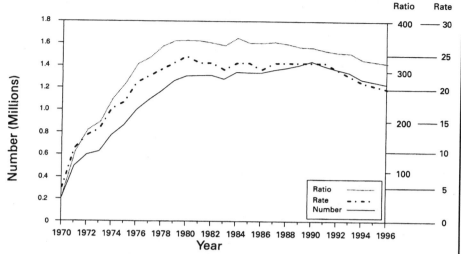

FIGURE 4.1

Number, ratio,* and rate† of legal abortions performed, by year — United States, 1970–1996

*Number of abortions per 1,000 live births.
†Number of abortions per 1,000 women 15–44 years of age.

Source: "Abortion Surveillance — United States, 1996," *Morbidity and Mortality Weekly Report*, vol. 48, no SS-4, July 30, 1999

TABLE 4.2

Number, ratio,* and rate† of legal abortions and source of reporting, by year — United States, 1970–1996

Year	Total no. of legal abortions	Ratio	Rate	Central health agency§	Hospital/Facilities¶
1970	193,491	52	5	18	7
1971	485,816	137	11	19	7
1972	586,760	180	13	21	8
1973	615,831	196	14	26	26
1974	763,476	242	17	37	15
1975	854,853	272	18	39	13
1976	988,267	312	21	41	11
1977	1,079,430	325	22	46	6
1978	1,157,776	347	23	48	4
1979	1,251,921	358	24	47	5
1980	1,297,606	359	25	47	5
1981	1,300,760	358	24	46	6
1982	1,303,980	354	24	46	6
1983	1,268,987	349	23	46	6
1984	1,333,521	364	24	44	8
1985	1,328,570	354	24	44	8
1986	1,328,112	354	23	43	9
1987	1,353,671	356	24	45	7
1988	1,371,285	352	24	45	7
1989	1,396,658	346	24	45	7
1990	1,429,577	345	24	46	6
1991	1,388,937	339	24	47	5
1992	1,359,145	335	23	47	5
1993	1,330,414	334	22	47	5
1994	1,267,415	321	21	47	5
1995	1,210,883	311	20	48	4
1996	1,221,585	314**	20	48	4

*Number of abortions per 1,000 live births.
†Number of abortions per 1,000 women aged 15–44 years.
§Abortion data reported by central health agencies, which include state health departments and the health departments of New York City and the District of Columbia.
¶Abortion data reported by hospitals and/or other medical facilities in state.
**Beginning in 1996, the ratio is based on births reported by CDC's National Center for Health Statistics.

Source: "Abortion Surveillance — United States, 1996," *Morbidity and Mortality Weekly Report*, vol. 48, no SS-4, July 30, 1999

quarter (23.3 percent) were obtained by those ages 25 to 29, and about one-fifth (19.2 percent) were obtained by 15- to 19-year-olds. Less than 1 percent were obtained by women younger than 15 years. (See Table 4.3.)

In 1996, teenagers and women 40 and older had the highest ratio of abortions to live births. Although less than 1 percent of all abortions were obtained by teenagers younger than 15 years of age, their abortion ratio (723 per 1,000 live births) was the highest. This means that within this age group, while the number of abortions (6,257) was small, of those adolescents who got pregnant, a very large percentage chose abortion. (See Chapter V for a full discussion of teen pregnancy and abortion.) For the oldest women (ages 40 to 44), the abortion ratio was 376 per 1,000 live births. (See Table 4.4 and Figure 4.3.) Women 40 years and over who selected abortion over delivering a child might not have wanted to raise a child in their later years or might have been concerned about the increased health risks of a late-life pregnancy to both mother and child.

For women in most age groups, the abortion ratio increased from 1974 through the early 1980s. It declined thereafter, especially for the youngest and oldest groups (Figure 4.3). From 1995 to 1996, although the abortion ratios for women younger than 15 and those ages 15 to 19 increased slightly, these ratios remained the lowest ever recorded for these age groups. The abortion ratio for the women with the highest fertility rate (ages 20-34) has remained stable since the mid-1980s. (See Table 4.4 for the 1996 abortion ratios for the different age groups.)

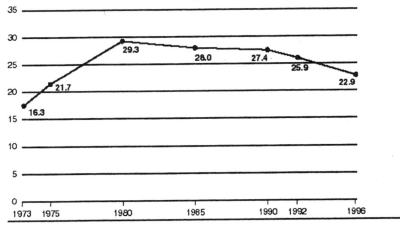

FIGURE 4.2

The number of abortions per 1,000 women aged 15–44, by year

Source: Reproduced with the permission of The Alan Guttmacher Institute from "Induced Abortion," *Facts in Brief*, New York, NY, 1998

TABLE 4.3

Reported legal abortions, by known race, age group, and marital status of women who obtained abortions — United States, 1996

| Age group (yrs)/ Marital status | Race | | | | Total | |
| | White | | Black/Other | | | |
	No.	%	No.	%	No.	%
Age group						
<15	2,019	0.6	2,500	1.0	4,519	0.8
15–19	69,406	20.0	43,073	17.9	112,479	19.2
20–24	109,177	31.5	79,378	33.0	188,555	32.1
25–29	77,783	22.4	59,270	24.7	137,053	23.3
30–34	48,371	13.9	33,950	14.1	82,321	14.0
35–39	30,403	8.8	17,223	7.2	47,626	8.1
≥40	9,631	2.8	5,036	2.1	14,667	2.5
Total*	**346,790**	**100.0**	**240,430**	**100.0**	**587,220**	**100.0**
Marital status						
Married	68,398	23.2	34,294	17.0	102,692	20.7
Unmarried	226,303	76.8	167,126	83.0	393,429	79.3
Total†	**294,701**	**100.0**	**201,420**	**100.0**	**496,121**	**100.0**

*Data from 34 states and New York City; excludes four states where unknown race was >15%.
†Data from 29 states and New York City; excludes six states where unknown race or marital status was >15%.

Source: "Abortion Surveillance — United States, 1996," *Morbidity and Mortality Weekly Report*, vol. 48, no SS-4, July 30, 1999

TABLE 4.4

Reported legal abortions, by age group of women who obtained abortions — United States, 1996

	\<15		15–19		20–24		25–29		30–34		35–39		≥40		Unknown		Total†	
	No.	%	No.	%	No.	%	No.	%	No.	%	No.	%	No.	%	No.	%	No.	%
Total	6,257	0.8	160,008	19.4	261,303	31.6	189,897	23.0	115,158	13.9	67,092	8.1	20,695	2.5	5,563	0.7	825,973	100.0
Ratio	723		415		355		227		165		220		376				271	
Rate	2		22		38		26		14		8		2				16	

Source: "Abortion Surveillance — United States, 1996," *Morbidity and Mortality Weekly Report*, vol. 48, no SS-4, July 30, 1999

FIGURE 4.3

Abortion ratio,* by age group† of women who obtained a legal abortion — United States, 1974–1996

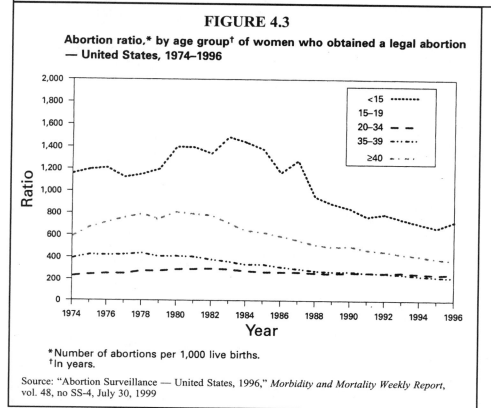

*Number of abortions per 1,000 live births.
†In years.

Source: "Abortion Surveillance — United States, 1996," *Morbidity and Mortality Weekly Report*, vol. 48, no SS-4, July 30, 1999

Over the past several years, the age at which women seek an abortion has remained fairly stable. In 1996, the abortion rate was highest for women ages 20 to 24 (38 per 1,000 women) and lowest for women less than 15 years and women 40 and older (2 per 1,000 women). (See Table 4.4.)

Race and Ethnicity

More than half (57 percent) of those who had an abortion were White, while one-third were Black (34 percent), and 5.5 percent were other races. The abortion ratio for Black women (555 per 1,000 live births) was about 2.7 times the ratio for White women (202 per 1,000 live births). Similarly, the abortion rate for Black women (31 per 1,000 women 15 to 44 years old) was approximately 2.6 times the rate for White women (12 per 1,000 women 15 to 44 years old). (See Table 4.5.)

For Hispanic women* (who may be of any race), the abortion ratio was only slightly lower than that for non-Hispanic women (276 versus 282 per 1,000 live births). However, the abortion rate for Hispanic women was higher than that for non-Hispanic women (20 versus 15 abortions per 1,000 women 15 to 44 years old). (See Table 4.6.) For women in all age groups, fertility was higher among Hispanic than non-Hispanic women.

Marital Status

Marital status was categorized as married or unmarried. The married-women category included those who were separated, while the unmarried-

---

* According to the CDC, its 1996 abortion data were based on geographic areas that represented approximately 34 percent of all Hispanic women of reproductive age. Hence, the number, ratio, and rate of abortions might not represent the overall Hispanic population.

TABLE 4.5

Reported legal abortions, by race of women who obtained abortions and state of occurrence — selected states,* United States, 1996

State	White No.	White %	Black No.	Black %	Other No.	Other %	Unknown No.	Unknown %	Total† No.	Total† %
Alabama	7,200	52.1	6,318	45.7	181	1.3	127	0.9	13,826	100.0
Arizona	8,466	76.9	553	5.0	837	7.6	1,160	10.5	11,016	100.0
Arkansas	3,745	63.7	1,992	33.9	92	1.6	53	0.9	5,882	100.0
Georgia	15,734	44.0	18,157	50.7	945	2.6	954	2.7	35,790	100.0
Hawaii	1,311	26.7	134	2.7	3,127	63.6	344	7.0	4,916	100.0
Idaho	971	95.0	9	0.9	39	3.8	3	0.3	1,022	100.0
Indiana	8,773	65.8	3,357	25.2	237	1.8	974	7.3	13,341	100.0
Kansas	8,215	76.9	1,821	17.0	595	5.6	54	0.5	10,685	100.0
Kentucky	5,183	74.0	1,397	20.0	288	4.1	132	1.9	7,000	100.0
Louisiana	5,663	47.7	5,925§	49.9	—	—	277	2.3	11,865	100.0
Maine	2,420	92.5	28	1.1	103	3.9	64	2.4	2,615	100.0
Maryland	5,033	40.7	6,384	51.6	745	6.0	201	1.6	12,363	100.0
Minnesota	10,636	74.9	1,836	12.9	1,444	10.2	277	2.0	14,193	100.0
Mississippi	1,340	31.9	2,805	66.7	54	1.3	7	0.2	4,206	100.0
Missouri	7,271	62.5	3,839	33.0	472	4.1	47	0.4	11,629	100.0
Montana	2,375	86.0	10	0.4	201	7.3	177	6.4	2,763	100.0
Nevada	5,726	82.2	527	7.6	373	5.4	339	4.9	6,965	100.0
New Jersey	11,250	35.3	14,235	44.7	5,035	15.8	1,340	4.2	31,860	100.0
New Mexico	4,315	85.7	165	3.3	553	11.0	0	0.0	5,033	100.0
New York City	42,267	38.7	53,338	48.8	4,681	4.3	9,045	8.3	109,331	100.0
North Carolina	17,215	51.3	13,715	40.9	1,890	5.6	734	2.2	33,554	100.0
North Dakota	1,162	90.0	19	1.5	109	8.4	1	0.1	1,291	100.0
Ohio	22,438	61.4	11,563	31.7	1,522	4.2	1,007	2.8	36,530	100.0
Oregon	11,913	86.5	738	5.4	966	7.0	150	1.1	13,767	100.0
Pennsylvania	22,102	58.2	14,727	38.8	1,144	3.0	31	0.1	38,004	100.0
Rhode Island	4,306	79.2	730	13.4	294	5.4	107	2.0	5,437	100.0
South Carolina	5,086	54.5	4,037	43.3	202	2.2	1	0.0	9,326	100.0
South Dakota	796	88.3	20	2.2	85	9.4	0	0.0	901	100.0
Tennessee	10,441	58.0	7,018	39.0	466	2.6	64	0.4	17,989	100.0
Texas	64,064	70.0	19,591	21.4	4,140	4.5	3,675	4.0	91,470	100.0
Utah	2,936	80.7	66	1.8	388	10.7	249	6.8	3,639	100.0
Vermont	2,074	97.0	21	1.0	40	1.9	4	0.2	2,139	100.0
Virginia	14,205	55.1	9,687	37.6	1,585	6.2	293	1.1	25,770	100.0
West Virginia	2,202	89.1	234	9.5	34	1.4	0	0.0	2,470	100.0
Wisconsin¶	9,561	72.9	2,835	21.6	703**	5.4	9**	0.1	13,108	100.0
Total	**348,395**	**57.0**	**207,831**	**34.0**	**33,570**	**5.5**	**21,900**	**3.6**	**611,696**	**100.0**
Ratio††	202		555§§		360§§				267	
Rate¶¶	12		31***		25***				15	

*Data from 34 states and New York City; excludes six areas where unknown race was >15%
†Percentages might not add to 100.0 because of rounding.
§Reported as black and "other" races.
¶Includes residents only.
**Women of some "other" races are included with "unknown."
††Calculated as the number of legal abortions obtained by women of a given race per 1,000 live births to women of the same race for these states. For each state, data for women of unknown race were distributed according to the known racial distribution for that state.
§§Ratios for black and "other" races exclude Louisiana because abortions for blacks and others were grouped together.
¶¶Calculated as the number of legal abortions obtained by women of a given race per 1,000 women aged 15–44 years of the same race for these states. For each state, data for women of unknown race were distributed according to the known racial distribution for that state.
***Rates for black and "other" races exclude Louisiana because abortions for blacks and others were grouped together.
— Not reported.

Source: "Abortion Surveillance — United States, 1996," *Morbidity and Mortality Weekly Report*, vol. 48, no SS-4, July 30, 1999

women category also included those divorced and widowed.

In 1996, as in the past, unmarried women comprised the greatest proportion of those who had an abortion (78 percent). The Alan Guttmacher Institute, during its periodic surveys, finds that women who are separated from their husbands are twice as likely as all women to have an abortion, while married women are much less likely to do so. In 1996, the abortion ratio for single women (655 per 1,000 live births) was about eight times the ratio for married women (78 per 1,000 live births). This is not surprising since teenagers and young adults, who had high abortion ratios, were more likely to be single.

TABLE 4.6

Reported legal abortions, by Hispanic ethnicity of women who obtained abortions and state of occurrence — selected states,* United States, 1996

State	Hispanic		Non-Hispanic		Unknown		Total†	
	No.	%	No.	%	No.	%	No.	%
Alabama	241	1.7	12,985	93.9	600	4.3	13,826	100.0
Arizona	2,693	24.4	7,163	65.0	1,160	10.5	11,016	100.0
Arkansas	47	0.8	5,457	92.8	378	6.4	5,882	100.0
Georgia	760	2.1	33,449	93.5	1,581	4.4	35,790	100.0
Idaho	96	9.4	918	89.8	8	0.8	1,022	100.0
Kansas	510	4.8	9,891	92.6	284	2.7	10,685	100.0
Minnesota	366	2.6	13,550	95.5	277	2.0	14,193	100.0
Mississippi	13	0.3	4,184	99.5	9	0.2	4,206	100.0
Missouri	211	1.8	11,043	95.0	375	3.2	11,629	100.0
New Jersey	5,930	18.6	24,602	77.2	1,328	4.2	31,860	100.0
New Mexico	2,195	43.6	2,838	56.4	0	0.0	5,033	100.0
New York City	29,237	26.7	66,716	61.0	13,378	12.2	109,331	100.0
North Dakota	25	1.9	1,142	88.5	124	9.6	1,291	100.0
Ohio	542	1.5	34,981	95.8	1,007	2.8	36,530	100.0
Oregon	991	7.2	12,727	92.4	49	0.4	13,767	100.0
Pennsylvania	1,391	3.7	36,591	96.3	22	0.1	38,004	100.0
South Carolina	121	1.3	9,203	98.7	2	0.0	9,326	100.0
South Dakota	25	2.8	876	97.2	0	0.0	901	100.0
Tennessee	191	1.1	17,769	98.8	29	0.2	17,989	100.0
Texas	27,157	29.7	60,638	66.3	3,675	4.0	91,470	100.0
Utah	397	10.9	3,173	87.2	69	1.9	3,639	100.0
Vermont	8	0.4	2,124	99.3	7	0.3	2,139	100.0
Wisconsin§	622	4.7	12,486	95.3	0	0.0	13,108	100.0
Total	**73,769**	**15.3**	**384,506**	**79.7**	**24,362**	**5.0**	**482,637**	**100.0**
Ratio¶	276		282				281	
Rate**	20		15				15	

*Data from 22 states and New York City; excludes 15 areas where unknown Hispanic ethnicity was >15%.

†Percentages might not add to 100.0 because of rounding.

§Includes residents only.

¶Calculated as the number of legal abortions obtained by women of a given ethnicity per 1,000 live births to women of the same ethnicity for these states. For each state, data for women of unknown ethnicity were distributed according to the known ethnicity distribution for that state.

**Calculated as the number of legal abortions obtained by women of a given ethnicity per 1,000 women aged 15–44 years of the same ethnicity for these states. For each state, data for women of unknown ethnicity were distributed according to the known ethnicity distribution for that state.

Source: "Abortion Surveillance — United States, 1996," *Morbidity and Mortality Weekly Report*, vol. 48, no SS-4, July 30, 1999

Contraceptive Use Prior to Pregnancy

A woman is fertile (capable of becoming pregnant) for almost half her life. She can get pregnant (once menstruation starts) years before she desires children. And years after she has had children, a woman continues to be fertile until menopause (occurring typically between the ages of 45 and 50).

Stanley K. Henshaw and Kathryn Kost, in "Abortion Patients in 1994-1995: Characteristics and Contraceptive Use (*Family Planning Perspectives*, vol. 28, no. 4, July/August 1996), reported that 6 in 10 (58 percent) abortion patients experienced contraceptive failures during the month in which they got pregnant. About 31 percent had used contraception before but not during the month they got pregnant, and 11 percent had never used contraception. Interestingly enough, similar proportions of women younger than 18 (55 percent) and those 18 and older (57 to 59 percent) were using contraception during the month they got pregnant. However, nearly twice as many abortion patients younger than 18 (19 percent) as those older than 18 (10 to 12 percent) had never used contraception.

Previous Live Births and Previous Abortions

In 1996, almost half (44.2 percent) of those who had an abortion had never had a live birth, while one-quarter (26.8 percent) had one previous live birth (Table 4.1). The abortion ratio was highest for women who had had three previous live births (315 abortions per 1,000 live births) and lowest for women who had had one previous live birth (223 per 1,000 live births).

More than half (53.6 percent) of women who obtained an abortion had never had an abortion before, while about one-fourth (26.4 percent) had had at least one previous abortion (Table 4.7). Statistically, as more women have first abortions, the proportion of women who have repeat abortions steadily increases each year.

TABLE 4.7

Reported legal abortions, by number of previous legal induced abortions and state of occurrence — United States, 1996

	No. of previous induced abortions										Total[†]	
	0		1		2		≥3		Unknown			
	No.	%	No.	%	No.	%	No.	%	No.	%	No.	%
Total	356,640	53.6	175,623	26.4	72,979	11.0	47,090	7.1	12,999	2.0	665,331	100.0

Source: "Abortion Surveillance — United States, 1996," *Morbidity and Mortality Weekly Report*, vol. 48, no SS-4, July 30, 1999

WHY DO WOMEN HAVE ABORTIONS?

Unplanned Pregnancy

Each year, more than six million women in the United States become pregnant. For about three million of these women, the pregnancies are unplanned (accidental). Nearly one and a half million of these women will obtain an abortion. According to the Alan Guttmacher Institute (AGI), approximately 14,000 women obtain an abortion because they have become pregnant as a result of rape or incest.

The AGI, based on its research of abortion all over the world, has found that "[t]hroughout the world, the reasons women give for deciding to end an unplanned pregnancy are similar." In *Sharing Responsibility: Women, Society and Abortion Worldwide* (New York and Washington, DC, 1999), the AGI lists the reasons generally given by women for choosing abortion. The woman

- Does not want any children at all, she wants to postpone having another child, or she has all the children that she wants.

- Cannot afford a baby now.

- Wants to complete her education or to work in order to help support her family.

- Has problems with a relationship or wants to avoid single parenthood.

- Thinks she is not mature enough to raise a child.

- Does not want her parents and/or others to know she is pregnant.

- Has health problems, such as AIDS, or she fears that the fetus is impaired.

- Is a victim of rape or incest.

WHERE DO WOMEN GO FOR AN ABORTION?

In State of Residence

In 1996, as in previous years, the largest numbers of abortions were performed in the most populated states — California (280,180), New York (152,991), and Texas (91,470). Together with Florida (80,040) and Illinois (53,613), these states accounted for more than half (54 percent) of all legal abortions in the United States. The fewest abortions were performed in Wyoming (208), South Dakota (901), Idaho (1,022), and North Dakota (1,291) (Table 4.8). For women whose state of residence was reported, about 92 percent had their abortion in the state where they lived.

Out of State

The percentage of abortions obtained by out-of-state residents ranged from 49.9 percent in the District of Columbia to less than 1 percent in Hawaii (Table 4.8). Abortion rates by state of occurrence do not necessarily reflect the number of abortions obtained by residents. Many women are forced to travel out of state for abortions because of a lack of providers or because of restrictive laws,

TABLE 4.8

Reported number,* ratio,[†] and rate[§] of legal abortions and percentage of abortions obtained by out-of-state residents,[¶] by state of occurrence — United States, 1996

State	Total no. of legal abortions	Ratio	Rate	Percentage of legal abortions obtained by out-of-state residents
Alabama	13,826	229	14	14.6
Alaska	2,139	213	15	0.8
Arizona	11,016	146	11	1.3
Arkansas	5,882	162	11	9.3
California	280,180**	519	39	—
Colorado	9,710	174	11	10.2
Connecticut	14,094	317	20	3.7
Delaware	4,482	441	26	—
Dist. of Columbia	13,674	—[††]	—[§§]	49.9
Florida	80,040	423	27	—
Georgia	35,790	314	20	9.4
Hawaii	4,916	267	19	0.3
Idaho	1,022	55	4	5.9
Illinois	53,613	293	20	7.2
Indiana	13,341	160	10	3.5
Iowa	7,602[¶]	205	12	—
Kansas	10,685	292	19	40.9
Kentucky	7,000	133	8	20.6
Louisiana	11,865	182	12	—
Maine	2,615	190	9	2.9
Maryland	12,363	173	10	5.6
Massachusetts	29,293	365	21	5.9
Michigan	30,208	226	14	4.3
Minnesota	14,193	223	13	9.2
Mississippi	4,206	103	7	5.3
Missouri	11,629	158	10	10.9
Montana	2,763	255	15	16.7
Nebraska	5,214	224	14	19.8
Nevada	6,965	267	20	11.4
New Hampshire	2,300[¶]	158	8	—
New Jersey	31,860	279	18	2.2
New Mexico	5,033	185	13	4.3
New York	152,991	580	37	—
City	109,331***	889	—	6.1[†††]
State	43,660	310	—	4.9[†††]
North Carolina	33,554	321	20	10.8
North Dakota	1,291	155	9	33.2
Ohio	36,530	241	15	7.4
Oklahoma	6,769[¶]	147	10	—
Oregon	13,767	315	20	12.2
Pennsylvania	38,004	256	15	4.9
Rhode Island	5,437	430	24	18.5
South Carolina	9,326	182	11	6.2
South Dakota	901	86	6	22.8
Tennessee	17,989	244	15	18.9
Texas	91,470	277	21	4.3
Utah	3,639	86	8	9.8
Vermont	2,139	316	16	20.9
Virginia	25,770	279	16	5.8
Washington	26,138	335	21	4.7
West Virginia	2,470	119	6	12.8
Wisconsin	13,673	204	12	4.1
Wyoming	208	33	2	6.3
Total	**1,221,585**	**314**	**20**	**8.1**

*Abortion data reported by central health agencies unless otherwise specified.
[†]Abortions per 1,000 live births. Number of live births was obtained from CDC's National Center for Health Statistics (7).
[§]Abortions per 1,000 women aged 15–44 years. The number of women in this age group was obtained from the U.S. Department of Commerce, Bureau of the Census (special unpublished tabulations).
[¶]Based on number of abortions for which residence of women was known.
**CDC estimate.
[††]>1,000 abortions per 1,000 live births.
[§§]>100 abortions per 1,000 women aged 15–44 years.
[¶]Reported by hospitals and/or other medical facilities in state.
***Reported by the New York City Department of Health.
[†††]Percentage based on number reported as "out-of-reporting area."
— Not available.

Source: "Abortion Surveillance — United States, 1996," *Morbidity and Mortality Weekly Report*, vol. 48, no SS-4, July 30, 1999

such as required parental notification and consent, waiting periods, as well as required counseling that involves more than one visit to the provider.

FEWER ABORTION PROVIDERS ARE AVAILABLE

According to the Alan Guttmacher Institute (AGI), in 1996, 86 percent of U.S. counties had no abortion providers, up from 84 percent in 1992. One-third (32 percent) of women of childbearing age (15 to 44 years old) lived in these counties with no known providers. In North Dakota, South Dakota, West Virginia, and Mississippi, approximately 4 of 5 women of reproductive age lived in counties with no abortion providers. (See Table 4.9.) Nearly one-third of the country's metropolitan areas lacked abortion services, and for many women in rural areas, obtaining an abortion entailed traveling hundreds of miles from their residence.

The 1996 AGI count of all known abortion facilities (2,042) indicated a 14 percent drop from 2,380 in 1992 (Table 4.9), or an average decrease of 85 providers each year. Between 1988 and 1992, the loss was 51 providers each year. Of the 2,042 providers in 1996, 34 percent (703 pro-

TABLE 4.9

Number of counties and number and percentage of counties without an abortion provider, and percentage of women aged 15–44 living in a county without a provider, 1996; and number of providers, 1982, 1992 and 1996, and change in number between 1992 and 1996; all by census division and state

Census division and state	Counties				No. of providers			
	N	Without provider, 1996			1982	1992	1996	Number change, 1992–1996
		N	%	% of women*				
Total	3,139	2,696	86	32	2,908	2,380	2,042	–338
New England	67	27	40	12	205	162	141	–21
Connecticut	8	2	25	10	46	43	40	–3
Maine	16	9	56	39	39	17	16	–1
Massachusetts	14	2	14	0	78	64	51	–13
New Hampshire	10	5	50	26	18	16	16	0
Rhode Island	5	3	60	37	5	6	5	–1
Vermont	14	6	43	23	19	16	13	–3
Middle Atlantic	150	78	52	16	516	458	421	–37
New Jersey	21	2	10	3	100	88	94	6
New York	62	26	42	8	302	289	266	–23
Pennsylvania	67	50	75	37	114	81	61	–20
East North Central	437	392	90	43	255	197	161	–36
Illinois	102	92	90	30	58	47	38	–9
Indiana	92	86	93	61	30	19	16	–3
Michigan	83	67	81	28	83	70	59	–11
Ohio	88	80	91	50	55	45	37	–8
Wisconsin	72	67	93	62	29	16	11	–5
West North Central	618	595	96	57	110	63	51	–12
Iowa	99	95	96	69	25	11	8	–3
Kansas	105	100	95	48	23	15	10	–5
Minnesota	87	83	95	57	20	14	13	–1
Missouri	115	110	96	53	29	12	10	–2
Nebraska	93	90	97	47	8	9	8	–1
North Dakota	53	52	98	80	3	1	1	0
South Dakota	66	65	98	79	2	1	1	0
South Atlantic	591	478	81	37	515	435	361	–74
Delaware	3	1	33	15	7	8	7	–1
District of Columbia	1	0	0	0	14	15	18	3
Florida	67	49	73	22	140	133	114	–19
Georgia	159	143	90	49	82	55	41	–14
Maryland	24	13	54	15	52	51	47	–4
North Carolina	100	74	74	39	114	86	59	–27
South Carolina	46	37	80	58	15	18	14	–4
Virginia	136	108	79	48	81	64	57	–7
West Virginia	55	53	96	84	10	5	4	–1
East South Central	364	347	95	65	116	70	48	–22
Alabama	67	62	93	58	45	20	14	–6
Kentucky	120	118	98	75	11	9	8	–1
Mississippi	82	79	96	82	13	8	6	–2
Tennessee	95	88	93	54	47	33	20	–13
West South Central	470	440	94	42	177	115	96	–19
Arkansas	75	73	97	78	13	8	6	–2
Louisiana	64	59	92	60	18	17	15	–2
Oklahoma	77	73	95	54	18	11	11	0
Texas	254	235	93	32	128	79	64	–15
Mountain	280	243	87	35	211	156	127	–29
Arizona	15	12	80	19	37	28	24	–4
Colorado	63	50	79	34	73	59	47	–12
Idaho	44	41	93	67	15	9	7	–2
Montana	56	50	89	41	20	12	11	–1
Nevada	17	14	82	12	25	17	14	–3
New Mexico	33	29	88	47	26	20	13	–7
Utah	29	27	93	49	7	6	7	1
Wyoming	23	20	87	75	8	5	4	–1
Pacific	162	96	59	7	803	724	636	–88
Alaska	25	19	76	23	14	13	8	–5
California	58	21	36	3	583	554	492	–62
Hawaii	4	0	0	0	51	52	44	–8
Oregon	36	29	81	38	60	40	35	–5
Washington	39	27	69	15	95	65	57	–8

*Population estimates are for 1995. *Sources:* **1982 and 1992**—reference 7. **Abortion and provider data, 1996**—AGI Abortion Provider Survey. **Population estimates**—Market Statistics, New York.

Source: Reproduced with the permission of The Alan Guttmacher Institute from: Stanley K. Henshaw, "Abortion Incidence and Services in the United States, 1995-1996," *Family Planning Perspectives*, 1998, 30(6): 263-270 & 287, Table 5.

viders) were hospitals, which accounted for only 7 percent of the abortions performed, similar to the 1992 figure. In contrast, in 1973, the year of the *Roe v. Wade* decision, hospitals made up 81 percent of all providers. In 1996, the 470 private physicians' offices (23 percent of providers) accounted for only 3 percent of the abortions performed, down from 4 percent in 1992.

In 1996, abortion clinics (452), which were 22 percent of all providers, performed 70 percent of all abortions. "Other clinics" (group practices, surgical centers, health maintenance organizations, family planning clinics, and facilities with clinic names), accounted for 20 percent of all abortion providers and performed 21 percent of the abortions.

Medical Training in Abortion

Abortion continues to be the most frequently performed surgical procedure in the United States. The AGI observes, "Traditionally, residency programs in obstetrics and gynecology have been the only programs to formally train residents in abortion procedures and in the management of complications from spontaneous and elective abortions." The legalization of abortion in 1973 did not bring about any marked increase in obstetrics and gynecology resident training in abortion. To the contrary, the number of residents being trained continues to decline.

The AGI believes that the decreasing number of residents trained in abortion procedures have contributed to provider shortage. In 1991-1992 (latest study conducted), the AGI surveyed program directors of obstetrics and gynecology residency programs in the United States to find out whether they offered abortion training to their residents (H. Trent MacKay and Andrea Phillips MacKay, "Abortion Training in Obstetrics and Gynecology Residency Programs in the United States, 1991-1992," *Family Planning Perspectives,* vol. 27, no. 3, May/June 1995).

The proportion of residency programs that offered routine first-trimester abortion training dropped from 26 percent in 1976 to 23 percent in 1985 and to just 12 percent in 1991-1992. For routine second-trimester abortion training, the percentage dropped significantly from 23 percent in 1976 to 21 percent in 1985 and to only 7 percent in 1991-1992.

The Accreditation Council for Graduate Medical Education (ACGME), which oversees medical education in the United States, has noticed the trend in the shortage of abortion providers. As a result of the impact of provider shortage on the already dwindling abortion services, the ACGME decided that, effective January 1996, induced abortion "must be part of residency training, except for residents with moral or religious objection." Teaching hospitals that do not train or arrange for abortion training risk losing accreditation, and consequently, federal reimbursements of services rendered by medical residents.

Under pressure from Catholic bishops and anti-abortion groups, the ACGME requirement was amended by Congress. The policy has become a "recommendation" that elective training in induced abortion be offered in residency training. So far, no medical school has lost accreditation for failing to do so.

The Alan Guttmacher Institute sees the training of family practice residents in abortion as one alternative in solving the shortage of abortion providers. Jody E. Steinauer et al., in "Training Family Practice Residents in Abortion and Reproductive Health Care: A Nationwide Survey" (*Family Planning Perspectives*, vol. 29, no. 5, September/ October 1997), observed that family doctors, more than any other medical practitioners, are in an ideal position to take an active role in the reproductive health care of their patients.

However, the AGI survey of program directors and chief residents at 244 family medicine residency programs found how ill-prepared family doctors were to perform abortions. Only 29 percent of the residency programs offered routine or optional first-trimester abortion training. Seventy-four percent of chief residents had no training in performing first-trimester abortions, while 85 percent of both chief residents and program directors had no clinical experience.

Family doctors trained in family planning methods are also better able to advise their patients, both women and men, on contraception. The use of effective contraception can mean less need for abortions. In most cases, poor women, especially in rural areas, have only the family doctor to turn to for reproductive health care. However, many of the chief residents had inadequate training in contraception and sterilization (tubal ligation and vasectomy). Although nearly 9 in 10 residents had managed oral contraceptive cases, most had managed just a minimal number of contraception (except for oral contraception) and sterilization cases.

While many obstetrics/gynecology residents and family practice residents are not getting adequate training in reproductive health care, many medical students are working to improve their reproductive health education. Medical Students for Choice, representing more than 5,000 medical students and residents, offers an intensive Reproductive Health Externship Program, wherein students "learn about reproductive health services, particularly abortion provision, in a clinical setting." Fourth-year medical students interested in reproductive health internships are also getting placement assistance from the American Medical Women's Association.

"Menstrual Extraction"

Access to abortion has become so limited in some areas that some women are resorting to "menstrual extraction," a do-it-yourself home technique once practiced before abortion was legalized. (Menstrual extraction involves inserting a flexible tube through the cervix and pumping a syringe to draw out the contents of the uterus through suction. It can be used through the eighth week of pregnancy.) Before *Roe v. Wade*, a women's group called JANE performed abortions by menstrual extraction. Today, Feminist Women's Health Centers offer the service to women who cannot afford abortions or who live too far from an abortion provider.

HOW MUCH DOES AN ABORTION COST?

Abortion fees vary, depending upon the stage of pregnancy and where the abortion is performed. A first-trimester abortion performed in a clinic usually costs anywhere from $200 to $400. The fees generally cover the examination, laboratory tests, local anesthesia, the procedure, and the follow-up visit.

The cost of an abortion increases after the first trimester. According to the National Abortion Federation, the professional association of abortion providers in the United States and Canada, a nonhospital abortion performed between the thirteenth and sixteenth week of pregnancy costs about $400 to $700. For an abortion done after the sixteenth week of pregnancy, the cost increases by about $100 per week of pregnancy.

Hospital abortions cost more than those performed in abortion clinics and doctors' offices. Besides the surgeon and anesthesiologist fees, the length of hospital stay, the type of anesthesia used, and additional tests and medications add to the expenses.

Obtaining an abortion is usually not a problem for women who can afford it and for those whose private-insurance plans cover abortion services. For those women who cannot afford an abortion and are not covered by insurance, having an abortion can present a financial burden. Women who live in states that mandate waiting periods suffer income loss from time taken from work and incur additional expenses for extra visits to the provider. Women who have to travel out of their area of residence have the additional costs of transportation and overnight accommodations.

Patricia Donovan, in *The Politics of Blame: Family Planning, Abortion and the Poor* (Alan

Guttmacher Institute, New York and Washington, DC, 1995), noted that women who have to raise the money to get an abortion end up having the procedure at a later stage in their pregnancy. This can only have a negative effect on their health since it is recognized that "the risks of an abortion increase with gestational age." (See Chapter III for public funding restrictions for abortion.)

WHEN ARE ABORTIONS PERFORMED?

Gestational Age

Part of the abortion debate concerns the gestational age of the fetus when abortion is performed. Physicians' estimates of gestation (pregnancy) start on the first day of a woman's last menstrual period. Ovulation (release of egg) actually takes place two weeks later, after which time the egg may be fertilized (united with a sperm). It will take almost one week for the fertilized egg to implant itself inside the uterine wall and another week for implantation to be completed. At this point, the physician considers a woman one month pregnant and the fetus four weeks old. But based on the time of fertilization, the fetus is actually only two weeks old.

Gestational age reported in abortion statistics is based on menstrual weeks. The length of pregnancy (hence, gestational age) has serious implications on whether the woman's decision to end her pregnancy is upheld, regulated, or prohibited by law.

The Data

According to the Centers for Disease Control and Prevention (CDC), in 1996, more than half of all abortions (54.6 percent) were performed at gestation of 8 weeks or less, and almost 9 in 10 abortions (88.3 percent) were performed before 13 weeks of pregnancy. Few abortions were performed after 15 weeks of gestation — 4.3 percent at 16 to 20 weeks and 1.5 percent at or after 21 weeks of pregnancy. (See Table 4.1.)

TABLE 4.10

Reported legal abortions, by known weeks of gestation, age group, race, and Hispanic ethnicity of women who obtained abortions — United States, 1996

Age group (yrs)/ Race/Hispanic ethnicity	Weeks of gestation												Total*	
	≤8		9–10		11–12		13–15		16–20		≥21			
	No.	%	No.	%	No.	%	No.	%	No.	%	No.	%	No.	%
Age group														
<15	1,741	35.9	1,080	22.3	760	15.7	560	11.5	462	9.5	246	5.1	4,849	100.0
15–19	55,869	45.2	29,902	24.2	16,931	13.7	10,172	8.2	7,697	6.2	3,113	2.5	123,684	100.0
20–24	107,128	53.2	46,629	23.1	23,363	11.6	12,824	6.4	8,535	4.2	2,945	1.5	201,424	100.0
25–29	86,139	58.5	32,232	21.9	14,216	9.7	7,463	5.1	5,306	3.6	1,846	1.3	147,202	100.0
30–34	54,252	60.3	19,068	21.2	8,232	9.1	4,157	4.6	3,205	3.6	1,092	1.2	90,006	100.0
35–39	31,823	61.1	10,826	20.8	4,546	8.7	2,238	4.3	2,032	3.9	652	1.3	52,117	100.0
≥40	10,072	63.3	3,091	19.4	1,200	7.5	647	4.1	705	4.4	200	1.3	15,915	100.0
Total†	347,024	54.6	142,828	22.5	69,248	10.9	38,061	6.0	27,942	4.4	10,094	1.6	635,197	100.0
Race														
White	158,278	55.9	64,049	22.6	29,677	10.5	15,504	5.5	11,289	4.0	4,235	1.5	283,032	100.0
Black	88,513	49.8	41,944	23.6	22,219	12.5	12,460	7.0	9,377	5.3	3,353	1.9	177,866	100.0
Other	17,557	61.5	5,394	18.9	2,226	7.8	1,495	5.2	1,405	4.9	451	1.6	28,528	100.0
Total§	264,348	54.0	111,387	22.8	54,122	11.1	29,459	6.0	22,071	4.5	8,039	1.6	489,426	100.0
Hispanic ethnicity														
Hispanic	39,151	56.0	15,073	21.6	7,053	10.1	4,413	6.3	3,247	4.6	971	1.4	69,908	100.0
Non-Hispanic	179,583	54.2	73,057	22.0	35,949	10.8	20,777	6.3	15,757	4.8	6,257	1.9	331,380	100.0
Total¶	218,734	54.5	88,130	22.0	43,002	10.7	25,190	6.3	19,004	4.7	7,228	1.8	401,288	100.0

* Percentages might not add to 100.0 because of rounding.
† Data from 37 states and New York City; excludes three states where unknown gestational age was >15%.
§ Data from 30 states and New York City; excludes six states where unknown gestational age or race was >15%.
¶ Data from 19 states and New York City; excludes 14 states where unknown gestational age or Hispanic ethnicity was >15%.

Source: "Abortion Surveillance — United States, 1996," *Morbidity and Mortality Weekly Report*, vol. 48, no SS-4, July 30, 1999

In 1996, teenagers were more likely to obtain abortions later in pregnancy than were older women. Black women were somewhat more likely than White women and women of other races to obtain an abortion later in pregnancy. There was virtually no difference for Hispanic and non-Hispanic women. (See Table 4.10.)

HOW ARE ABORTIONS PERFORMED?

Surgical Abortion

Abortion can be performed using surgical or other medical methods. Physicians use the following surgical methods to induce (bring about) abortion:

- Suction curettage (also known as vacuum aspiration) — Nearly all abortions performed in the first trimester are done by this method (Table 4.1). The physician dilates (widens) the cervix (opening of the uterus) and then inserts a small tube into the uterus. This tube is connected to an aspirator or suction machine that empties the contents of the uterus through the tube. The procedure takes about 5 to 10 minutes. It requires local anesthesia, but some patients prefer general anesthesia.

- Dilation and evacuation (D&E) — This is the method generally used in the second trimester. The physician dilates the cervix. Since the fetus is larger (for example, a 14-week fetus weighs about four ounces and is five inches long), the cervix must be dilated more than during the first trimester. Dilation can take several hours or even overnight. Once the cervix is dilated, the physician uses vacuum aspiration. Then forceps may be used to ensure that the fetus has been totally removed. Finally, the physician scrapes the wall of the uterus with a curette (a spoon-shaped surgical instrument) to remove any remaining fetal and placental tissue. This method is referred to as "sharp curettage" in the CDC data tables. The surgical procedure takes from 10 to 30 minutes.

- Instillation or induction method — This method is used late in the second trimester. The physician injects saline solution or a solution of urea with prostaglandins into the uterus to induce contractions. With saline solution, the patient goes into labor after about 24 hours, causing the fetus to be expelled. The use of urea and prostaglandins results in labor after about 12 hours.

The CDC has found the surgical methods used for abortion over the past two decades have changed somewhat. From 1972 to 1996, the percentage of abortions performed by curettage (which includes D&E) increased from 88.6 to 98.8 percent. Meanwhile, the percentage of abortions performed by instillation or induction declined sharply from 10.4 to 0.4 percent. (See Table 4.1.)

From 1974 through 1996, the percentage of second-trimester abortions using D&E increased from 31 to 93 percent, while the percentage using instillation decreased from 57 to 2 percent. The increasing use of D&E can be attributed to the lower risk of complications using this procedure.

Deaths from Surgical Abortion

In 1992 (the most recent year for which such data were available), 27 women died from abortion-related causes. Ten deaths were associated with legal induced abortion, and 17 deaths resulted from spontaneous abortion (miscarriage). As in previous years, abortion-related deaths in 1992 were a rare occurrence — about one death per 100,000 abortions. (See Table 4.11.) The CDC, in "Achievements in Public Health, 1900-1999: Healthier Mothers and Babies" (*Morbidity and Mortality Weekly Report*, vol. 48, no. 38, October 1, 1999), reported that "[t]he legalization of induced abortion beginning in the 1960s contributed to an 89 percent decline in deaths from septic (causing infection that may lead to fatal blood poisoning) illegal abortions during 1950-1973."

Although abortion-related deaths are rare, legal abortions are still surgical procedures and entail some risk. An abortion performed at or before eight weeks of gestation is the safest. Similarly, the abortion method used also has a bearing on risk. Vacuum aspiration, used during the first trimester of pregnancy, carries the least risk.

Medical Abortion

RU-486

Women in the early stage of pregnancy (up to 49 days from the last menstrual period) have a medical alternative to early surgical abortion. Mifepristone, popularly known as RU-486, was developed in 1980 by a French pharmaceutical firm, Roussel-Uclaf (thus the RU designation of the patented name).

Mifepristone is an antiprogestin. It prevents the hormone progesterone from doing its function, which is to prepare the uterus lining for the implantation of a fertilized egg and to maintain the pregnancy. When used alone, mifepristone, which disintegrates the uterus lining, has been found effective 65 to 80 percent of the time. However, combined with misoprostol (a drug already available in the United States), it is 95 percent effective. Administered two days after mifepristone, miso-prostol causes the uterus to contract and to expel the fertilized egg. If the woman does not abort completely (2 percent of women), surgical abortion is performed.

Mifepristone is effective only in the earliest stage of pregnancy. Up to the end of the sixth week of pregnancy, progesterone is produced by the ovaries. After this, the placenta itself produces progesterone in large quantities, making mifepristone ineffective.

Women opting for this method of abortion report side effects not unlike those of spontaneous abortion (miscarriage) — cramps, abdominal pain, bleeding, nausea, and fatigue. Advantages cited include privacy, a non-invasive procedure that does not require anesthesia, a high percentage of effectiveness, safety (no risk of cervix and uterine damage), affordabilty, and greater control over one's body.

RU-486 in the United States

RU-486 was approved for use in France in September 1988. Since then, it has been introduced in China, England, Sweden, Scotland, and other countries. Fearing boycotts and protests, Roussel-Uclaf has never tried to market the drug in the United States.

TABLE 4.11

Number of deaths and case-fatality rates* for abortion-related deaths reported to CDC, by type of abortion — United States, 1972–1992

	No. of deaths					
	Type of abortion					
	Induced					Case-fatality
Year	Legal	Illegal	Spontaneous†	Unknown	Total	rate*
1972	24	39	25	2	90	4.1
1973	25	19	10	3	57	4.1
1974	26	6	21	1	54	3.4
1975	29	4	14	1	48	3.4
1976	11	2	13	1	27	1.1
1977	17	4	16	0	37	1.6
1978	9	7	9	0	25	0.8
1979	22	0	8	0	30	1.8
1980	9	1	6	2	18	0.7
1981	8	1	3	0	12	0.6
1982	11	1	5	0	17	0.8
1983	11	1	7	0	19	0.9
1984	12	0	5	0	17	0.9
1985	11	1	8	1	21	0.8
1986	11	0	5	2	18	0.8
1987	7	2	8	0	17	0.5
1988	16	0	7	0	23	1.2
1989	12	1	3	0	16	0.9
1990	5	0	5	0	10	0.3
1991	11	1	6	0	18	0.8
1992	10	0	17	0	27	0.7
Total	**297**	**90**	**201**	**13**	**601**	**1.2**

*Legal induced abortion-related deaths per 100,000 legal induced abortions.
†In 1978, CDC defined "spontaneous abortion-related deaths" as those deaths that occurred at <20 weeks of estimated gestational age. Deaths that occurred at an estimated gestational age of ≥20 weeks were classified as stillbirths. Before 1978, criteria for gestational age were unspecified.

Source: "Abortion Surveillance — United States, 1996," *Morbidity and Mortality Weekly Report*, vol. 48, no SS-4, July 30, 1999

In 1989, President Bush, through the Food and Drug Administration (FDA), banned the importation of RU-486. Upon taking office in January 1993, President Clinton directed the Department of Health and Human Services to promote the testing and licensing of RU-486/mifepristone. In September 1993, the Institute of Medicine recommended an application to the FDA for the use of mifepristone for early abortion, as well as its other uses as a contraceptive and emergency contraceptive and as treatment for breast cancer and other disorders. (The Institute of Medicine, established by the National Academy of Sciences, examines policy matters pertaining to public health.)

In 1994, Roussel-Uclaf donated its American patent rights to a nonprofit family planning research group, the Population Council. Shortly after, the Council began clinical trials involving 2,121 women in several American cities. On April 30,

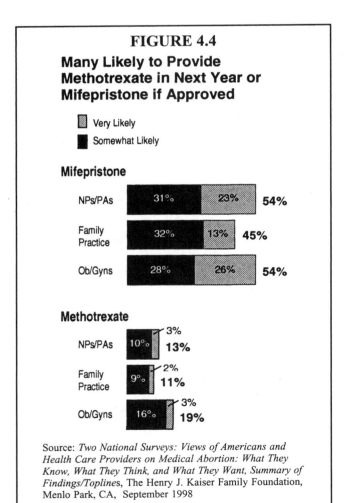

FIGURE 4.4

Many Likely to Provide Methotrexate in Next Year or Mifepristone if Approved

Very Likely
Somewhat Likely

Mifepristone

NPs/PAs   31%   23%   **54%**
Family Practice   32%   13%   **45%**
Ob/Gyns   28%   26%   **54%**

Methotrexate

NPs/PAs   10%   3%   **13%**
Family Practice   9%   2%   **11%**
Ob/Gyns   16%   3%   **19%**

Source: *Two National Surveys: Views of Americans and Health Care Providers on Medical Abortion: What They Know, What They Think, and What They Want, Summary of Findings/Toplines*, The Henry J. Kaiser Family Foundation, Menlo Park, CA, September 1998

1998, the *New England Journal of Medicine* reported on the results of these clinical trials that were submitted to the FDA (Irving M. Spitz et al., "Early Pregnancy Termination with Mifepristone and Misoprostol in the United States, vol. 338, no. 18). The study found that the mifepristone-misoprostol combination was effective in inducing abortion in 92 percent of pregnancies with a 49-day duration or less.

In March 1996, the Council applied for licensing from the FDA. It did not take long for the advisory committee of the FDA (July 19, 1996) to recommend that mifepristone be approved for use in the United States. Mifepristone awaits formal approval by the FDA. The Danco Group (New York) has been licensed by the Population Council to manufacture and market mifepristone.

In the meantime, methotrexate, a drug approved by the FDA for cancer treatment in 1953, has been used in combination with misoprostol for medical abortion. According to the Alan Guttmacher Institute, in 1996 and during the first half of 1997, about 8,500 such abortions were performed in the United States.

Will Physicians Offer Mifepristone or Methotrexate?

A survey of health care providers (*Two National Surveys: Views of Americans and Health Care Providers on Medical Abortion: What They Know, What They Think, and What They Want,* The Henry J. Kaiser Family Foundation, Menlo Park, California, 1998) found that, if the FDA approves mifepristone, 54 percent of obstetricians/gynecologists (ob/gyns) would offer mifepristone abortions. Family practice physicians (45 percent) and nurse practitioners/physician assistants (NPs/PAs; 54 percent) also indicated they would offer such abortions. (See Figure 4.4.) Nearly half (45 percent) of ob/gyns who do not ever perform surgical abortions reported they would offer mifepristone if approved by the FDA. (See Chapter IX for the views of Americans on medical abortion.)

Although methotrexate (see above) is available for use in medical abortions, many providers would rather wait for mifepristone to be approved to perform medical abortions. Nonetheless, 19 percent of ob/gyns, 13 percent of NPs/PAs, and 11 percent of family practice physicians indicated they are likely to offer methotrexate abortions in the next year. (See Figure 4.4.)

Proponents and Opponents

The nation's largest pro-life group, the National Right to Life Committee (NRLC), has threatened to boycott any drug company that sells mifepristone. In the early 1980s, the NRLC successfully pressured the Upjohn Company to discontinue developing an abortion-inducing drug through a two-year boycott of its products. Ms. Wanda Franz, president of the NRLC, claims that "[w]omen who use mifepristone are exposing themselves to the emotional sharp edges of the event. Our concern is for the psychological well-being of these women." Pro-lifers argue that "chemical" abortion would leave serious intangible scars on women who would experience real labor pains and see their aborted fetuses.

Dr. Jeannie Rosoff, the past president of the Alan Guttmacher Institute, which supports abortion rights, believes that the legalization of mifepristone may help defuse the violence that has visited many abortion clinics. The mifepristone pill is taken at the doctor's office, but the abortion usually occurs at home or in a private place after the vaginal insertion of misoprostol.

NEW ABORTION TECHNIQUE

Abortions can now be performed as early as eight to ten days after conception, before a woman misses a menstrual period. Dr. Jerry Edwards of Planned Parenthood in Houston developed a procedure that uses a hand-held syringe to suction out the contents of the uterus. The procedure takes about two minutes.

Using ultrasensitive pregnancy testing, a physician can detect pregnancy eight to 10 days after conception, when the embryo has just implanted in the uterus. Then, guided by ultrasound, the physician locates the gestational sac, a clump of tissue "the size of a matchstick head," and suctions it out of the uterus.

Abortion advocates say the earlier an abortion is performed, the less traumatic it is for a woman. In addition, abortions performed during the early stages of pregnancy are safer. Physicians report that women are already choosing Dr. Edwards' procedure over mifepristone (see above). Those who believe that human life begins at conception see no moral difference between an abortion performed a week after conception or that performed at a later time.

CHAPTER V

TEEN PREGNANCY AND ABORTION

TEEN PREGNANCY

Teen pregnancy is a serious problem in America. Each year approximately 900,000 teenagers ages 15 to 19 get pregnant. Nearly 3 in 5 (62 percent) of these pregnancies occur among 18- to 19-year-olds. (See Table 5.1.)

While there has been a decline in teen pregnancy since 1990 (see below), the United States still has the highest rate of teen pregnancy among the developed countries, although the number of sexually active teens is about the same in all these countries. The U.S. teen pregnancy rate is nearly twice as high as the next highest country, Great Britain, and nine times as high as the Netherlands or Japan (Figure 5.1). An estimated 4 of 10 American teenagers become pregnant at least once before they turn 20 (Figure 5.2).

Declining Teen Pregnancy

Some analysts ascribe the declining trend of teen pregnancy to the increasing use of birth control methods, especially the longer-lasting contraceptives Norplant® and Depo Provera®. The increasing use of condoms (see below), due to fear of contracting AIDS, is also thought to contribute to the lower teen pregnancy rate. James G. Kahn, Claire D. Brindis, and Dana A. Glei, in "Pregnancies Averted Among U.S. Teenagers by the Use of Contraceptives" (*Family Planning Perspectives*, vol. 31, no. 1, January/February 1999), based on the *1995 National Survey of Family Growth*, concluded that, in 1995, contraceptive use among teens ages 15 to 19 averted an estimated one million pregnancies, with a range of 750,000 to 1.25 million.

Conservative analysts discount the increasing use of contraception as responsible for the lower pregnancy rates. Instead, they attribute the drop in teen pregnancy to the increasing practice of abstinence (see below). Some observers note that young people have become more conservative in their attitudes toward casual sex. The survey *The American Freshman: National Norms for Fall 1998*, prepared by the Higher Education Research Institute of the University of California, Los Angeles (UCLA), found that acceptance of casual sex has been dropping. Freshmen were asked if they agreed that "if two people really like each other, it's all right for them to have sex even if they've known each other for a very short time." An all-time record low of 39.6 percent agreed with this statement, compared with 42.2 percent in 1997 and a high of 51.9 percent in 1987. (See Chapter IX for the freshmen's attitudes toward abortion.)

Consequences of Pregnancy

Douglas Kirby, in *No Easy Answers: Research Findings on Programs to Reduce Teen Pregnancy* (National Campaign to Prevent Teen Pregnancy, Washington DC, 1997), pointed out the serious consequences that high teen pregnancy rates have on teenagers, their children, and society at large. (The National Campaign is a nonprofit, nonpartisan initiative launched in 1996 in response to President Bill Clinton's call for a national effort against teen pregnancy.) According to Kirby,

When adolescent girls give birth, their future prospects decline.... [T]een mothers complete less school, are more likely to have large families, and are more likely to

54

TABLE 5.1

Number of pregnancies among women aged 15-19, by state of residence, according to age-group, 1996

State	15-17	18-19	15-19	State	15-17	18-19	15-19
U.S. total	**337,530**	**542,640**	**880,170**	**U.S. total**	**337,530**	**542,640**	**880,170**
Alabama	6,400	10,120	16,520	Montana	790	1,440	2,230
Alaska	640	1,130	1,770	Nebraska	1,350	2,520	3,870
Arizona	7,050	10,600	17,650	Nevada	2,690	4,150	6,840
Arkansas	3,660	6,430	10,090	New Hampshire*	720	1,410	2,130
California*	49,110	77,190	126,300	New Jersey	9,420	14,280	23,700
Colorado	4,660	7,270	11,930	New Mexico	3,010	4,390	7,400
Connecticut	3,440	4,790	8,230	New York	23,960	37,740	61,700
Delaware*	910	1,310	2,220	North Carolina	9,770	15,470	25,240
Dist. of Columbia†	1,400	2,000	3,400	North Dakota	390	840	1,230
Florida*	18,300	29,990	48,290	Ohio	11,510	20,270	31,780
Georgia	11,270	16,950	28,220	Oklahoma*	3,950	7,090	11,040
Hawaii	1,510	2,440	3,950	Oregon	3,740	6,310	10,050
Idaho	1,240	2,430	3,670	Pennsylvania	10,090	17,040	27,130
Illinois	17,380	25,130	42,510	Rhode Island	930	1,690	2,620
Indiana	6,650	12,020	18,670	South Carolina	5,160	7,830	12,990
Iowa*	2,200	4,010	6,210	South Dakota	640	1,130	1,770
Kansas	2,720	4,760	7,480	Tennessee	6,800	11,360	18,160
Kentucky	4,600	8,070	12,670	Texas	31,800	48,690	80,490
Louisiana	6,700	10,650	17,350	Utah	2,070	4,140	6,210
Maine	840	1,580	2,420	Vermont	420	790	1,210
Maryland	6,550	9,930	16,480	Virginia	6,960	12,080	19,040
Massachusetts	5,160	9,010	14,170	Washington	6,220	10,110	16,330
Michigan	11,350	18,490	29,840	West Virginia	1,730	3,230	4,960
Minnesota	3,480	5,960	9,440	Wisconsin	4,250	7,300	11,550
Mississippi	4,940	7,150	12,090	Wyoming	580	930	1,510
Missouri	6,060	10,350	16,410				

*Abortion estimates are based on the proportion of abortions obtained by women of the same age in neighboring or similar states. †Distribution of abortions among teenagers into age-groups 15-17 and 18-19 is based on the proportion among all black teenagers nationally. *Notes:* Data are tabulated according to the woman's age at the pregnancy outcome. Even though abortions have been tabulated according to state of residence where possible, in states with parental notification or consent requirements for minors, the number of pregnancies shown may be too low because minors may have traveled to other states for abortion services. Pregnancies include estimates of the number of miscarriages. Numbers are rounded to the nearest 10.

Source: Reproduced with the permission of The Alan Guttmacher Institute from The Alan Guttmacher Institute, *Teenage Pregnancy: Overall Trends and State-by-State Information, April 1999*, <http://www.agi-usa.org/pubs/teen_preg_stats.html>, accessed December 28, 1999, Table 3.

be single parents. The children born to teens bear the brunt of their mother's young age: … [they] have less supportive and stimulating home environments, poorer health, lower cognitive development, worse edu-

cational outcomes, higher rates of behavior problems, and higher rates of teen childbearing themselves. There is also considerable cost to the taxpayers and society more generally. After adjusting for other

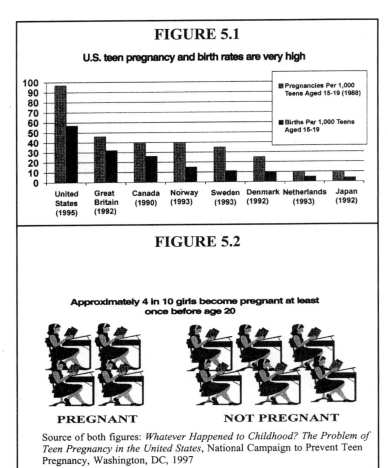

FIGURE 5.1

U.S. teen pregnancy and birth rates are very high

- ■ Pregnancies Per 1,000 Teens Aged 15-19 (1988)
- ■ Births Per 1,000 Teens Aged 15-19

United States (1995) · Great Britain (1992) · Canada (1990) · Norway (1993) · Sweden (1993) · Denmark (1992) · Netherlands (1993) · Japan (1992)

FIGURE 5.2

Approximately 4 in 10 girls become pregnant at least once before age 20

PREGNANT   NOT PREGNANT

Source of both figures: *Whatever Happened to Childhood? The Problem of Teen Pregnancy in the United States*, National Campaign to Prevent Teen Pregnancy, Washington, DC, 1997

Abstinence Education

The 1996 federal welfare reform law, the Personal Responsibility and Work Opportunity Reconciliation Act (PL 104-193), provided an annual $50 million allocation over a five-year period (1998 to 2002) to states for abstinence-education programs. The purpose of these programs is "… to enable the State to provide abstinence education, and at the option of the State, where appropriate, mentoring, counseling, and adult supervision to promote abstinence from sexual activity, with focus on those groups which are most likely to bear children out of wedlock." Funded programs are prohibited from teaching birth control, although students requesting information may be given referrals. In addition, the law included an incentive provision, allotting $20 million to be distributed to the top five states that reduce their out-of-wedlock births without increasing abortions during the previous two years (see Chapter III).

Some observers are concerned that *abstinence-only* sex education programs may not be effective in reducing teen pregnancy. They advocate a comprehensive curriculum that is *abstinence-based* (also called *abstinence-plus*) yet provides information about contraception, including condom use, especially because of the prevalence of sexually transmitted diseases (STDs) among adolescents. According to the Institute of Medicine, every year about three million teenagers are newly infected with STDs. More than half of all teenagers ages 15 to 19 have had sexual intercourse (based on the *1995 National Survey of Family Growth* and the *1995 National Survey of Adolescent Males* by the Centers for Disease Control and Prevention). The latest study by the Alan Guttmacher Institute found that three-fourths (78 percent) of teen pregnancies in 1994 were unintended (Stanley K. Henshaw, "Unintended Pregnancy in the United States," *Family Planning Perspectives*, vol. 30, no. 1, January/February 1998).

factors related to teen parenthood, the estimated annual cost to taxpayers … is at least $6.9 billion in lost tax revenues and increased spending on public assistance, health care for the children, foster care, and the criminal justice system.

PREVENTING TEEN PREGNANCY

There is little agreement, however, on how to accomplish teen pregnancy prevention and what the role of sex education and the availability of contraception should be. While countries, such as France, Germany, and the Netherlands, try to prevent teenage pregnancy through education about sexuality and safe sex, the United States tries to prevent teenage sex. Many Americans consider the promotion of birth control as an encouragement to teens to be promiscuous and advocate abstinence instead.

As of January 1999, 20 states required schools to provide sexuality education. Of these 20 states, half provided information on contraception. Of the 34 states and the District of Columbia that mandated STD, HIV, and/or AIDS education, 21 required the inclusion of abstinence and contraception education. (See Table 5.2.) Supporters of a comprehensive abstinence-based sex education program (discouraging premarital sex but also teaching birth control methods) believe adolescents need more information about sexuality and safe sex.

Characteristics of Effective Sexuality Education Programs

Douglas Kirby (see above) noted that more research needs to be conducted because very few sexuality education programs have been evaluated as to their impact in delaying sexual intercourse among adolescents. Kirby observed that those programs that "show modest behavioral effects share nine important characteristics." These programs (the author's words)

- Focus clearly on reducing one or more sexual behaviors that lead to unintended pregnancy or HIV/STD infection.

- Incorporate behavioral goals, teaching methods, and materials that are appropriate to the age, sexual experience, and culture of the students.

- Are based upon theoretical approaches that have been demonstrated to be effective in influencing other health-related risky behaviors.

- Last long enough to allow participants to complete important activities.

- Provide basic, accurate information about the risks of unprotected intercourse and methods of avoiding unprotected intercourse.

- Employ a variety of teaching methods designed to involve the participants and have them personalize the information.

- Include activities that address social pressures related to sex.

- Provide models of and practice in communication, negotiation, and refusal skills.

- Select teachers or peers who believe in the program and then provide them with training, which often includes practice sessions.

A 1999 report *Teenage Girls on Sex, School, and Self*, prepared by the American Association

---

TABLE 5.2

Information about sexuality education and STD and/or HIV/AIDS education current as of January 1999:

- **Sexuality Education Mandates:** Only 20 states, including the District of Columbia, require schools to provide sexuality education (AL, DE, DC, GA, HI, IL, IA, KS, KY, MD, MN, NV, NJ, NC, RI, SC, TN, UT, VT, WV).

- **Content Requirements of Sexuality Education Mandates:** Of the 20 states that require schools to provide sexuality education, four require that sexuality education teach abstinence but do not require the inclusion of information about contraception (AL, IL, KY, UT). Ten require that sexuality education teach abstinence and provide information about contraception (DE, GA, HI, NJ, NC, RI, SC, TN, VT, WV).

- **STD/HIV Education Mandates:** Thirty-five states, including the District of Columbia, require schools to provide STD, HIV, and/or AIDS education (AL, CA, CT, DE, DC, FL, GA, HI, IL, IN, IA, KS, KY, MD, MI, MN, MO, NV, NH, NJ, NM, NY, NC, OH, OK, OR, PA, RI, SC, TN, UT, VT, WA, WV, WI).

- **Content Requirements of STD/HIV Mandates:** Of the 35 states that require schools to provide STD, HIV, and/or AIDS education, one requires that AIDS education teach abstinence until marriage but does not require the inclusion of other AIDS prevention methods (IN). Twenty-one require that STD, HIV, and/or AIDS education teach abstinence and other methods of prevention (AL, CA, DE, FL, GA, HI, IL, KY, MI, NJ, NM, NY, NC, OK, OR, PA, RI, TN, VT, WA, WV).

Source: *State Sexuality and STD/HIV Education Regulations*, NARAL Factsheet, The National Abortion and Reproductive Rights Action League Foundation, Washington, DC, 1999

TABLE 5.3

HHS Programs and Funding Streams That Support Teen Pregnancy Prevention

Program or funding stream	Description	Fiscal year 1997 funding	Administering agency
TPP-specific programs			
Adolescent Family Life Demonstration and Research Program	Directly funds local abstinence-based programs that emphasize abstinence but include information on reproductive health; beginning fiscal year 1997, provides funding for abstinence-only programs following the welfare law's abstinence definition.	$14.2 million through Office of Secretary (up to $8 million may be awarded to state or local grantees, with the remainder awarded to localities)	Office of Population Affairs (OPA)
Community Coalition Partnership Program for the Prevention of Teen Pregnancy	CDC's 5-year program (now in its third year) funds 13 communities to demonstrate that they can mobilize community resources to support comprehensive prevention programs. CDC also provides support for national nongovernmental education organizations to help schools implement TPP programs. This effort is just beginning.	$13.7 million	CDC
Abstinence Education Program	Legislated under welfare reform, awards grants to states for abstinence-only programs. The legislation prescribes the parameters of acceptable abstinence-only programming. There is a required match of 3 nonfederal dollars for every 4 federal dollars awarded.	$50 million a year for 5 years, beginning fiscal year 1998 ($250 million total); additional $6 million for evaluation	Health Resources and Services Administration (HRSA)
Block grant funding			
Maternal and Child Health Services Block Grant	Funding to monitor and improve the health status of women, infants, children, and teens. States receive funding directly from the federal government to fund various programs, including TPP programs.	$681 million total (could not isolate TPP)	HRSA
Social Services Block Grant	Funding directly to states for social services. Up to 10% of the grant may be transferred to other block grant programs, including those that support health services.	$2.5 billion total (could not isolate TPP)	Administration for Children and Families (ACF)
Preventive Health and Health Services Block Grant	Funds state activities to meet Healthy People 2000 goals. States can use the funds for programs to reduce teen pregnancy for ages 15 to 17 and to reduce unintended pregnancies. In 1997, 9 states funded teen pregnancy prevention.	$148 million total, with $2.8 million used for TPP	CDC
Community Services Block Grant	Funding for states to address poverty. Teen pregnancy prevention is not a specific activity, but programs can fund family planning, job counseling, substance abuse treatment, and general equivalency diploma education.	$487 million total (could not isolate TPP)	ACF
TANF	Funding directly to states to serve needy families and children (replaces Aid to Families With Dependent Children). Funds can be used for preventing out-of-wedlock births, especially to teens.	$13 billion total (could not isolate TPP)	ACF

(continued)

of University Women (AAUW) Educational Foundation (Washington, DC), tends to bear out Kirby's model sexuality education program. According to the report, sex and pregnancy are the number one issues confronting girls today. Sharon Schuster, president of AAUW, observed, "Girls want to learn how to say 'yes' to relationships without automatically saying 'yes' to sex."

Media Cooperation

In May 1997, at a hearing on television viewing and sexual behavior before the Senate Com-

mittee on Governmental Affairs' Subcommittee on Government Management, Restructuring, and the District of Columbia, Director Sarah Brown of the National Campaign to Prevent Teen Pregnancy observed,

Kids and adults alike say that one of [the] factors that lies behind the nation's high rates of teen pregnancy is that the current media environment is quite accepting of teen sexual activity and pregnancy. How can we encourage teens to postpone pregnancy and childbearing when their idols

TABLE 5.3 (Continued)

Program or funding stream	Description	Fiscal year 1997 funding	Administering agency
Key categorical and entitlement programs			
Title X Family Planning Program	Family planning education, counseling, and clinical services, with priority given to ensuring services are available to individuals up to 250 percent of the federal poverty level. The prevention of unintended pregnancy is a major program goal. About 30% of clients are under age 20, and clinics can have programs that target teens.	$198 million total through HRSA, with an estimated $59 million for teens[a]	OPA
Male research grants	Grants awarded to 10 local organizations in 8 states to support male-oriented organizations in developing, implementing, and testing approaches to involve young men in family planning and reproductive health programs.	$1.8 million through HRSA (fiscal year 1998)	OPA
Medicaid	Provides medical assistance for low-income individuals, and requires states to provide family planning services to eligible individuals of childbearing age (including sexually active minors).	$67,181,220 (family planning for ages 19 and under)	Health Care Financing Administration
Other programs or funding sources related to TPP			
Health education in schools	Provides funding to all states, 19 of the nation's largest cities, and relevant national nongovernmental organizations to support schools and other agencies that serve youth to provide HIV prevention education, including training teachers and developing and distributing educational materials. The goal is to prevent HIV, but sexual risk behaviors that also put teens at risk of unintended pregnancy are targeted.	$38 million total (could not isolate TPP)	CDC
Healthy Schools, Healthy Communities	Grants to local communities to establish school-based health centers that provide comprehensive primary health care services to at-risk youth. Reproductive health services could be included.	$5.1 million for 26 centers in 20 states (could not isolate TPP)	HRSA
Community Schools Program	Funds after-school programs in communities with high poverty and delinquency to help youth aged 5 to 18 achieve academic and employment success.	$13 million total (could not isolate TPP)	ACF
Girl Neighborhood Power	Targets girls aged 10 to 14 to promote successful futures; teaches prevention for multiple risks, including pregnancy. Nationally, there are 4 projects in low-income neighborhoods.	$1 million total through the Maternal and Child Health Services Block Grant (could not isolate TPP)	HRSA
Direct health care services for American Indian and Alaskan Natives	Provides direct care to native American Indians and Alaskans, including teen pregnancy prevention and family planning services.	$5.6 million estimated for TPP and family planning services	Indian Health Service
High-Risk Youth Program	Supports 117 projects focusing on female teen drug prevention. Teen pregnancy is a risk factor associated with drug use; teen pregnancy prevention is a goal of some of the projects.	$15 million total, with $750,000 for TPP	Substance Abuse and Mental Health Services Administration (SAMHSA)
Pregnant and Postpartum Substance Abuse Prevention	Program for pregnant and postpartum women also provides services for girls and women of childbearing age to prevent unwanted pregnancies that could result in a drug-exposed infant.	$883,000 total, with $45,000 for TPP	SAMHSA

(continued)

and role models in sports and the media engage in sex with little enduring meaning? Sex with no serious consequences?

Brown believes that the media can be part of the solution by showing teens the real consequences of pregnancy through public service announcements and the content of their programming. Some television networks and other media have developed programs relevant to teen pregnancy prevention. In July 1999, the United Paramount Network (UPN) aired a documentary called *The Truth About Sex*, which profiled teens around the country who were faced with issues about sex, pregnancy, and STDs. The Black Entertainment Television (BET) cable show *Teen Summit* features regular programs on teen sexuality — a May 1999 show focused on male responsibility and involve-

TABLE 5.3 (Continued)

Program or funding stream	Description	Fiscal year 1997 funding	Administering agency
Independent Living Initiatives Program	Assists teens in transitioning from foster care to independent living. Pregnancy prevention is not specifically addressed in the legislation, but some programs fund teen pregnancy prevention.	$70 million total (could not isolate TPP)	ACF
Healthy Start	Demonstration to reduce infant mortality. Teen pregnancy contributes to higher rates of infant mortality, so projects have developed approaches to prevent teen pregnancy.	$96 million total (could not isolate TPP)	HRSA
Community health centers	Provide health services (including family planning) to low-income individuals in medically underserved areas. Teen pregnancy prevention is not an explicit goal.	$645 million total (could not isolate TPP)	HRSA
Migrant health centers	Provide medical and support services to migrant farmworkers and their families in about 400 clinics, including family planning services.	$69 million total (could not isolate TPP)	HRSA
National Youth Sports Program	National Collegiate Athletic Association sports program for 70,000 low-income youth aged 10 to 16.	$12 million total (could not isolate TPP)	ACF
Basic Center Program for Runaway and Homeless Youths	Supports local agencies that provide crisis intervention services and social and health services to runaway and homeless youth outside the traditional juvenile justice and law enforcement systems.	$43.7 million total (could not isolate TPP)	ACF
Street Outreach Program	Sexual abuse and exploitation prevention program for runaway, homeless, and street youth.	$8 million total (could not isolate TPP)	ACF
Transitional Living for Older Homeless Youth	Provides services for homeless youth aged 16 to 21 to transition to self-sufficiency.	$14.9 million total (could not isolate TPP)	ACF
Empowerment Zone/Enterprise Community Initiative	Federal governmentwide effort to enable the self-revitalization and growth of distressed urban and rural areas; 105 designated communities receive enhanced federal funds through Social Services Block Grant funds, tax incentives, special consideration for competitive federal grants, and technical assistance.	$1 billion total in Social Services Block Grant funds; $2.5 billion in tax incentives (could not isolate TPP)	HHS and other federal agencies, with the Departments of Agriculture and Housing and Urban Development as lead program managers

aEstimate based on the proportion of title X clients under age 20.

Source: *Teen Pregnancy: State and Federal Efforts to Implement Prevention Programs and Measure Their Effectiveness*, U.S. General Accounting Office, Washington, DC, 1998

ment in teen pregnancy. BET reaches about half a million people each week. The *Channel One News*, a nationwide school-based news program involving over eight million students and 400,000 educators, covers issues affecting America's teenagers. *Teen People* magazine has continuing editorial coverage of teen pregnancy, while *Sports Illustrated,* BET's *Heart and Soul* magazine, and *Parenting* magazine have featured teen pregnancy prevention in their public service messages.

Federal and State Initiatives

The U.S. Department of Health and Human Services is the primary federal agency involved in teen pregnancy prevention. In fiscal year 1997, the department spent about $164 million in related programs. (See Table 5.3 for a listing of the various programs.)

The Alan Guttmacher Institute reports that a number of states are implementing a curriculum called the PSI (Postponing Sexual Involvement) program. Designed to delay sexual activity among middle school teens, it helps them understand the social pressures that lead to sexual activity. Through the PSI program, adolescents learn "skills that will enable them to set limits, resist peer pressure, be assertive in saying 'no' to sex, and develop nonsexual ways to express their feelings."

Some states have implemented the Teen Outreach Program (TOP) for high school students. A school-based program, TOP is designed to reduce problem behaviors, including academic suspension, school failure and dropout, and teen pregnancy. The program does not focus on the problem behaviors. Instead, it helps youth develop socially through interaction with supportive adults

TABLE 5.4

Percentage of high school students who reported sexual risk behaviors, by sex, grade, race/ethnicity, and survey year — United States, Youth Risk Behavior Survey, 1991, 1993, 1995, 1997

	Survey year	Ever had sexual intercourse		Four or more sex partners during lifetime		Currently sexually active*		Condom use during last sexual intercourse†	
		%	(95% CI§)	%	(95% CI)	%	(95% CI)	%	(95% CI)
Sex									
Male	1991	57.4	(±4.1)	23.4	(±3.0)	36.8	(±3.4)	54.5	(± 3.8)
	1993	55.6	(±3.5)	22.3	(±2.7)	37.5	(±3.0)	59.2	(± 3.8)
	1995	54.0	(±4.7)	20.9	(±2.6)	35.5	(±3.5)	60.5	(± 4.3)
	1997	48.8	(±3.4)	17.6	(±1.5)	33.4	(±2.6)	62.5	(± 2.8)
Female	1991	50.8	(±4.0)	13.8	(±1.8)	38.2	(±3.4)	38.0	(± 4.3)
	1993	50.2	(±2.5)	15.0	(±1.9)	37.5	(±1.8)	46.0	(± 2.8)
	1995	52.1	(±5.0)	14.4	(±3.5)	40.4	(±4.2)	48.6	(± 5.2)
	1997	47.7	(±3.7)	14.1	(±2.0)	36.5	(±2.7)	50.8	(± 3.0)
Grade									
9	1991	39.0	(±5.0)	12.5	(±2.9)	22.4	(±3.9)	53.3	(± 6.2)
	1993	37.7	(±4.2)	10.9	(±2.0)	24.8	(±3.2)	61.6	(± 5.7)
	1995	36.9	(±5.9)	12.9	(±3.0)	23.6	(±4.0)	62.9	(± 5.5)
	1997	38.0	(±3.8)	12.2	(±2.5)	24.2	(±3.3)	58.8	(± 5.6)
10	1991	48.2	(±5.7)	15.1	(±2.8)	33.2	(±4.6)	46.3	(± 4.7)
	1993	46.1	(±3.6)	15.9	(±2.0)	30.1	(±3.0)	54.7	(± 4.5)
	1995	48.0	(±5.1)	15.6	(±2.0)	33.7	(±3.1)	59.7	(± 4.6)
	1997	42.5	(±4.3)	13.8	(±2.7)	29.2	(±2.9)	58.9	(± 3.6)
11	1991	62.4	(±3.2)	22.1	(±3.6)	43.3	(±3.6)	48.7	(± 5.8)
	1993	57.5	(±3.5)	19.9	(±3.1)	40.0	(±3.6)	55.3	(± 3.0)
	1995	58.6	(±5.0)	19.0	(±3.7)	42.4	(±4.4)	52.3	(± 6.2)
	1997	49.7	(±5.2)	16.7	(±2.9)	37.8	(±4.8)	60.1	(± 5.2)
12	1991	66.7	(±4.4)	25.0	(±4.0)	50.6	(±4.5)	41.4	(± 3.6)
	1993	68.3	(±4.6)	27.0	(±3.6)	53.0	(±3.9)	46.5	(± 4.0)
	1995	66.4	(±4.0)	22.9	(±3.5)	49.7	(±3.9)	49.5	(± 4.4)
	1997	60.9	(±6.5)	20.6	(±3.5)	46.0	(±5.0)	52.4	(± 3.5)
Race/Ethnicity¶									
Non-Hispanic white	1991	50.0	(±3.2)	14.7	(±1.8)	33.9	(±2.8)	46.5	(± 4.6)
	1993	48.4	(±2.8)	14.3	(±2.1)	34.0	(±2.1)	52.3	(± 3.9)
	1995	48.9	(±5.0)	14.2	(±2.4)	34.8	(±3.9)	52.5	(± 4.0)
	1997	43.6	(±4.2)	11.6	(±1.5)	32.0	(±3.1)	55.8	(± 2.0)
Non-Hispanic black	1991	81.4	(±3.2)	43.1	(±3.5)	59.3	(±3.8)	48.0	(± 3.8)
	1993	79.7	(±3.2)	42.7	(±3.8)	59.1	(±4.4)	56.5	(± 3.8)
	1995	73.4	(±4.5)	35.6	(±4.4)	54.2	(±4.7)	66.1	(± 4.8)
	1997	72.6	(±2.8)	38.5	(±3.6)	53.6	(±3.2)	64.0	(± 2.8)
Hispanic	1991	53.1	(±3.5)	16.8	(±2.6)	37.0	(±3.6)	37.4	(± 6.2)
	1993	56.0	(±4.1)	18.6	(±3.1)	39.4	(±3.7)	46.1	(± 4.4)
	1995	57.6	(±8.6)	17.6	(±3.7)	39.3	(±7.1)	44.4	(±11.1)
	1997	52.2	(±3.6)	15.5	(±2.4)	35.4	(±3.9)	48.3	(± 5.6)
Total	**1991**	**54.1**	**(±3.5)**	**18.7**	**(±2.1)**	**37.4**	**(±3.1)**	**46.2**	**(± 3.3)**
	1993	**53.0**	**(±2.7)**	**18.7**	**(±2.0)**	**37.5**	**(±2.1)**	**52.8**	**(± 2.7)**
	1995	**53.1**	**(±4.5)**	**17.8**	**(±2.6)**	**37.9**	**(±3.4)**	**54.4**	**(± 3.5)**
	1997	**48.4**	**(±3.1)**	**16.0**	**(±1.4)**	**34.8**	**(±2.2)**	**56.8**	**(± 1.6)**

* Sexual intercourse during the 3 months preceding the survey.
†Among currently sexually active students.
§Confidence interval.
¶Numbers of students in other racial/ethnic groups were too small for meaningful analysis.

Source: "Trends in Sexual Risk Behaviors Among High School Students — United States, 1991-1997," *Morbidity and Mortality Weekly Report*, vol. 47, no. 36, September 18, 1998

and peers, community services, and a classroom curriculum that focuses on life options and decision-making.

A 1997 nationwide evaluation found that TOP students who participated in a nine-month program had an 11 percent lower rate of school course failure, 14 percent fewer academic suspensions, and a 60 percent lower dropout rate. In addition, these students also had 33 percent fewer pregnancies.

TRENDS IN SEXUAL RISK BEHAVIORS

Unprotected sexual intercourse and multiple sex partners place young people at risk for pregnancy, as well as the human immunodeficiency virus (HIV) infection and other sexually transmitted diseases (STDs).

In "Trends in Sexual Risk Behaviors Among High School Students — United States, 1991-

1997" (*Morbidity and Mortality Weekly Report*, vol. 47, no. 36, September 18, 1998), the Centers for Disease Control and Prevention (CDC) reported that, in 1997, fewer high school students were engaging in sexual behaviors that would put them at risk for pregnancy, HIV infection, and other STDs. In 1997, for the first time in the 1900s, a majority of students (51.6 percent) reported that they had never had sexual intercourse. The proportion of students who reported having multiple partners dropped somewhat from 18.7 percent in 1991 to 16 percent in 1997. Among currently sexually active students, condom use increased from 46.2 percent in 1991 to 56.8 percent in 1997. The proportion of students who reported current sexual activity fell from 37.4 percent in 1991 to 34.8 percent in 1997. (See Table 5.4.)

The decline in risk behaviors among high school students between 1991 and 1997 corresponded with the increase in the proportion of students who participated in HIV/AIDS education in school — from 83.3 percent in 1991 to 91.5 percent in 1997. Dr. Lloyd Kolbe, director of the CDC's Division of Adolescent and School Health, claims that the survey findings show that teaching teenagers about safe sex does not result in more promiscuity.

TEEN ABORTION

Teenagers account for one-fifth (20.3 percent; see Chapter IV, Table 4.1) of all abortions obtained in the United States. Stanley K. Henshaw, in *Teenage Pregnancy: Overall Trends and State-by-State Information* (The Alan Guttmacher Institute, April 1999), reported on trends in the rates of pregnancies, births, and abortions among American teens ages 15-19 from 1986 through 1996. In 1996, 97.3 pregnancies occurred per 1,000 teens, down 9 percent from 106.7 pregnancies in 1986 and 17 percent from a peak of 117.1 pregnancies in 1990. (See Table 5.5.)

In 1996, of the 880,170 pregnancies among women ages 15 through 19 (Table 5.1), 34.9 percent (307,179) ended in abortion, a 24 percent drop

from 10 years earlier in 1986. (The Alan Guttmacher Institute defines the *abortion ratio* as the number of abortions per 100 pregnancies, while the Centers for Disease Control and Prevention defines it as the number of abortions per 1,000 live births; see Chapter IV.) The abortion rate fell 31 percent from 42.3 to 29.2 abortions per 1,000 women ages 15 to 19. (See Table 5.5.) (See below for the latest data on teen birth rates.)

Race and Ethnicity

Racial groups were categorized as Whites, non-Whites, and Blacks. According to Henshaw, no data were given separately for non-White teens other than Blacks because of the small numbers and the heterogeneity (dissimilarity) of the groups. In 1996, Black teenagers had more than twice (178.9 pregnancies per 1,000 Black women ages 15 to 19) the pregnancy rate of White teenagers (82.6 per 1,000 White women ages 15 to 19). Between 1990 and 1996, the pregnancy rate for Black teens declined 20 percent, while that for White teens fell 16 percent. In 1996, 32 percent of pregnancies among White adolescents were terminated by abortion, compared to 40.8 percent among Black adolescents. (See Table 5.5.)

In 1996, Hispanic teenagers, who can be of any race, had a pregnancy rate of 164.6 pregnancies per 1,000 Hispanic women ages 15 to 19, down 6.5 percent from 1992 (176 pregnancies) and about the same as that in 1990 (163.4 pregnancies). In 1996, the abortion rate (101.8 abortions per 1,000 Hispanic women 15 to 19 years old) was down 5 percent from the rate in 1992 (107.1 abortions). About 28 percent of the pregnancies ended in abortions.

Pregnancy Rates, Abortion Rates, and Abortion Ratios by State and the District of Columbia

Not surprisingly, Henshaw found that, in 1996, the number of pregnancies in each state reflected the size of the teenage population. California (126,300), Texas (80,490), and New York (61,700)

TABLE 5.5

Pregnancy, birth and abortion rates per 1,000 women aged 15-19, and abortion ratio (abortions per 100 pregnancies), by race, 1986-1996

Race and measure	1986	1987	1988	1989	1990	1991	1992	1993	1994	1995	1996
Total											
Pregnancy rate*											
All women 15-19	106.7	106.6	111.4	114.9	117.1	115.8	111.9	109.3	106.1	101.1	97.3
Sexually active women 15-19	210.7	206.7	212.2	219.5	224.3	222.4	215.5	211.1	205.4	196.3	189.5
Birthrate	50.2	50.6	53.0	57.3	60.4	62.1	60.7	59.6	58.9	56.8	54.4
Abortion rate	42.3	41.8	43.5	42.0	40.6	37.6	35.5	34.3	32.2	30.0	29.2
Abortion ratio†	45.7	45.2	45.1	42.3	40.2	37.7	36.9	36.5	35.3	34.6	34.9
White											
Pregnancy rate*	90.0	89.6	93.0	95.8	98.3	97.0	93.0	90.9	88.9	86.0	82.6
Birthrate	42.3	42.5	44.4	47.9	50.8	52.8	51.8	51.1	51.1	50.1	48.1
Abortion rate	35.6	35.1	36.1	34.8	33.9	30.5	28.1	26.9	25.1	23.5	22.6
Abortion ratio†	45.7	45.2	44.9	42.1	40.1	36.6	35.2	34.5	33.0	32.0	32.0
Nonwhite											
All											
Pregnancy rate*	180.7	180.1	189.1	193.4	189.6	189.6	185.2	180.4	172.5	158.7	153.3
Birthrate	84.8	85.5	89.2	95.9	96.5	98.4	95.5	92.5	89.1	82.2	78.1
Abortion rate	71.8	70.4	74.6	71.3	67.1	65.1	64.2	63.1	59.6	54.6	54.2
Abortion ratio†	45.8	45.2	45.5	42.6	41.0	39.8	40.2	40.5	40.1	39.9	41.0
Black											
Pregnancy rate*	u	u	u	u	224.3	223.7	218.7	212.7	202.1	184.8	178.9
Birthrate	95.8	97.6	102.7	111.5	113.1	115.5	112.4	108.6	104.5	96.1	91.4
Abortion rate	u	u	u	u	80.5	77.4	76.2	74.9	69.7	63.2	62.9
Abortion ratio†	u	u	u	u	41.6	40.1	40.4	40.8	40.0	39.7	40.8

*Includes estimated number of pregnancies ending in miscarriages. †Denominator excludes miscarriages. *Notes:* Data are tabulated according to the woman's age at the pregnancy outcome and, for births, according to the mother's race (not the child's). No data are presented separately for nonwhite women other than blacks because of small numbers and the heterogeneity of the group. u=unavailable.

Source: Reproduced with the permission of The Alan Guttmacher Institute from The Alan Guttmacher Institute, *Teenage Pregnancy: Overall Trends and State-by-State Information, April 1999*, <http://www.agi-usa.org/pubs/teen_preg_stats.html>, accessed December 28, 1999, Table 3.

TABLE 5.6

Ranking of pregnancy, birth and abortion rates per 1,000 women aged 15-19, these rates by age-group, and abortion ratio (abortions per 100 pregnancies), all according to state, 1996

State	Pregnancy rate*				Birthrate				Abortion rate				Abortion ratio‡
	Rank†	15-19	15-17	18-19	Rank†	15-19	15-17	18-19	Rank†	15-19	15-17	18-19	
U.S. total	na	97	62	153	na	54	34	86	na	29	19	45	35
Alabama	12	106	69	160	7	69	45	104	24	21	13	32	23
Alaska	35	75	46	117	29	46	26	75	33	18	13	25	28
Arizona	3	118	80	176	3	74	49	111	16	27	19	39	27
Arkansas	8	108	65	174	2	75	45	122	37	16	10	25	18
California§	2	125	80	196	14	63	39	99	5	45	30	70	42
Colorado	21	90	58	141	25	50	30	80	15	28	20	41	36
Connecticut	29	86	58	131	42	37	24	58	8	37	26	55	50
Delaware§	20	95	65	137	18	57	41	80	20	24	15	37	30
Dist. of Columbia**	na	256	185	349	na	102	79	133	na	121	82	173	54
Florida§	4	115	71	185	16	59	37	94	6	40	24	65	40
Georgia	7	109	72	167	8	68	45	103	19	25	16	39	27
Hawaii	15	101	66	149	26	48	28	76	7	39	30	53	45
Idaho	38	70	40	114	27	47	26	78	45	12	7	19	20
Illinois	11	106	70	164	17	57	36	91	10	34	25	50	38
Indiana	25	88	52	143	19	56	33	91	30	19	11	30	25
Iowa§	46	58	34	96	41	38	21	64	46	12	7	18	23
Kansas	34	79	47	130	24	50	28	84	35	18	12	26	26
Kentucky	24	89	54	140	15	61	37	98	43	14	9	21	18
Louisiana	19	97	62	148	9	67	43	102	41	15	10	23	19
Maine	47	57	32	96	48	31	17	55	34	18	11	28	36
Maryland	13	106	68	165	30	46	30	72	4	46	30	71	50
Massachusetts	33	79	48	126	46	32	20	51	9	37	22	59	53
Michigan	27	87	54	140	28	46	28	75	14	29	18	45	38
Minnesota	49	56	33	93	47	32	19	54	38	16	10	25	33
Mississippi	10	108	74	160	1	75	52	110	39	16	10	25	17
Missouri	30	86	52	140	20	54	31	90	29	19	13	30	27
Montana	40	65	38	107	40	39	21	66	36	17	11	26	31
Nebraska	41	62	36	101	39	39	22	64	42	14	8	22	26
Nevada	1	140	90	220	6	70	42	114	2	51	36	76	42
New Hampshire§	48	57	31	100	50	29	15	51	25	20	12	35	42
New Jersey	18	97	63	152	44	35	23	55	3	50	32	78	58
New Mexico	6	110	73	168	5	71	46	111	22	22	16	32	24
New York	9	108	70	166	36	42	26	66	1	53	36	78	56
North Carolina	14	105	68	161	11	63	41	97	18	26	17	40	29
North Dakota	50	50	26	88	45	32	16	58	49	10	6	17	24
Ohio	32	81	48	131	22	50	30	83	32	18	11	29	27
Oklahoma§	23	90	53	149	12	63	37	105	44	13	7	21	17
Oregon	22	90	55	146	21	51	29	85	17	26	18	40	34
Pennsylvania	39	70	42	112	38	39	24	63	26	20	12	34	34

(continued)

TABLE 5.6 (Continued)

State	Pregnancy rate*				Birthrate				Abortion rate				Abortion ratio‡
	Rank†	15-19	15-17	18-19	Rank†	15-19	15-17	18-19	Rank†	15-19	15-17	18-19	
Rhode Island	28	87	51	142	35	42	27	66	11	32	16	57	43
South Carolina	17	98	65	145	13	63	41	94	27	20	14	29	24
South Dakota	45	59	35	95	37	39	22	66	48	10	7	15	20
Tennessee	16	100	62	158	10	66	40	106	31	18	12	28	22
Texas	5	113	74	174	4	73	49	111	21	23	14	36	24
Utah	44	60	34	95	34	43	24	69	50	8	5	12	15
Vermont	43	60	34	103	49	30	15	54	23	22	14	35	42
Virginia	26	87	54	136	31	46	28	72	12	30	19	46	40
Washington	31	85	54	135	32	45	26	74	13	29	20	42	39
West Virginia	37	73	43	117	23	50	29	82	47	11	8	17	19
Wisconsin	42	61	37	100	43	37	22	61	40	15	10	24	29
Wyoming	36	74	46	120	33	44	25	75	28	20	15	27	31

*Includes estimated number of pregnancies ending in miscarriages. †Based on rates for women aged 15-19. ‡Denominator excludes miscarriages. §Abortion estimates are based on the proportion of abortions obtained by women of the same age in neighboring or similar states. **Distribution of abortions among teenagers into age-groups 15-17 and 18-19 is based on the proportion among all black teenagers nationally. *Notes:* Data are tabulated according to the woman's age at the pregnancy outcome. Even though abortions have been tabulated according to state of residence where possible, in states with parental notification or consent requirements for minors, the pregnancy and abortion rates may be too low because minors may have traveled to other states for abortion services. na=not applicable.

Source: Reproduced with the permission of The Alan Guttmacher Institute from The Alan Guttmacher Institute, *Teenage Pregnancy: Overall Trends and State-by-State Information, April 1999*, <http://www.agi-usa.org/pubs/teen_preg_stats.html>, accessed December 28, 1999, Table 3.

had the most pregnancies, while Wyoming (1,510), North Dakota (1,230), and Vermont (1,210) had the least. (See Table 5.1.) The teenage pregnancy rate was highest in the District of Columbia (256 pregnancies per 1,000 women ages 15 to 19), followed by Nevada (140), California (125), Florida (115), and Texas (113). (See Table 5.6.)

Abortion rates were highest in the District of Columbia (121 abortions per 1,000 women ages 15 to 19), New York (53), Nevada (51), Maryland (46), and California (45). The rates were lowest in Utah (8), North and South Dakota (10 each), West Virginia (11), and Idaho and Iowa (12 each). (See Table 5.6.)

The abortion ratio also varied by state. In New Jersey, almost 6 in 10 (58 percent) of teen pregnancies were terminated by abortion; over 5 in 10 in New York (56 percent), the District of Columbia (54 percent), and Massachusetts (53 percent);

and 50 percent in Connecticut and Maryland. On the other hand, in Utah, just 15 percent of teenage pregnancies ended in abortion. The abortion ratio was also below 20 percent in Mississippi and Oklahoma (17 percent each), Arkansas and Kentucky (18 percent each), and Louisiana and West Virginia (19 percent). (See Table 5.6.)

Factors That Affect Pregnancy and Abortion

The Alan Guttmacher Institute (AGI), in *Sex and America's Teenagers* (New York, 1994), discussed the outcomes of adolescent pregnancies that are unintended. A teenager faced with an unintended pregnancy can either choose parenthood, adoption, or an abortion. Most teenagers choose to raise the infant or to have an abortion (about one-fifth of all abortions performed annually are obtained by teens). Very few choose to give up the baby for adoption (see Chapter VII).

65

Number of births to women under 20 years by age, race, and Hispanic origin of mother: United States, 1998; birth rates, 1991–98; and percent change in rates, 1991–98

[Rates per 1,000 women in specified group]

Age, race, and Hispanic origin of mother	Number of births, 1998[1]	Birth rates								Percent change in rates, 1991–98
		1998[1]	1997	1996	1995	1994	1993	1992	1991	
10–14 years										
Total	9,481	1.0	1.1	1.2	1.3	1.4	1.4	1.4	1.4	–28.6
White, total	4,821	0.7	0.7	0.8	0.8	0.8	0.8	0.8	0.8	–12.5
Non-Hispanic white	2,145	0.4	0.4	0.4	0.4	0.5	0.5	0.5	0.5	–20.0
Black	4,291	2.9	3.3	3.6	4.2	4.6	4.6	4.7	4.8	–39.6
American Indian[2]	195	1.6	1.7	1.7	1.8	1.9	1.4	1.6	1.6	0.0
Asian or Pacific Islander	174	0.4	0.5	0.6	0.7	0.7	0.6	0.7	0.8	–50.0
Hispanic[3]	2,721	2.1	2.3	2.6	2.7	2.7	2.7	2.6	2.4	–12.5
15–19 years										
Total	484,975	51.1	52.3	54.4	56.8	58.9	59.6	60.7	62.1	–17.7
White, total	340,894	45.4	46.3	48.1	50.1	51.1	51.1	51.8	52.8	–14.0
Non-Hispanic white	212,292	35.2	36.0	37.6	39.3	40.4	40.7	41.7	43.4	–18.9
Black	126,865	85.3	88.2	91.4	96.1	104.5	108.6	112.4	115.5	–26.1
American Indian[2]	8,174	71.8	71.8	73.9	78.0	80.8	83.1	84.4	85.0	–15.5
Asian or Pacific Islander	9,043	23.1	23.7	24.6	26.1	27.1	27.0	26.6	27.4	–15.7
Hispanic[3]	121,455	93.7	97.3	101.8	106.7	107.7	106.8	107.1	106.7	–12.2
15–17 years										
Total	173,252	30.4	32.1	33.8	36.0	37.6	37.8	37.8	38.7	–21.4
White, total	116,699	25.9	27.1	28.4	30.0	30.7	30.3	30.1	30.7	–15.6
Non-Hispanic white	68,657	18.4	19.4	20.6	22.0	22.8	22.7	22.7	23.6	–22.0
Black	50,062	56.8	60.8	64.7	69.7	76.3	79.8	81.3	84.1	–32.5
American Indian[2]	3,155	44.3	45.3	46.4	47.8	51.3	53.7	53.8	52.7	–15.9
Asian or Pacific Islander	3,336	13.7	14.3	14.9	15.4	16.1	16.0	15.2	16.1	–14.9
Hispanic[3]	48,265	62.3	66.3	69.0	72.9	74.0	71.7	71.4	70.6	–11.8
18–19 years										
Total	311,724	82.0	83.6	86.0	89.1	91.5	92.1	94.5	94.4	–13.1
White, total	224,195	74.7	75.9	78.4	81.2	82.1	82.1	83.8	83.5	–10.5
Non-Hispanic white	150,635	60.6	61.9	63.7	66.1	67.4	67.7	69.8	70.5	–14.0
Black	76,803	126.8	130.1	132.5	137.1	148.3	151.9	157.9	158.6	–20.1
American Indian[2]	5,019	118.0	117.6	122.3	130.7	130.3	130.7	132.6	134.3	–12.1
Asian or Pacific Islander	5,707	38.2	39.3	40.4	43.4	44.1	43.3	43.1	43.1	–11.4
Hispanic[3]	73,189	140.2	144.3	151.1	157.9	158.0	159.1	159.7	158.5	–11.5

[1] Data for 1998 are preliminary.
[2] Includes births to Aleuts and Eskimos.
[3] Includes all persons of Hispanic origin of any race.

Source: Stephanie J. Ventura, T. J. Mathews, and Sally C. Curtin, "Declines in Teenage Birth Rates, 1991-98: Update of National and State Trends," *National Vital Statistics Reports*, vol. 47, no. 26, October 25, 1999

According to the AGI, factors that affect pregnancy and abortion include

- Marital status — Married teens with unintended pregnancies are less likely than unmarried teens to have an abortion. These teens generally have the support of their spouse and family to carry the pregnancy to term. In addition, married couples are more likely to be employed, have higher incomes, and are more willing to have children. Even so, about one-fourth of married teens with unintended pregnancies obtain an abortion.

- Expectations for the future — In general, teenagers who have a plan for their future are more likely to end their pregnancy. In contrast, teenagers who are ambivalent about their future tend to carry their pregnancy to term.

- Socioeconomic status and parents' education — Teens who come from families that are better off financially and whose parents are more educated tend to have abortions. Those from poor or low-income families and whose parents are less educated tend to choose childbirth.

- The age of the teen's partner — Teenagers with partners who are older are more likely to bear a child.

- Race and ethnicity — White teenagers whose pregnancies are unintended are more likely to have an abortion than Black and Hispanic teens.

- Medicaid coverage — Teenagers whose health care is covered by Medicaid are less likely to have an abortion. Most states pay for prenatal care and childbirth, but not for abortion.

BIRTH RATE

According to preliminary data from the Centers for Disease Control and Prevention (CDC), for the seventh straight year since 1991, the birth rate among teenagers ages 15 to 19 has declined ("Declines in Teenage Birth Rates, 1991-1998: Update of National and State Trends," *National Vital Statistics Report*, vol. 47, no. 26, October 25, 1999). In 1998, the birth rate was 51.1 births per 1,000 women ages 15 to 19, down 18 percent from 1991 (62.1 births). Despite the declining trend, nearly one-half million babies were born to teenagers in 1998. (See Table 5.7 and Figure 5.3.)

The highest recorded teenage birth rate was 96.3 births per 1,000 women ages 15 to 19 in 1957. In 1960, the teen birth rate was down to 89.1 births per 1,000 women ages 15 to 19. After 1965 (70.5 births), the teen birth rate steadily decreased. In 1988, the birth rate started rising sharply, increasing from 53 births to 62.1 births in 1991, the highest recorded in 20 years (64.5 in 1971). (See Figure 5.3.)

Racial and Ethnic Differences

Between 1991 and 1998, the birth rates for females ages 15 to 19 decreased for all racial and ethnic groups — a 15.7 percent drop for Asians/ Pacific Islanders, 15.5 percent for American Indians, 14 percent for Whites, and 12.2 percent for Hispanics. The most significant decline was for

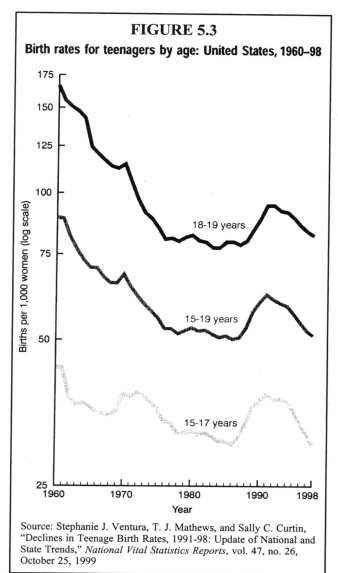

FIGURE 5.3

Birth rates for teenagers by age: United States, 1960–98

Source: Stephanie J. Ventura, T. J. Mathews, and Sally C. Curtin, "Declines in Teenage Birth Rates, 1991-98: Update of National and State Trends," *National Vital Statistics Reports*, vol. 47, no. 26, October 25, 1999

Blacks — 26.1 percent. In 1998, the birth rate for Black teenagers (85.3 births per 1,000 Black women ages 15 to 19) was the lowest ever reported. (See Table 5.7 and Figure 5.4.)

Births to Unmarried Teenagers

In 1998, births to unmarried teenagers ages 15 to 19 accounted for 78.5 percent of the births to all teenagers of the same ages. Although the proportion of nonmarital births continued to increase, most births to unmarried women were not to teenagers. Seventy percent were to women age 20 and older. (See Table 5.8.)

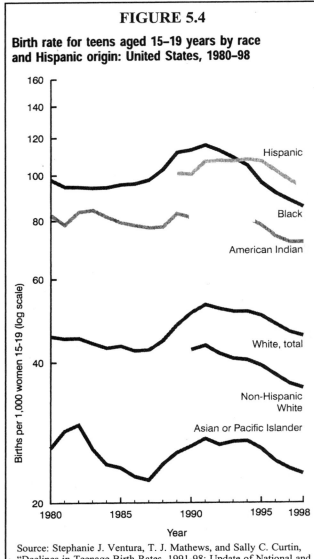

FIGURE 5.4

Birth rate for teens aged 15–19 years by race and Hispanic origin: United States, 1980–98

Births per 1,000 women 15-19 (log scale)

Hispanic

Black

American Indian

White, total

Non-Hispanic White

Asian or Pacific Islander

Year

Source: Stephanie J. Ventura, T. J. Mathews, and Sally C. Curtin, "Declines in Teenage Birth Rates, 1991-98: Update of National and State Trends," *National Vital Statistics Reports*, vol. 47, no. 26, October 25, 1999

PARENTAL INVOLVEMENT IN ABORTION DECISIONS

Parental Consent and Notification

Most state laws require minors to either obtain their parents' consent or notify their parents of their intent to get an abortion before they undergo the procedure. These laws generally include judicial bypass provisions if the young woman does not want to or cannot tell her parents of her decision. In a judicial bypass (waiver), the court decides if the minor is mature enough to make the decision on her own or if the abortion would be in her best interests.

As of December 1999, 42 states had laws requiring a minor seeking an abortion to obtain the consent of or to notify an adult, usually a parent. Thirty-two of these laws are currently enforced. Among the laws enforced, Idaho, Maryland, and Utah did not provide a judicial bypass to enable a minor to bring her case before the court. Delaware, Maryland, and West Virginia allowed a minor to get an abortion without parental notification in certain situations if a specified health professional waived the requirement. Some states— Delaware, Illinois, Iowa, Maine, North Carolina, Ohio, Pennsylvania, South Carolina, and Wisconsin — permitted a minor to seek the consent of or give notice to an adult family member, such as a grandparent or a sibling. (See Table 5.10.)

State-Specific Birth Rates

State-specific birth rates varied greatly from 1991 to 1997, depending on the compositions of the teenage populations by race and ethnicity. The rates per 1,000 women ages 15 to 19 ranged from 26.9 births in Vermont to 73.7 births in Mississippi. Birth rates declined significantly in most of the states and the District of Columbia, except for Rhode Island. The birth rates declined 20 percent or more in 10 states and the District of Columbia, 16 to 19.9 percent in 11 states, 13 to 15.9 percent in 16 states, and less than 13 percent in 14 states (See Table 5.9.)

TABLE 5.8

Number of total births and percent of births to unmarried women, all ages and women under 20 years: United States, final 1997 and preliminary 1998

Age of mother	Total births		Births to unmarried women		Percent unmarried	
	1998	1997	1998	1997	1998	1997
All ages.	3,944,046	3,880,894	1,292,534	1,257,444	32.8	32.4
Under 20 years . . .	494,456	493,341	389,721	385,802	78.8	78.2
Under 15 years . .	9,481	10,121	9,152	9,685	96.5	95.7
15–19 years	484,975	483,220	380,569	376,117	78.5	77.8
15–17 years . .	173,252	180,154	151,445	156,253	87.4	86.7
18–19 years . .	311,724	303,066	229,124	219,864	73.5	72.5

Source: Stephanie J. Ventura, T. J. Mathews, and Sally C. Curtin, "Declines in Teenage Birth Rates, 1991-98: Update of National and State Trends," *National Vital Statistics Reports*, vol. 47, no. 26, October 25, 1999

TABLE 5.9

Birth rates for teenagers aged 15–19 years by age group and State, and percent change by age: United States and each State, 1991 to 1997

[Rates per 1,000 women in specified group]

State	1991 15–19 years	1991 15–17 years	1991 18–19 years	1997 15–19 years	1997 15–17 years	1997 18–19 years	Percent change, 1991–97 15–19 years	Percent change, 1991–97 15–17 years	Percent change, 1991–97 18–19 years
United States[1]	62.1	38.7	94.4	52.3	32.1	89.1	−15.8	−17.2	−5.6
Alabama	73.9	47.7	109.5	66.6	43.4	100.2	−9.9	−9.1	−8.5
Alaska	65.4	35.3	111.7	44.6	25.1	73.6	−31.8	−29.0	−34.1
Arizona	80.7	51.4	122.6	69.7	44.0	111.2	−13.6	−14.4	−9.3
Arkansas	79.8	49.4	122.8	72.9	42.9	119.2	−8.6	−13.1	−2.9**
California	74.7	46.9	113.6	57.3	36.2	90.5	−23.3	−22.9	−20.3
Colorado	58.2	35.3	91.4	48.2	29.9	77.2	−17.2	−15.5	−15.5
Connecticut	40.4	26.3	59.4	36.1	22.5	58.1	−10.6	−14.5	−2.2**
Delaware	61.1	40.3	87.1	55.8	36.8	83.3	−8.7	−8.6**	−4.3**
District of Columbia	114.4	102.8	125.5	91.0	65.9	122.4	−20.5	−35.9	−2.5**
Florida	68.8	44.0	102.9	57.7	35.1	94.2	−16.1	−20.2	−8.4
Georgia	76.3	50.6	110.9	67.2	44.0	102.8	−11.9	−13.0	−7.3
Hawaii	58.7	34.7	91.5	43.8	25.3	69.6	−25.4	−27.1	−23.9
Idaho	53.9	29.3	90.8	43.3	23.3	72.5	−19.7	−20.6	−20.2
Illinois	64.8	40.6	99.1	54.7	34.4	87.6	−15.6	−15.2	−11.7
Indiana	60.5	35.2	95.2	54.2	32.1	87.6	−10.4	−8.7	−7.9
Iowa	42.6	22.8	71.5	35.7	20.1	60.4	−16.2	−12.1	−15.5
Kansas	55.4	29.4	94.1	48.5	27.5	81.7	−12.5	−6.4**	−13.2
Kentucky	68.9	42.6	105.5	59.6	35.4	95.0	−13.5	−17.0	−9.9
Louisiana	76.1	51.1	111.4	66.3	42.1	101.4	−12.9	−17.6	−9.0
Maine	43.5	23.8	70.1	32.0	15.4	58.3	−26.4	−35.0	−16.8
Maryland	54.3	35.2	79.8	43.9	28.2	68.8	−19.2	−19.9	−13.7
Massachusetts	37.8	25.2	52.9	31.7	19.1	50.8	−16.1	−24.3	−4.0**
Michigan	59.0	35.5	91.1	43.9	25.4	72.2	−25.6	−28.4	−20.8
Minnesota	37.3	20.7	61.4	32.0	17.8	55.1	−14.2	−14.1	−10.2
Mississippi	85.6	60.1	120.4	73.7	50.2	108.8	−13.9	−16.4	−9.6
Missouri	64.5	38.7	100.7	51.5	29.6	86.3	−20.2	−23.7	−14.2
Montana	46.7	23.6	83.0	37.6	20.1	65.2	−19.5	−14.8	−21.4
Nebraska	42.4	23.6	69.2	37.2	21.3	61.6	−12.3	−9.8**	−10.9
Nevada	75.3	43.9	119.1	67.7	42.2	109.1	−10.1	−3.8**	−8.4
New Hampshire	33.3	17.1	53.8	28.6	14.0	53.0	−14.1	−18.2	−1.4**
New Jersey	41.6	26.3	62.9	35.0	21.3	56.7	−15.9	−19.0	−9.9
New Mexico	79.8	50.0	124.4	68.4	44.4	106.3	−14.3	−11.2	−14.5
New York	46.0	29.1	69.0	38.8	23.4	62.3	−15.7	−19.4	−9.8
North Carolina	70.5	46.2	101.7	61.3	37.7	97.3	−13.0	−18.5	−4.3
North Dakota	35.6	18.1	62.4	30.1	14.3	55.0	−15.4	−20.9	−11.8
Ohio	60.5	36.2	93.8	49.8	28.6	82.6	−17.7	−21.1	−12.0
Oklahoma	72.1	41.7	115.6	64.3	37.3	107.4	−10.8	−10.7	−7.1
Oregon	54.9	31.3	90.7	46.9	27.0	78.2	−14.6	−13.7	−13.8
Pennsylvania	46.9	29.2	70.5	37.3	21.9	61.3	−20.5	−25.0	−13.0
Rhode Island	45.4	30.1	63.6	42.7	27.6	65.6	−5.9**	−8.2**	3.2**
South Carolina	72.9	48.0	105.4	61.4	40.0	93.0	−15.8	−16.6	−11.8
South Dakota	47.5	26.3	79.2	39.7	21.8	66.3	−16.4	−17.2	−16.3
Tennessee	75.2	47.8	112.1	64.5	38.5	103.8	−14.2	−19.4	−7.4
Texas	78.9	50.4	119.3	71.7	47.1	110.1	−9.1	−6.6	−7.7
Utah	48.2	27.0	79.8	42.6	23.7	68.3	−11.6	−12.3	−14.5
Vermont	39.2	21.3	62.0	26.9	12.1	51.2	−31.4	−43.3	−17.6
Virginia	53.5	31.8	81.2	44.2	26.1	70.8	−17.4	−17.8	−12.8
Washington	53.7	31.0	86.5	42.5	24.5	70.7	−20.9	−20.8	−18.2
West Virginia	57.8	32.4	93.2	49.1	27.5	80.3	−15.1	−15.1	−13.9
Wisconsin	43.7	24.8	71.2	35.9	21.4	58.8	−17.8	−13.7	−17.4
Wyoming	54.2	26.4	98.6	43.3	23.3	75.8	−20.1	−12.1**	−23.1
Puerto Rico	72.4	50.8	105.9	77.8	57.6	106.6	7.5	13.4	0.7**
Virgin Islands	77.9	48.6	124.0	66.0	45.6	96.7	−15.3	−6.2**	−22.0
Guam	95.7	55.0	156.1	106.3	61.4	178.2	11.1**	11.6**	14.2**
American Samoa	· · ·	· · ·	· · ·	43.9	20.7	81.5	· · ·	· · ·	· · ·

** Not signficant at p<0.05.

· · · Data not available.

[1]Excludes data for Puerto Rico, Virgin Islands, Guam, and American Samoa.

NOTE: Birth rates by State in this table are based on population estimates provided by the U.S. Bureau of the Census and, therefore, the rates shown here may differ from rates computed on the basis of other population estimates.

Source: Stephanie J. Ventura, T. J. Mathews, and Sally C. Curtin, "Declines in Teenage Birth Rates, 1991-98: Update of National and State Trends," *National Vital Statistics Reports*, vol. 47, no. 26, October 25, 1999

TABLE 5.10

RESTRICTIONS ON MINOR'S ACCESS TO ABORTION

State	One Parent	Two Parent	Consent	Notice	Judicial Bypass	Enjoined/ Not Enforced	Enforced
Alabama	X		X		X		X
Alaska	X		X		X	X[1]	
Arizona	X		X		X	X[1]	
Arkansas		X		X	X		X
California	X		X		X	X[1]	
Colorado	X[11]			X		X	
Delaware	X[2]			X[3]	X		X
Florida	X			X	X	X[1]	
Georgia	X			X	X		X
Idaho		X[4]		X			X
Illinois	X[5]			X	X	X[1]	
Indiana	X		X		X		X
Iowa	X[2]			X	X		X
Kansas	X			X	X		X
Kentucky	X		X		X		X
Louisiana	X		X		X		X
Maine	X[6]		X[7]		X		X
Maryland	X			X[3]			X
Massachusetts	X[8]		X		X		X
Michigan	X		X		X		X
Minnesota		X		X	X		X
Mississippi		X	X		X		X
Missouri	X		X		X		X
Montana	X			X	X	X[1]	
Nebraska	X			X	X		X
Nevada	X			X	X	X[1]	
New Jersey	X			X	X	X[12]	
New Mexico	X		X			X[1]	

(continued)

Both abortion rights groups and anti-abortionists dislike judicial bypasses. Abortion supporters claim that the law does not promote family communication and requires young women to travel to counties or states where the bypasses are available. The delay generally results in young women getting second-trimester abortions. (Physicians agree that first-trimester abortions are the safest.) On the other hand, a spokesman for the Right-to-Life Committee calls the judicial waiver "... a monstrosity. The average hearing takes 12 minutes and it's a rubber stamp."

Opinion polls (see Chapter IX) indicate that a large majority (74 percent) of the public approves of a parental-consent requirement for a minor to get an abortion. Most Americans feel that parents have a right and a duty to guide their children's decisions and that a teenager needs her parents' support when faced with a stressful situation, such as an unplanned pregnancy. Furthermore, many parents think that, if they are going to be financially and legally responsible for the child, they should have some say in the decision.

Minors' Rights

In 1967, the U.S. Supreme Court, in *In re Gault* (387 U.S. 1), ruled that "constitutional rights do not mature and come into being magically only

TABLE 5.10 (Continued)

RESTRICTIONS ON MINOR'S ACCESS TO ABORTION

State	One Parent	Two Parent	Consent	Notice	Judicial Bypass	Enjoined/ Not Enforced	Enforced
North Carolina	X^2		X		X		X
North Dakota		X	X		X		X
Ohio	X^9			X	X		X
Pennsylvania	X^9			X	X		X
Rhode Island	X		X		X		X
South Carolina	X^2		X		X		X
South Dakota	X			X	X		X
Tennessee	X		X		X		X^{13}
Texas	X			X	X		X
Utah		X^4		X			X
Virginia	X			X	X		X
West Virginia	X			X^3	X		X
Wisconsin	X^{10}		X		X		X
Wyoming	X		X		X		X
TOTAL	36	6	20	22	37	10	32

1. This statute has been declared unenforceable by a court or attorney general.
2. This statute also allows consent of or notice to a grandparent under certain circumstances.
3. This requirement may be waived by a specified health professional under certain circumstances.
4. This statute requires notice to a minor's parents, if possible.
5. This statute also allows consent of or notice to a grandparent or step-parent.
6. This statute also allows consent of an adult family member.
7. This statute offers mandatory counseling as an alternative to one-parent or adult famil[member consent with a judicial bypass.
8. This statute requires two-parent consent, but a court has issued an order that the law b[enforced as requiring the consent of one parent.
9. This statute also allows notice to a grandparent, step-parent or adult sibling over the a[of 21 under certain circumstances.
10. This statute allows consent of or notice to a grandparent or certain other adult family members over the age of 25.
11. This statute requires notice to both parents, but allows notice to one parent, if the min[requests, and if the parents do not reside together.
12. A court has ruled that this law is unconstitutional under the state constitution, but the][has been stayed pending an appeal to the state supreme court.
13. Pursuant to a court order, the Tennessee law is scheduled to become effective January 2000.

Source: *Who Decides? A State-by-State Review of Abortion and Reproductive Rights*, The National Abortion and Reproductive Rights Action League Foundation, Washington, DC, 2000

when one attains the state-defined age of majority." Based on this decision, the Supreme Court, in *Planned Parenthood of Central Missouri v. Danforth* (428 U.S. 52, 1976) and *Belloti v. Baird* (433 U.S. 622, 1979), upheld the constitutional right of privacy for minors, which includes the right to obtain contraceptives and the right to terminate pregnancies. (See Chapter II.)

States generally recognize that minors are capable of giving informed consent to their own medical care in such areas as prenatal care and delivery services, contraceptive services, alcohol/drug addiction, and treatment for sexually transmitted diseases. Abortion rights supporters point out that, while some states allow minors to give consent to major medical procedures such as a

Caesarian delivery, many of these same states require parental consent for abortion.

Most Teenagers Tell Their Parents

Stanley Henshaw and Kathryn Kost, in "Parental Involvement in Minors' Abortion Decisions" (*Family Planning Perspectives*, vol. 24, no. 5, September/October 1992), studied a nationally representative sample of 1,500 unmarried teens having abortions. In 61 percent of the cases, the parents were either told by the minor (45 percent) or had found out some other way (15 percent). Mothers were far more likely to be told about the abortion than fathers were (43 percent compared to 12 percent). The younger the teen, the more likely the parents were to know. Half or more teens 15 years and younger told their mothers about the abortion, while two-fifths of the older teens told their mothers.

The researchers found that the teens most likely to discuss the abortion with their parents were younger, not employed, not in school, and living with at least one parent. In addition, those who felt comfortable talking with their mothers, those whose mothers had encouraged them to use contraceptives, and those whose mothers had left decisions about sexual activity up to the teen were more likely to inform a parent.

Teens were asked why they either did or did not tell their parents. The most common reason for telling a parent was that the teen "wouldn't have felt right not telling" him/her (48 percent of those who told their mothers and 39 percent of those who told their fathers). Other common reasons for telling were the need for assistance in deciding what to do, the belief that the parent would be sympathetic, and the need for help in getting an abortion. The minors' most frequently cited reasons for not telling their mothers were the desire not to disappoint them (73 percent), the fear that they would be angry (55 percent), and not wanting them to know that the daughters had had sex (32 percent). The proportions of those who did not tell their fathers for those reasons were 60 percent, 51 percent, and 38 percent, respectively.

All minors reported that at least one other person had taken part in their decision to get an abortion. Aside from parents, the individual most likely to have been involved was the minor's boyfriend (78 percent) — he was more than three times as likely as her father to be involved. Half (54 percent) reported that someone had tried to convince them to get an abortion, while 40 percent reported that someone had tried to convince them to see the pregnancy to term.

TEENAGERS CROSS STATE LINES

In April 1998, Representative Ileana Ros-Lehtinen (R-FL) introduced the Child Custody Protection Act (CCPA; H.R. 3682), which would make it a federal offense to transport a minor across state lines to obtain an abortion to avoid state laws requiring the involvement of parents in abortion decisions. The House of Representatives passed the bill by a 276-to-150 vote, but the Senate never considered the bill. In March 1999, Representative Ros-Lehtinen reintroduced the bill (H.R. 1218), which passed the House by a 270-to-159 vote. (Nine abortion rights advocates had then been elected to the House). As of November 1999, the Senate had not taken final action on the bill.

Chairman Henry Hyde of the House Judiciary Committee claims that "the CCPA is not a federal parental involvement law; it merely ensures that state laws are not evaded through interstate activity. The CCPA does not encroach on state powers, but rather reinforces state powers." A violation of the law would result in a fine of up to $100,000, or a prison term of up to one year, or both. The law would not apply in abortions obtained to save the life of the minor. In addition, the minor's parent (including a guardian, a legal custodian, or a person who has care and control of a minor) is exempted from the prohibition of the law.

Minors do cross state lines to obtain abortions. Proponents of the Child Custody Protection Act point out that the legislation would protect minors from those who might not have their best interests. Abortion rights supporters argue that the

CCPA would criminalize a family member or a clergyman (who is not a guardian or legal custodian) who may come to a minor's aid. (See Chapters XI and XII for the arguments for and against passage of the bill during the House Judiciary Committee hearings in 1998 and 1999.)

WHAT DO TEENS KNOW ABOUT ABORTION?

Rebecca Stone and Cynthia Waszak, of the Center for Population Options, an organization that supports abortion as an alternative, conducted focus-group studies of teens across the country to understand adolescent attitudes on abortion. The authors wanted to learn where teens got their information, how they formed their opinions on abortion, how they felt about speaking to their parents about the issue or having to turn to them for consent for the procedure, and whether there were gender, ethnic, or cultural differences in attitude. The results of the discussions (published in "Adolescent Knowledge and Attitudes About Abortion," *Family Planning Perspectives*, vol. 24, no. 2, March/April 1992) revealed surprising consistency in the responses. Four themes were consistent among the 11 focus groups.

First, most teens held negative attitudes toward abortion, but they felt that women still needed the right to choose. Second, the teenagers did not think that mandatory parental involvement was helpful no matter how strongly the teenagers opposed abortion. Third, teenagers lacked knowledge about abortion and related laws. They relied on anecdotal evidence and often believed that abortion is medically dangerous, emotionally damaging, and widely illegal. Fourth, teens' attitudes toward abortion were generally shaped by anti-abortion views, conservative morality, and religion.

The teens, regardless of sex, mentioned "murder, killing a baby, or death" when asked about what the word "abortion" brought to mind. Many felt abortion was something done out of fear of being found out. Most of the females agreed that the male had a right to know if his girlfriend was pregnant and to be included in the decision. Although the participants generally disliked abortion, they condoned abortion in cases of rape and incest. Moreover, they approved of keeping abortion legal either because they felt women would do it anyway and it was better that it was done right, or because they did not feel it was right to dictate ideas to others.

Although the teens generally disapproved of abortion, they did not approve of requiring parental permission for abortion. Even those who reported open relationships with their parents (mothers in particular) and claimed they could discuss sex with their parent(s) felt they would have a hard time telling their parents that they wanted an abortion. Even those who felt they could discuss abortion with their parents could imagine circumstances for other teens where it would be very difficult or impossible.

The focus groups revealed teens' lack of understanding about abortion. Teens in the focus groups knew little about the legality of abortion. Only a few were aware of *Roe v. Wade* or its significance. The participants did not know that abortion is legal in all 50 states, although they seemed to know that it is legal in their own state. The teens held misconceptions about the physical and mental effects of abortion. Many believed that abortion, especially multiple abortions, made a woman sterile and that it was some kind of cutting procedure that hurt. They also thought it was emotionally devastating.

Stone and Waszak believed that "from a public health perspective, assessing adolescents' views on abortion is critical to devising effective ways to deliver information and services to teenagers in need of pregnancy prevention or pregnancy option counseling." They further believed that, with the high incidence of pregnancies among American teens, there is a need for educating young people not only about pregnancy prevention, but also about early, safe abortion.

CHAPTER VI

ABORTION CLINICS

ACTIONS AGAINST ABORTION CLINICS

Violence and Disruption

The National Abortion Federation (NAF, Washington, DC) is the professional association of abortion providers in the United States and Canada. Its members (approximately 350) include non-profit clinics, private physicians' offices, for-profit surgicenters, feminist women's health centers, Planned Parenthood affiliates, and hospital-based clinics.

Since 1977, NAF has tracked incidents of violence and disruption against abortion providers across the country. NAF members report incidents on an ongoing basis. Their reports are supplemented with information from newspaper reports, law enforcement agencies, and abortion provider organizations. A yearend survey is conducted to complete each year's presentation.

On January 29, 1998, a week after the twenty-fifth anniversary of *Roe v. Wade*, the Supreme Court decision legalizing abortion, a bomb exploded at the New Woman All Women Health Care Clinic in Birmingham, Alabama. The explosion killed an off-duty police officer, Robert Sanderson, who was moonlighting as a security guard at the clinic, and seriously injured the clinic nurse and counselor, Emily Lyons. Authorities said that the bomb was obviously intended to kill and maim. Eric Rudoph, who has been charged with the attack, remains in hiding.

Over the years, many abortion clinics throughout the nation have been bombed, but this was the first time anyone was killed in an explosion. Since 1993, seven physicians and other clinic employees have been murdered (see below).

The number of violent incidents against abortion providers dropped from 223 in 1997 to 65 in 1999. In 1999, one bombing was reported, while arsons doubled from four incidents in 1998 to eight in 1999. Abortion clinics also reported 40 incidents of vandalism. Death threats decreased to seven in 1999, from 25 in 1998 and a peak of 78 in 1993. (See Table 6.1.)

The NAF first collected data on stalking (the persistent following, threatening, and harassing of an abortion provider, staff member, or patient *away from* the clinic) in 1993, reporting a record high of 188 cases that year. The number of stalkings dropped from 67 cases in 1997 to three in 1999 (Table 6.1).

In 1997 (latest data available), abortion clinics incurred over $1 million in damages caused by arsons and bombings. Between 1990 and 1997, the monetary damages from arsons and bombings amounted to $8.5 million. In addition, individual clinics have spent many thousands of dollars on protective measures, such as bulletproof windows, metal detectors, security cameras, and armed guards.

After the passage of the Freedom of Access to Clinic Entrances Act (FACE, PL 103-259; see below) in 1994, the number of blockades dropped sharply, from 25 that year to five in 1995, seven in 1996, and two in both 1998 and 1999. Picketing is, by far, the major activity of pro-life activists.

TABLE 6.1

Incidents of Violence and Disruption Against Abortion Providers, 1999 [1]

VIOLENCE	'77-83	1984	1985	1986	1987	1988	1989	1990	1991	1992	1993	1994	1995	1996	1997	1998	1999	TOTAL
Murder	0	0	0	0	0	0	0	0	0	0	1	4	0	0	0	2	0	7
Attempted Murder	0	0	0	0	0	0	0	0	2	0	1	8	1	1	2	1	0	16
Bombing	8	11	2	3	0	0	1	1	1	0	1	1	1	2	6	1	1	40
Arson	13	14	9	7	8	5	8	10	8	19	12	11	14	3	8	4	8	161
Attempted Bombing/Arson	5	6	10	4	7	3	2	3	1	13	7	3	1	4	2	5	1	77
Invasion	68	34	47	53	14	6	25	19	29	26	24	26	4	0	7	5	2	365
Vandalism	35	35	49	43	29	29	24	26	44	116	113	42	31	29	105	46	40	836
Assault and Battery	11	7	7	11	5	5	12	6	6	9	9	7	2	1	9	4	1	112
Death Threats	4	23	22	7	5	4	5	7	3	8	78	59	41	13	11	25	7	322
Kidnapping	2	0	0	0	0	0	0	0	0	0	0	0	0	0	0	1	0	3
Burglary	3	2	2	5	7	1	0	2	1	5	3	3	3	6	6	6	2	57
Stalking [2]	0	0	0	0	0	0	0	0	0	0	188	22	61	52	67	13	3	406
TOTAL	149	132	148	133	75	53	77	74	95	196	437	162	159	111	223	113	65	2,402
DISRUPTION																		
Hate Mail & Harassing Phone Calls	9	17	32	53	32	19	30	21	142	469	628	381	255	605	2829	915	242	6679
Bomb Threats	9	32	75	51	28	21	21	11	15	12	22	14	41	13	79	31	27	502
Picketing	107	160	139	141	77	151	72	45	292	2898	2279	1407	1356	3932	7518	8402	4259	33235
TOTAL	125	209	246	245	137	191	123	77	449	3379	2929	1802	1652	4550	10426	9348	4528	40416
CLINIC BLOCKADES																		
No. Incidents	0	0	0	0	2	182	201	34	41	83	66	25	5	7	25	2	2	675
No. Arrests [3]	0	0	0	0	290	11732	12358	1363	3885	2580	1236	217	54	65	29	16	2	33827

1. Numbers represent incidents reported to NAF as of 12/17/99 and classified by the ATF; actual incidents are most likely higher.

2. Stalking is defined as the persistent following, threatening, and harassing of an abortion provider, staff member, or patient *away from* the clinic. Tabulation of stalking incidents began in 1993.

3. The "number of arrests" represents the total number of arrests, not the total number of *persons* arrested. Many blockaders are arrested multiple times.

Source: National Abortion Federation, Washington, DC, 2000, www.prochoice.org

The number of incidents of picketing peaked at 8,402 in 1998, dropping to 4,259 in 1999. (See Table 6.1.)

Many protests at abortion clinics have been under the direction of Operation Save America (formerly Operation Rescue National), an organization that seeks to shut down clinics completely, but denies promoting the use of violence. In the late 1980s and early 1990s, Operation Rescue members staged massive clinic blockades.

Operation Save America believes that the United States, in permitting abortion, has lost its morality. Demonstrators claim that they are not only saving the lives of the unborn, but also preventing the judgment of God from being passed on the United States for murder committed through abortion.

Tactics Against Pro-Choice Individuals

Over the past several years, a growing number of pro-life activities has been directed at individuals. Some anti-abortionists have used high-powered surveillance microphones to listen in on conversations and obtain the names of future clinic patients. They believe that if the patients can be intercepted ahead of time, perhaps they can be convinced to carry their fetuses to term. Some abortion opponents have traced the automobile license numbers of clinic patients and then called them at home, accusing them of being baby killers. Some have even contacted the patients' parents and employers.

Clinic employees have been stalked and harassed at their workplaces and homes. In January 2000, before the twenty-seventh anniversary of *Roe*

75

v. Wade, several clinics received packages said to contain the bacterium that causes the potentially deadly disease anthrax. The packages were empty.

"Wanted" posters featuring doctors' faces have been distributed throughout the doctors' hometowns. In some parts of the country, pro-lifers have harassed doctors and their family members. Those focusing upon the doctors and their families have concluded that they are the weak link in the abortion chain. If doctors can be forced to give up their practices, abortion will be stopped.

Jury Verdict Against Anti-Abortion Protesters

On January 28, 2000, the U.S. Fifth Circuit Court of Appeals upheld an $11 million jury verdict against the Dallas Pro-Life Action League whose harassment campaign forced Dr. Norman T. Tompkins, an abortion provider, to move his practice out of the Dallas area. Starting in 1992, the pro-life group picketed the home and offices of Dr. Tompkins and his wife, Carolyn, distributing anti-abortion literature in their neighborhood. The protesters trespassed on the couple's property, conducted surveillance, and placed crosses in their yard. They confronted the couple in their church and other public places and made threatening phone calls.

Judge E. Grady Jolly, delivered the court's opinion, stating,

> We cannot say that the amount of the damages is demonstrably out of line with the harm. Because of both the defendants' conduct and the Tompkinses' particular susceptibility, the Tompkinses lived in genuine fear for their lives for an extended period of time. The evidence supports the conclusion that the protestors turned their lives into a hellish, torturous experience. The ten-month episode permanently affected their life-style, their professional lives, their enjoyment of life, their personalities, their economic well-being, and their general emotional well-being....

Internet Tactics

In February 1999, a federal jury in Portland, Oregon, unanimously ruled that it is illegal for pro-life activists to threaten abortion providers through Wild West "wanted posters" and an Internet site called the "Nuremberg Files." The "Nuremberg Files" listed the names of abortion doctors accused of committing "crimes against humanity." The list included the doctors' addresses and other family information. Murdered doctors were listed with lines drawn through their names.

The jury ordered the defendants (American Coalition of Life Activists, Advocates for Life Ministries, and 12 individuals) to pay the plaintiffs (Planned Parenthood, the Portland Feminist Women's Health Center, and four abortion doctors) over $109 million in damages. The jury found all defendants guilty of violating or conspiring to violate FACE (see below) and all but two defendants of violating or conspiring to violate RICO (see below).

Murder and Attempted Murder

The most serious instances of clinic violence have been the murder and attempted murder of abortion doctors and clinic workers. In 1993, Michael Griffin shot and killed Dr. David Gunn in Pensacola, Florida. Mainstream anti-abortion groups and the Catholic Church condemned the murder. The United States Catholic Conference declared,

> The violence of killing in the name of pro-life makes a mockery of the pro-life cause. As we abhor the violence of abortion, we abhor violence as a dangerous and deplorable means to stop abortion. It is not enough to say, "We sympathize with Mr. Griffin's motivation but disagree with his actions." In the name and the true spirit of pro-life, we call on all in the pro-life movement to condemn such violence in no uncertain terms.

Some of the more radical anti-abortion groups were more ambivalent in their reactions to the murder. In a television interview, then-director of Operation Rescue, Randall Terry, said, "While we grieve for him and for his widow and for his children, we must also grieve for the thousands of children that he has murdered." At least 32 anti-abortion leaders, including pastors, Catholic priests, and Operation Rescue leaders, signed a declaration prepared by the Defensive Action group headed by Reverend Paul Hill (see below), stating that the murder of Dr. Gunn was justified and endorsing the use of violence against doctors.

In July 1996, John Burt, regional director of Rescue America, settled a lawsuit filed by Dr. Gunn's family. The lawsuit charged that Burt had incited Griffin to murder Dr. Gunn by giving him inflammatory literature and videos, pointing out the doctor during a protest, and showing Griffin an effigy of Dr. Gunn with a rope around its neck.

Rachelle Shannon thought Griffin was a hero, sending him at least 25 letters in prison. Four months later, on August 19, 1993, Shannon shot and wounded Dr. George Tiller as he left his clinic in Wichita, Kansas.

On July 29, 1994, Paul Hill shot and killed Dr. John Bayard Britton and James H. Barrett, a retired Air Force lieutenant colonel who had volunteered to be a clinic escort. Mr. Barrett's wife, also an escort, was wounded in this attack in Pensacola, Florida.

Many mainstream anti-abortion leaders insisted that Hill acted as a lone maniac. Nevertheless, three months before the murder, at a meeting of about a hundred anti-abortion leaders in Chicago, there had been significant support for Hill's endorsement of violence. After the double murders, Operation Rescue publicly denied any support for Hill's action. Operation Rescue's director, the Reverend Philip "Flip" Benham, labeled Hill's call for violence a "heresy" and a "sin."

The pro-choice National Abortion and Reproductive Rights Action League (NARAL) dismissed Operation Rescue's disavowal of violence. "Opponents of choice who call physicians 'baby killers' one day have no credibility the next when they issue polite statements of regret after physicians and escorts have been gunned down in cold blood."

On December 30, 1994, John Salvi III shot and killed Shannon Lowney and Lee Ann Nichols, receptionists at two abortion clinics in Brookline, Massachusetts. He also shot and wounded five other people. Salvi then drove to Norfolk, Virginia, where he was arrested for firing into another clinic.

On December 18, 1996, Dr. Calvin Jackson was repeatedly stabbed as he entered his New Orleans clinic. Later that day, the same assailant, Donald Cooper, was apprehended in a Baton Rouge clinic as he waited for the clinic physician to arrive. Cooper had a knife in his possession.

On October 23, 1998, a sniper killed Dr. Barnett A. Slepian, a Buffalo, New York, abortion provider. Authorities charged James C. Kopp, an anti-abortion activist, with murder and the federal crime of violence. Kopp remains a fugitive.

FREEDOM OF ACCESS TO CLINIC ENTRANCES ACT (FACE)

The Freedom of Access to Clinic Entrances Act (FACE; PL 103-259) was signed into law on May 26, 1994 in response to increasing violence against abortion clinics. FACE prohibits whoever "by force or threat of force or by physical obstruction, intentionally injures, intimidates or interferes with or attempts to injure, intimidate or interfere with any person ... obtaining or providing reproductive health services." It further forbids the intentional destruction of a medical facility where reproductive health services are offered. The term "reproductive health services" was specifically chosen to include agencies that provide abortion services or counseling centers that offer alternatives to abortion.

The legislation received support from both abortion proponents and opponents. Pro-life advocate Senator Harry Reid (D-NV) said that despite his conviction against abortion, FACE's aim was "not to restrict the rights of people to demonstrate but to protect the rights of people to be free from the fear of violence against them."

Opponents of FACE have challenged its constitutionality on a number of grounds. Some charge that FACE violates the freedom of speech and religion protections under the First Amendment, while others claim that Congress lacks the power to pass such a law under the Commerce Clause (to regulate interstate commerce) of the Constitution. However, the U.S. Supreme Court has affirmed the constitutionality of FACE by refusing to hear challenges to the law.

Is FACE Effective?

The U.S. General Accounting Office (GAO), in *Abortion Clinics: Information on the Effectiveness of the Freedom of Access to Clinic Entrances Act* (Washington, DC, 1998), studied the occurrence of clinic incidents before and after FACE. The GAO surveyed 42 clinics that experienced relatively high levels of incidents before FACE was enacted. Most of the clinics (34) reported experiencing fewer types of incidents during the two years after FACE than they had before FACE became law. Nonetheless, almost all clinics indicated no change in the occurrences of picketing and hate mail/harassing phone calls before and after FACE. (See Table 6.2.) However, 35 respondents reported a decrease in the severity of the incidents, particularly of picketing. Overall, most respondents felt that FACE had deterred or reduced clinic incidents.

Most Clinics Were Generally Satisfied with Local Law Enforcement of FACE

Most police departments surveyed told the GAO that after FACE was passed, they had taken steps to reduce and better respond to clinic incidents. These included increasing patrols at clinics during high-risk times, such as at the anniversary of *Roe v. Wade* or on Saturdays, when more protesters were present; providing training about clinic incidents; and conducting outreach or education with clinic staff.

Most (35) clinic respondents were generally satisfied with the effectiveness of their local law enforcement in protecting their clinics during the two-year period after FACE. Five of the 7 dissatisfied respondents cited the officers' poor response (slow response or lack of response) to incidents. Eleven of the 15 police departments surveyed reported that "police officers' personal ideologies or religious beliefs about abortion did not interfere with their carrying out their duties when violent or disruptive incidents occurred at abortion clinics." The four

TABLE 6.2

Number of Clinics Experiencing Specific Types of Incidents During 2-Year Period Preceding FACE (June 1992 Through May 1994) and 2-Year Period Preceding GAO Survey (April 1996 Through March 1998)

Type of incident	Clinics reporting incident occurred before FACE (6/92 to 5/94)	Clinics reporting incident occurred more recently (4/96 to 3/98)	Change in number of clinics reporting incident
Blockades	27	6	−21
Vandalism	36	19	−17
Invasions	25	10	−15
Bomb threats	29	14	−15
Death threats	31	16	−15
Assault	23	10	−13
Stalking	25	12	−13
Burglary	6	2	−4
Arson	5	1	−4
Hate mail/ harassing calls	40	37	−3
Bombings	2	0	−2
Attempted arson	5	4	−1
Attempted bombings	2	1	−1
Picketing	41	42	+1

n=42

Source: *Abortion Clinics: Information on the Effectiveness of the Freedom of Access to Clinic Entrances Act*, U.S. General Accounting Office, Washington, DC, 1998

departments who had problems with officers' not wanting to be involved with abortion clinics resolved the problems by not assigning them to such duties. (See Table 6.3 for the clinics' satisfaction with local law enforcement by type of incident.)

CASES INVOLVING CLINICS

Do Abortion Protesters Violate the Civil Rights Act?

Prior to the enactment of FACE, although states had laws limiting anti-abortion demonstrations, many abortion rights groups felt that the scale of the protests frequently overwhelmed local law enforcement. Believing that federal law would be more effective in prohibiting the more threatening anti-abortion behaviors, the National Organization for Women (NOW) filed a lawsuit in 1989, charging that various anti-abortion organizations, including Operation Rescue and the Pro-Life Action League, violated the Civil Rights Act of 1871 (the Ku Klux Klan Act).

The act, originally passed to protect the newly freed Blacks in the South from mob violence, prohibits conspiracies to deprive people of their civil rights. Up until then, the court had interpreted the law to apply only to particular groups or classes of people and to instances when the conspiracy was motivated by a "discriminatory animus" (ill will) against those people. The Supreme Court never ruled on whether the law protected gender-based classes.

In *Bray v. Alexandria Women's Health Clinic* (506 U.S. 263, 1993), the Supreme Court, in a 6-3 ruling, held that the civil rights statute cannot be used to pre-vent abortion protesters from blocking access to clinics. The majority opinion, written by Justice Scalia and joined by Justices Rehnquist, White, Kennedy, and Thomas, rejected the claims that women's equal rights were infringed upon by the anti-abortion protesters.

The justices held that the Civil Rights Act does not protect women seeking abortions as a class. A protected class must be something more than a group of individuals who seek to engage in an activity that an alleged violator of the act opposes. Opposition to abortion is not opposition to women because both men and women are represented on both sides of the issue, and opposing abortion is not, by itself, sex discrimination.

The High Court cited an earlier case (*Geduldig v. Aiello* — 417 U.S. 484, 1974) in which it ruled, "While it is true that only women can become pregnant, it does not follow that every legislative classification concerning pregnancy is a sex-based classification." Further, the High Court referred to the district court observation that the protesters defined their "rescues" (preventing women from entering clinics), not in reference to women, but as a physi-

TABLE 6.3

Clinic Respondents' Satisfaction with Local Law Enforcement, by Type of Incident (April 1996 Through March 1998)

Type of incident	Number reporting contact with local law enforcement	Level of satisfaction		
		Generally satisfied	Neither satisfied nor dissatisfied	Generally dissatisfied
Picketing	41	30	4	7
Hate mail/ harassing calls	22	13	4	5
Blockades	6	4	1	1
Invasions	10	8	0	2
Vandalism	17	12	3	2
Burglary	2	0	0	2
Arson	1	1	0	0
Attempted arson	4	2	1	1
Bomb threats	12	9	2	1
Assaults	10	7	2	1
Stalking	10	5	3	2
Death threats	12	7	4	1

n=42

Source: *Abortion Clinics: Information on the Effectiveness of the Freedom of Access to Clinic Entrances Act*, U.S. General Accounting Office, Washington, DC, 1998

cal intervention for the "innocent victims" (the fetuses).

Justices Stevens and O'Connor (with Justice Blackmun concurring) submitted their own separate dissenting opinions. They felt that the Court ignored the original intent of the Civil Rights Act. Justice Stevens took issue with the notion that the demonstrations did not reflect class-based animus because the protesters were saving fetuses. The justice argued that those who were affected were women, and they were targeted "*because* of their sex, specifically, because of their capacity to become pregnant and to have an abortion." In reaction to the Court's decision, Congress moved quickly to pass FACE.

Just hours after passing FACE, the Senate approved the Driver's Privacy Protection Act (PL 103-322), making it a federal crime for state motor vehicle bureaus to routinely release personal information obtained in connection with car registration and driver's license issuance. Relative to abortion, the legislation is intended to prevent anti-abortion protesters from obtaining the home addresses of those who visit clinics and then harassing them at their homes.

Setting Limits — Fixed Buffer Zones

In 1993, a court injunction forbade demonstrators from blocking the driveway and the entrance to a Melbourne, Florida, abortion clinic. The protestors were also banned from using bullhorns to shout at patients and clinic workers.

When the demonstrators ignored the original injunction, the judge broadened the injunction, ordering a 36-foot buffer zone around the clinic's property line and prohibiting disruptive noises and visual displays. In addition, he established a 300-foot buffer zone around the clinic and the homes of its staff.

The Florida Supreme Court upheld the lower court decision. Three anti-abortion protesters appealed the ruling. In *Madsen v. Women's Health*

Center, Inc. (114 S. Ct. 2516, 1994), the Supreme Court, in a 6-3 ruling, upheld the noise restrictions (abortion clinics are medical facilities where noise control is important) and allowed the 36-foot buffer zone in front of the clinic. The protesters had argued that because the injunction silenced only one side of the abortion debate, it violated their First Amendment rights by discriminating against speech based on its content. Chief Justice Rehnquist, writing for the majority, disagreed.

An injunction, by its very nature, does not address the general public, but applies only to particular parties, regulating their activities, and perhaps their speech, because of their past action in the context of a specific dispute…. [T]he injunction imposed incidental restriction on petitioners' message [against abortion] because they repeatedly violated the original injunction. That the injunction covers people who all share the same viewpoint suggests only that those in the group *whose conduct* violated the court's order happen to share that viewpoint.

Justice Scalia, joined by Justices Kennedy and Thomas, argued that the injunction was intended not for the violators of the earlier injunction but for the protesters who were speaking out against abortion.

Because I believe that the judicial creation of a 36-foot zone in which only a particular group, which had broken no law, cannot exercise its rights of speech, assembly, and association, and the judicial enactment of a noise prohibition, applicable to that group and that group alone, are profoundly at odds with our First Amendment precedents and traditions, I dissent.

What About Floating Buffer Zones?

On February 19, 1997, the Supreme Court handed down a 6-3 decision on a three-part injunction against clinic protesters in Buffalo, New York.

In *Schenck v. Pro-Choice Network* (117 S. Ct. 855), the justices upheld a lower court's order keeping demonstrators at least 15 feet away from the clinics' doorways. The justices' reassertion of their support for fixed buffer zones was very important to abortion proponents since about one-third of the approximately 900 abortion clinics in the country are safeguarded by fixed buffer zones.

The High Court struck down the second provision of the injunction forbidding demonstrators to come within 15 feet of people entering or leaving the clinics. This 15-foot space around a person is known as a "floating buffer zone." Chief Justice Rehnquist, writing for the majority, stated,

> The floating buffer zones prevent defendants except for two sidewalk counselors … from communicating a message … or handing leaflets to people entering or leaving the clinics…. Leafletting and commenting on matters of public concern are classic forms of speech that lie at the heart of the First Amendment, and speech in public areas is at its most protected on public sidewalks, a prototypical example of a traditional public forum.

The Court also struck down the floating buffer zones around vehicles. Finally, the Court upheld the third provision, "cease and desist"— two protesters at a time could enter the fixed buffer zone to peacefully dissuade women from having an abortion. However, these "sidewalk counselors" had to stop counseling and leave the buffer zone upon request. Justice Scalia, dissented, stating, "If our First Amendment jurisprudence has stood for anything, it is that courts have *an obligation* 'to enhance speech rights' and *a duty* 'to bend over backwards to accommodate speech rights.' "

Anti-Abortion Protesters as Racketeers

In 1994, the Supreme Court gave clinics a potentially powerful tool against protesters in *National Organization for Women, Inc., v. Joseph Scheidler et al.* (114 S. Ct. 798). In March 1986, the National Organization for Women (NOW) had filed a lawsuit against Joseph Scheidler, his Pro-Life Action League, and other anti-abortionists, alleging a "conspiracy in restraint of interstate commerce." In 1988, NOW broadened the scope of its lawsuit to include then-Director Randall Terry and his Operation Rescue. NOW charged that the anti-abortion groups were members of a "nationwide conspiracy to shut down abortion clinics through a pattern of racketeering activity" in violation of the Racketeer-Influenced and Corrupt Organizations (RICO) chapter of the Organized Crime Control Act of 1970 (PL 91-452). RICO was originally intended to curb organized crime.

Two lower courts denied abortion clinics the right to use RICO as the basis of the NOW lawsuit, claiming that RICO applied only to activities motivated by economic gain. The courts cited Section 1962 (c) of RICO, which makes it unlawful "for any person employed by or associated with any enterprise engaged in, or the activities of which *affect,* interstate or foreign commerce, to conduct or participate … in the conduct of such enterprise's affair through a pattern of racketeering activity or collection of unlawful debt."

In a unanimous ruling, the Supreme Court allowed NOW's lawsuit to proceed, using RICO as its basis. The High Court focused on "affect," citing the definition of *Webster's Third New International Dictionary*, "to have a detrimental influence on" — used especially in the phrase *affect commerce*. In denying the need for an economic motive, Chief Justice Rehnquist wrote,

> An enterprise surely can have a detrimental influence on interstate or foreign commerce without having its own profit-seeking motives…. Respondents and the two courts of appeals, we think, overlook the fact that … the alleged extortion may not benefit the protesters financially but still may drain money from the economy by harming businesses such as the clinics.

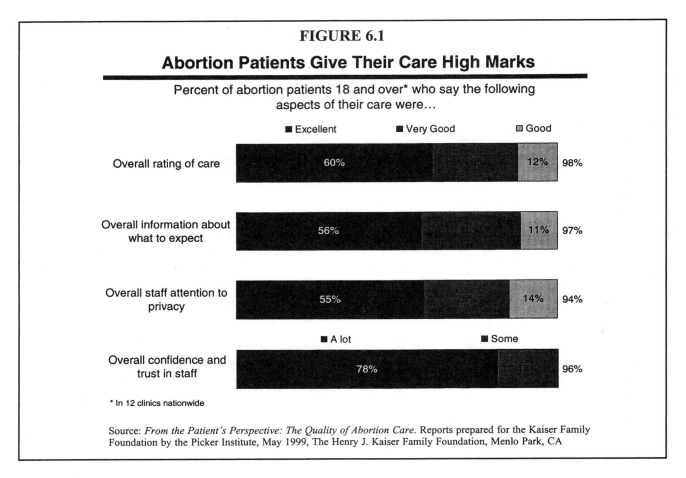

FIGURE 6.1

Abortion Patients Give Their Care High Marks

Percent of abortion patients 18 and over* who say the following aspects of their care were…

■ Excellent   ■ Very Good   ▨ Good

Overall rating of care	60% · 12% · 98%
Overall information about what to expect	56% · 11% · 97%
Overall staff attention to privacy	55% · 14% · 94%

■ A lot   ■ Some

Overall confidence and trust in staff	78% · 96%

* In 12 clinics nationwide

Source: *From the Patient's Perspective: The Quality of Abortion Care.* Reports prepared for the Kaiser Family Foundation by the Picker Institute, May 1999, The Henry J. Kaiser Family Foundation, Menlo Park, CA

ABORTION PATIENTS' PERSPECTIVE ON CARE

In 1998, in the first study about the quality of abortion care from the patients' perspective, the Kaiser Family Foundation surveyed over 2,200 abortion patients age 18 and over in clinics nationwide. The patients were "women who successfully located a provider, could afford the procedure, and were able to get to the clinic."

Three in 5 (60 percent) patients reported their care to be "excellent," and nearly 2 in 5 (38 percent) thought their abortion care "very good" or "good." Over half the patients indicated the information they received (56 percent of patients) and the staff's attention to their privacy (55 percent) were excellent. The remaining 40 percent rated these two aspects of their care as very good or good. Three-quarters (78 percent) of the patients felt "a

lot" of confidence and trust in the staff who cared for them, and about one-fifth (18 percent) reported "some" confidence and trust. (See Figure 6.1.) Almost all patients (96 percent) said they would recommend their abortion provider to family or friends.

Patients Ranked the Adequacy of Information the Most Important

The adequacy of information about the abortion was the most important issue to the patients. Almost all (98 percent) of the patients reported that the clinic staff explained the procedure, and 99 percent thought the explanation was clear. Nearly 9 in 10 (87 percent) stated they received all the information they wanted about what to expect during the procedure. More than 9 in 10 (93 percent) reported receiving information about emotional or physical reactions that might follow the abortion.

CHAPTER VII

SOME MEDICAL ETHICS QUESTIONS CONCERNING ABORTION

IS ABORTION DANGEROUS TO A WOMAN'S HEALTH?

Abortion was widely practiced during the Colonial Period and early years of the United States until it was eventually criminalized between the early 1800s and 1973 (see Chapter I). After abortion was legally banned, women of means were generally able to find doctors willing to perform "therapeutic (medically necessary) abortions" allowed by law. Many poor women, on the other hand, died or developed medical complications from self-induced abortions or abortions performed by untrained practitioners.

Since the 1973 Supreme Court ruling on the legality of abortion in *Roe v. Wade* (see Chapter II), a number of studies have been made on the physical, emotional, and psychological impact of abortion on women. In 1975, in its first major study of abortion (*Legalized Abortion and the Public Health*, National Academy of Sciences, Washington, DC), the Institute of Medicine concluded that "evidence suggests that legislation and practices that permit women to obtain abortions in proper medical surroundings will lead to fewer deaths and a lower rate of medical complications than [will] restrictive legislation and practices."

In 1987, President Ronald Reagan promised the various right-to-life groups that he would investigate the health effects of abortion. The president instructed Surgeon General C. Everett Koop to prepare such a report. After meetings with experts and thorough reviews of many studies for almost a year and a half, Dr. Koop refused to release a report.

In a January 1989 letter to President Reagan, Dr. Koop reported that "in spite of a diligent review on the part of many in the Public Health Service and in the private sector, the scientific studies do not provide conclusive data about the health effects of abortion on women." Dr. Koop added that the physical health effects following abortion — infertility, a damaged cervix, premature birth, low birthweight babies — can develop were the pregnancy carried to term. In March 1989, testifying before the U.S. House of Representatives, Dr. Koop reported that, while psychological problems may result from having an abortion, the problem is "miniscule from a public health perspective."

Morbidity and Mortality

In *Safety of Abortion,* (National Abortion Federation, Washington, DC, 1995), Susan Dudley reported that, like any other surgical procedure, abortion carries risks of complications. (The National Abortion Federation is the professional association of abortion providers in the United States and Canada.) Major complications from abortions performed before 13 weeks of pregnancy are rare. About 89 percent of women who have an abortion are less than 13 weeks pregnant. Of these women, 97 percent do not develop complications; 2.5 percent have minor complications that are treatable at the doctor's office or at the abortion clinic; and less than 0.5 percent requires hospitalization.

Besides the length of pregnancy, other factors that determine the likelihood of complications include the physician's skill and training, the use of general anesthesia, the abortion method used, and the woman's overall health.

Dudley pointed out that, "although rare, possible complications from an abortion" include

- Blood clots in the uterus, which require a repeat suctioning — occur in less than 1 percent of cases.

- Infections, most of which are easy to identify and treat if the woman follows the post-operative instructions — occur in less than 3 percent of cases.

- A tear in the cervix, which may be repaired with stitches — occurs in less than 1 percent of cases.

- A tear in the uterine wall and/or other organs, which may heal by itself or require surgery or, rarely, hysterectomy (removal of the uterus) — occurs in less than one-half of 1 percent of cases.

- Missed abortion, which does not terminate the pregnancy and requires a repeat abortion — occurs in less than one-half of 1 percent of cases.

- Incomplete abortion, in which tissue from the pregnancy remains in the uterus and requires a repeat abortion — occurs in less that 1 percent of cases.

- Too much bleeding, caused by failure of the uterus to contract, which may require a blood transfusion — occurs in less than 1 percent of the cases.

The legalization of abortion has resulted in a significant decrease in abortion-related deaths. In 1989, following Dr. Koop's refusal to release his report and because of his admission of bias against abortion, the House Committee on Government Operations relied instead on research done by the Centers for Disease Control and Prevention (CDC) and concluded that childbirth was seven times more likely to result in the mother's death than was abortion. As of 1992 (the most recent year for which such data were available), one death occurred per 100,000 abortions performed in the United States (see Chapter IV).

Post-Abortion Stress Syndrome

Dr. Koop's investigation of the psychological effects of abortion was as inconclusive as his findings of its physical health effects. In the same letter to President Reagan, Koop observed that "the data do not support the premise that abortion does or does not cause or contribute to psychological problems." Many anti-abortion groups, however, claim that, for many women, having an abortion can lead to serious psychological problems, most notably post-abortion syndrome. Some have compared this with the post-traumatic stress disorder suffered by many Vietnam veterans.

Following Dr. Koop's findings, an American Psychological Association (APA) expert, Dr. Nancy Adler of the University of California at San Francisco, testified before the Human Resources and Intergovernmental Relations Subcommittee of the House Committee on Government Operations. Dr. Adler reported that an APA expert panel on the psychological effects of abortion found no evidence of the so-called "post-abortion syndrome" of psychological trauma or deep depression. In fact, the APA investigation found "the predominant feelings following abortion to be relief and happiness. Some women report feelings of sadness, regret, anxiety, or guilt, but these tend to be mild." According to the Planned Parenthood Federation of America, some women experience these short-term feelings due to the abrupt hormonal changes caused by abortion.

Nancy F. Russo and Amy J. Dabul, in "The Relationship of Abortion to Well-Being: Do Race and Religion Make a Difference?" (*Professional Psychology: Research and Practice*, vol. 28, no. 1, 1997), reported that their eight-year longitudinal study of about 5,000 women found that the women's abortion experience had no ill effect on their psychological well-being. Rather, the women's level of self-esteem before their pregnancy determined their sense of well-being after abortion. This remained true regardless of the women's race, religious affiliation, or their religious groups' attitude towards abortion. The researchers also observed that although some women exhibited a higher level of distress after abortion, their distress was more likely to be traced to events and conditions that occurred prior to their pregnancy and not to their having had an abortion.

Others Disagree

Abortion opponents insist that they have ample anecdotal evidence of psychological stress following abortion. According to the Pro-Life Action Ministries, in *What They Won't Tell You at the Abortion Clinic* (St. Paul, Minnesota, undated),

Most often a woman will feel the consequences of her decision within days of her abortion. If they don't appear immediately, they will appear as she gets older. Emotional scars include unexplained depression, a loss of the ability to get close to others, repressed emotion, a hardening of the spirit, thwarted maternal instincts (which may lead to child abuse or neglect later in life), intense feelings of guilt and thoughts of suicide.

Dr. E. Joanne Angelo, an assistant clinical professor of psychiatry at the Tufts University School of Medicine and a psychiatrist in private practice in Boston, has participated in Project Rachel, an outreach program for women and men who have experienced abortion. In *A Special Word to Women Who Have Had an Abortion* (National Conference of Catholic Bishops, Washington, DC, 1999), Dr. Angelo observed,

TABLE 7.1

Among children born to never-married women under 45 years of age, percent who were relinquished for adoption, by race, according to year of birth

Race	Before 1973	1973–81	1982–88[1]	1989–95 (standard error)
All women[2]	8.7	4.1	2	0.9 (.03)
Black	1.5	0.2	1.1	–
White	19.3	7.5	3.2	1.7 (0.55)

– Quantity zero.

[1]Percentages for before 1973 through 1988 are based on combined data from the 1982 and 1988 NSFG (12).
[2]Includes women of other races, not shown separately.

NOTE: Categories "Black" and "White" include women of Hispanic origin.

Source: Anjani Chandra et al., "Adoption, Adoption Seeking, and Relinquishment for Adoption in the United States," *Advance Data*, no. 306, May 11, 1999

Women who have had abortions ... may turn to alcohol or drugs to get to sleep at night or to deaden the pain of their waking hours, or throw themselves into feverish activity in an attempt to forget their sorrow, guilt and shame. Deep feelings of loneliness and emptiness may lead to binge eating, alternating with purging and anorexia, or intense efforts to repair intimate relationships or develop new ones inappropriately, or to an insatiable need to replace the lost child at any cost.

ADOPTION

Adoption is often offered as the preferable solution to an unwanted pregnancy rather than abortion. To pro-lifers, adoption offers obvious advantages over abortion — it permits the fetus to live and provides infertile couples with a much longed-for baby. Although adoption would seem to be the clear solution, the relinquishment of children for adoption has never been common. For most women, adoption is emotionally very complicated. Married women and those who are already mothers are highly unlikely to consider adoption for their child.

Over the past few decades, the placement of infants for adoption among never-married women has grown increasingly rare. Before the 1973 *Roe v. Wade* decision, 8.7 percent of children of never-married women were relinquished for adoption —

1.5 percent of Black infants and 19.3 percent of White infants. Between 1989 and 1995, barely 1 percent of babies born to never-married women were placed for adoption. While Black infants were consistently less likely to be placed for adoption, the proportion of White infants given up for adoption dropped to just 1.7 percent in the first half of the 1990s. (See Table 7.1.)

Although abortion and adoption are both "resolutions" to an unwanted pregnancy, experts point out that adoption is rarely experienced as a resolution. The pregnancy and birth are experienced fully, allowing time for the woman to form an attachment to the infant. Women frequently feel ambivalence about the adoption process, and their loss is profound.

Adoption advocates worry that focusing on the pain of giving up a child will discourage women from choosing adoption. Furthermore, controversies over open adoption (in which the child can find out who his/her birth parents are), interracial adoption, adoption by gay persons, and situations where parents change their minds after giving up the child contribute to the negative impression of adoption. (See Chapter III for information about the promotion of adoption in Title X clinics.)

ETHICAL QUESTIONS

Scientific advances have been happening very quickly, often developing faster than medical ethics can respond to them. As science continually redefines the limits to life and medicine, fetal tissue research, stem cell research, genetic manipulation, infertility treatments, and other medical issues have raised troubling ethical questions.

Fetal Tissue Research

The ethical controversy of fetal tissue research has arisen because the source of fetal tissue is induced abortion. Fetal tissue research is not a recent medical development. It dates back to the 1930s and has been responsible, in the mid-twentieth century, for the development of the vaccines against poliomyelitis and rubella (German measles), as well as the preventive treatment of Rh incompatibility (a condition in which a mismatch between the blood of a pregnant woman and of her fetus can harm the fetus).

Fetal Tissue Transplantation

Advances in medical technology have led to the potential usefulness of fetal tissue transplantation for the treatment of neurological disorders (Parkinson's disease, Alzheimer's disease, Huntington's disease), blood disorders (leukemia, aplastic anemia, hemophilia), spinal cord injuries, diabetes, and stroke. Scientists have found that transplanted fetal tissue is not only less likely to be rejected by the recipient, it also has the unique capabilities of maturing and functioning as any kind of tissue (muscle or organ) and of taking over the functions of a diseased tissue.

Although fetal tissue research has been taking place since the early part of the twentieth century, it was not until after the 1973 *Roe v. Wade* decision legalizing abortion that controversies about the use of aborted fetuses erupted. Anti-abortion groups oppose fetal tissue research because they believe it encourages abortion. Would a daughter become pregnant in order to produce fetal tissue that could be transplanted to her father who has Alzheimer's disease? Would a woman get pregnant and then get an abortion in order to sell her aborted fetus?

In March 1988, the U.S. Department of Health and Human Services (HHS) imposed a moratorium on the use of federal funds for fetal tissue transplantation research until an expert panel could study the ethical implications of such research. In November 1989, despite the panel's finding that the use of fetal tissue in research is acceptable public policy, Secretary Louis Sullivan of the HHS continued the moratorium. In 1992, President George Bush vetoed Congress' efforts to restore public funding of fetal tissue research, fearing "its potential for promoting and legitimizing abortion."

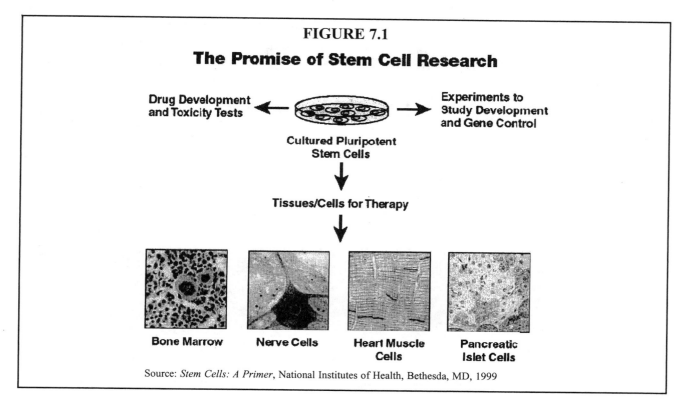

FIGURE 7.1

The Promise of Stem Cell Research

Drug Development and Toxicity Tests

Cultured Pluripotent Stem Cells

Experiments to Study Development and Gene Control

Tissues/Cells for Therapy

Bone Marrow   Nerve Cells   Heart Muscle Cells   Pancreatic Islet Cells

Source: *Stem Cells: A Primer*, National Institutes of Health, Bethesda, MD, 1999

When Bill Clinton took office in 1993, one of his first actions was to lift the ban on federally funded research using fetal tissue from induced abortion. That same year, the National Institutes of Health (NIH) Revitalization Act (PL 103-43) legalized fetal tissue research and transplantation.

Human Embryo Research

In 1995, Congress first banned the NIH from using appropriated funds to create, destroy, discard, or subject to risk of injury or death human embryos for research purposes. Human embryo research, which is not illegal in the United States, has been conducted in private in vitro fertilization (IVF) clinics (see below) seeking to improve the efficiency of IVF. IVF researchers rely on embryos donated by couples who no longer need them for implantation ("spare embryos") or because the embryos have abnormalities.

Embryonic Stem Cell Research

In November 1998, two groups of privately funded researchers reported growing pluripotent (capable of evolving into most tissues of the body) stem cells outside the human body. Scientists be-

lieve these stem cells could provide numerous therapeutic benefits. Pluripotent stem cells could help scientists understand normal cell biology, enabling them to correct the abnormal cell processes that occur in such conditions as cancer and birth defects. Human stem cells could also help in the development of more effective drugs. Scientists could use stem cells to produce human cell lines possessing the characteristics of a disease against which the potential drug would be tested. As a result, only drugs that are safe and appear to be beneficial would be tested on humans. (See Figure 7.1.)

The NIH reports, "Perhaps the most far-reaching potential application of human pluripotent stem cells is the generation of cells and tissue that could be used for so-called cell therapies." These stem cells could be stimulated to grow replacement cells and tissues, with the potential for treating various conditions and diseases. Scientists could grow heart cells to replace damaged hearts, brains cells for patients with Parkinson's and Alzheimer's diseases, insulin-producing cells for diabetics, and nerve cells for victims of spinal cord injury. (See Figure 7.1.)

The Abortion Debate and Stem Cell Research

The potential benefits of pluripotent stem cells have added to the abortion debate. One source of stem cells is human embryos, and extracting stem cells results in the destruction of these embryos. To pro-lifers, this is no different from induced abortion, the taking of human life. In January 1999, the U.S. Department of Health and Human Services (HHS) ruled that stem cell research does not fall within the congressional ban on embryo research. According to the HHS Office of the General Counsel, since the stem cells by themselves are not capable of developing into a human being, they could not be considered embryos.

Interestingly, Dr. John Gearhart of Johns Hopkins University, one of the two researchers who succeeded in keeping stem cell cultures alive in a laboratory, derived primordial germ cells (similar to embryonic stem cells; see below) from fetuses legally aborted between the fifth and ninth week after conception. (Dr. Gearhart's research could have been federally funded because federal laws are already in place that govern fetal tissue research; see above). The second researcher, Dr. James Thomson of the University of Wisconsin-Madison, isolated pluripotent stem cells from surplus early-stage embryos (blastocysts) donated by people undergoing infertility treatments in IVF clinics. Cells from the inner cell mass of the blastocyst are the ones that will form the tissues of the human body. (See Figure 7.2.)

On January 26, 1999, Richard M. Doerflinger, associate director for Policy Development at the Secretariat for Pro-Life Activities of the National Conference of Catholic Bishops (Washington, DC), appearing before the Senate Appropriations Subcommittee on Labor, Health, and Education, testified that, instead of destroying embryos for their stem cells, other "morally acceptable" alternatives exist. These include the use of adult stem cells and the enzyme teleromase for tissue regeneration purposes.

Doerflinger pointed out that, while the HHS had ruled that the embryonic stem cell is not an "organism," or a human being, Dr. Gearhart's experiments found that some of the stem cells might have joined together to form an embryo. Doerflinger argued, "In other words, a stem cell is not an organism — but the possibility must be explored that groups of stem cells may recongregate to form an entity that is, however briefly, a living organism."

Other opponents of stem cell research noted that, although government-proposed guidelines require that no public monies may be used to destroy an embryo — a necessary step to harvesting

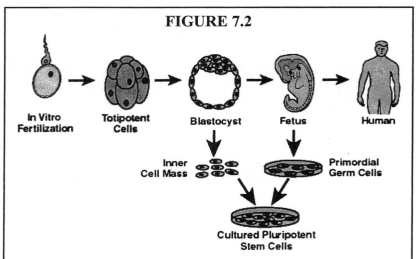

FIGURE 7.2

NOTE:
When a sperm fertilizes an egg, the resulting single cell has the potential to form an entire human being — it is *totipotent*, meaning that its potential is total. After approximately four days, the totipotent cells become a blastocyst. The blastocyst consists of an outer layer of cells and a cluster of cells (inner cell mass) found inside the hollow sphere.

The outer layer of cells will form the placenta and other supporting tissues needed for fetal development in the uterus. The inner cell mass cells will form virtually all of the tissues of the human body. Although the inner cell mass cells can form virtually every type of cell found in the human body, they cannot form a human being because they are unable to give rise to the placenta and supporting tissues necessary for development in the human uterus. These inner cell mass cells are ***pluripotent*** — they can give rise to many types of cells but not all types of cells.

Source: *Stem Cells: A Primer*, National Institutes of Health, Bethesda, MD, 1999

stem cells — the rules allow federal researchers to use embryo-derived stem cells created by scientists supported by private funds. They believe that this is an inconsistency in federal policy that should be stopped.

Genetic Testing

Gender Selection

Progress in prenatal testing has raised a number of questions about the possible reasons for obtaining an abortion. Sonography (also called ultrasound scanning, in which images of the fetus are made using sound waves) and amniocentesis (removal of a small amount of amniotic fluid from a pregnant woman to gain information about the fetus) can determine the sex of a fetus.

In some countries of the world, such as China and India, parents often prefer boys, sometimes using abortion to prevent the birth of daughters (see Chapter VIII.) In the United States, women have not been generally known to have abortions for reasons of sex preference in a child. Interestingly, a new technology called sperm sorting has become very popular with couples who want a daughter. Originally developed by the Genetics and I.V.F. Institute, a fertility clinic in Fairfax, Virginia, to increase significantly the chances of couples who are carriers of chromosomal disorders to produce daughters (females are not carriers of the 350 X-linked genetic disorders), sperm sorting is now offered for "family balancing." According to the clinic, more daughters than sons have been selected.

Screening for Birth Defects and Hereditary Diseases

Prenatal testing through amniocentesis or sonogram can also accurately recognize severe defects in the fetus, such as anencephaly (congenital absence of part or all of the brain), spina bifida (a condition in which part of the spinal cord protrudes through a gap in the backbone, leading to serious, often fatal, infections and paralysis), and Down's syndrome (mental retardation).

In addition, genetic (hereditary) testing has allowed parents to determine if the child they are carrying has the gene for certain diseases, such as Huntington's disease, Tay-Sachs disease, cystic fibrosis, or the genes *BRCA1* and *BRCA2* that increase a female's risk of breast and ovarian cancer. Women who discover in the second or third trimester of pregnancy that the fetuses they are carrying are seriously impaired or will develop debilitating diseases can face an agonizing decision whether to have an abortion or not.

Some persons have no problem with genetic testing if it makes possible the use of preventive therapy for a predisposed condition or an acceptance of the child who may be born with abnormalities. However, since most genetic tests are for untreatable disorders, some fear that the screening techniques may be used for eugenic (selective breeding) purposes, preventing the birth of children affected by hereditary anomalies.

Many handicapped persons take issue with those who advocate abortions in cases of fetal defects and potential diseases. They argue that had late-term abortions been available to their mothers during pregnancy, they might very well have never had the chance for life. Many disabled resent those who feel one can mandate a certain quality of life or place an economic value on it. Some observers are also wary that the genetic information obtained from prenatal testing might eventually result in preventing the birth of children with certain traits or behavioral tendencies.

Infertility Treatments

Multiple Births

Many women, unable to bear children, have turned to assisted reproductive technology (ART). About 15 percent of American women of childbearing age (ages 15 to 44) have undergone infertility treatments. In vitro fertilization (IVF) is the most widely used method to help women achieve pregnancy. IVF is performed by removing the woman's eggs, fertilizing them in the laboratory,

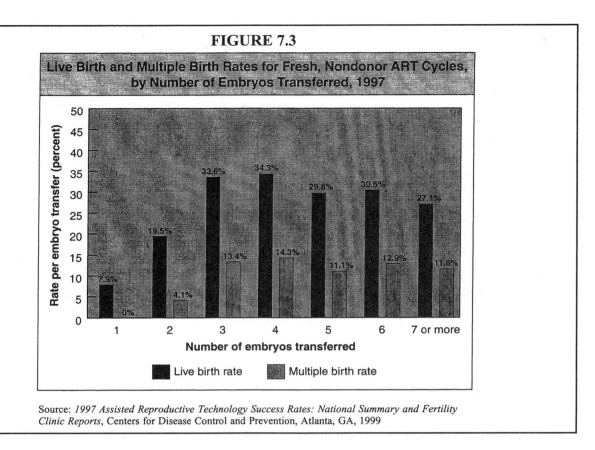

FIGURE 7.3

Live Birth and Multiple Birth Rates for Fresh, Nondonor ART Cycles, by Number of Embryos Transferred, 1997

Source: *1997 Assisted Reproductive Technology Success Rates: National Summary and Fertility Clinic Reports*, Centers for Disease Control and Prevention, Atlanta, GA, 1999

and transferring the resulting embryo or embryos back into her uterus. In 1997, 71.8 percent of ART cycles involved IVF that used fresh embryos developed from the woman's own eggs. In 1997, 24,582 infants were born as a result of assisted reproductive technology.

The pregnancy success rate in ART decreases as the woman's age increases. Therefore, in order to increase the chances of success in older women, doctors are likely to implant more embryos. In a number of cases, many well-publicized multiple births have resulted. Figure 7.3 shows the multiple birth rate, depending on the number of embryos transferred. Although the figure shows the results only for women younger than 35, the trends are the same across all age groups.

Multiple Births and Abortion

In 1997 and 1998, the birth of septuplets and octuplets, respectively, in the United States brought criticisms from the medical profession who thought the parents and their fertility doctors had acted ir-

responsibly. Some believed the mothers had taken a tremendous risk with their health and that of their children. Siblings in multiple births are at a high risk for prematurity, low birthweight, long-term mental and physical disabilities, and death.

Other people thought the parents should have resorted to "selective reduction," a euphemism for abortion. Fetal reduction involves selectively aborting some fetuses to limit the risk to the remaining fetuses. Ethicists ask if it is justifiable behavior to abort some fetuses so that the remaining ones could live. Many physicians believe the fertility doctors should have stopped the treatment cycle as soon as they saw the maturation of too many eggs in the mothers.

Those against selective reduction warn that the acceptance of abortion in cases of multiple births will eventually make it too easy in the future to "selectively reduce" other members of society, such as the elderly or the disabled. They further cite the case of the McCaughey septuplets of Iowa, all delivered alive and thriving, as proof that doctors are wrong when they advise the abortion of some fetuses to save the others. In November 1999, it was reported that some of the two-year-old septuplets were having health problems. Two children have developmental problems, unable to walk or sit up without assistance. Tests also showed that some areas in their brains are underdeveloped. Some of the other children have minor health problems but are said to be talking and walking.

The Catholic Church has taken a strong stand against in vitro fertilization. Ethicist Sister Mary Brady, though sympathetic to infertile couples, noted that "IVF might be motivated by love, but it is often motivated by something else — a presumed right to have a child. The Church has great compassion for those who are infertile. You can have compassion without thinking these things are all right."

IS A FETUS A PERSON?

Prenatal Substance Use Is Considered Child Abuse

In November 1997, the South Carolina Supreme Court, in *Whitner v. South Carolina* (492 S.E.2d 777, 778 [S.C. 1997]), ruled that pregnant women who use drugs can be criminally prosecuted for child maltreatment. The court found that a viable fetus is a "person" covered by the state's child abuse and neglect laws. The ruling was handed down in a case appealed by Cornelia Whitner, who was sentenced to eight years in prison in 1992 for pleading guilty to child neglect. Her infant tested positive for cocaine.

In 1998, the U.S. Supreme Court (*Whitner v. South Carolina*, *cert. denied*, 118 S. Ct. 1857 [1998]) refused to review Whitner's case, letting the ruling stand. The Supreme Court observed,

As the courts of numerous sister states have unequivocally recognized, efforts to expand the reach of pre-existing child endangerment statutes to cover a woman's conduct during pregnancy necessarily renders these laws unconstitutionally vague....

... [T]he South Carolina Legislature ..., like every other state legislature that has considered expanding its child neglect statute to reach pregnant women or creating special penalties for women who become pregnant while substance addicted, deliberately chose not to do so.... [T]he Legislature ... acknowledged the conclusion of every leading medical group, that threatening women with arrest for conduct engaged in during pregnancy will endanger both fetal and maternal health by frightening women away from prenatal and other needed care.

Forceful Confinement of a Pregnant Woman

In 1998, Wisconsin revised its child protection statute, stating that an unborn child is a human being from fertilization to birth. Therefore, a pregnant woman suspected of substance abuse may be forcefully subjected to treatment in a confined environment if the law believes she is endangering the unborn child's health. That same year, South Dakota enacted a similar law, further mandating the reporting of "child abuse" by substance-ingesting pregnant women to law enforcement officers instead of to social services. Failure to report such cases of child abuse would constitute a crime punishable by up to six months in prison.

Drinking Alcohol While Pregnant

In 1996, the state of Wisconsin charged Deborah Zimmerman with attempted first-degree intentional homicide and first-degree reckless injury because she drank alcohol while pregnant. The state claimed she was trying to kill her unborn child by using alcohol. Zimmerman requested that the case against her be dismissed, but her motion was denied. She appealed to the state Court of Appeals. Because this was an issue of first impression (a case with no existing precedent) in Wisconsin, the Court of Appeals referred the case to the state Supreme Court (*State v. Deborah J.Z.*, 219 Wis.2d 926, 584 N.W.2d 125 [1998]).

The state Supreme Court, in *State v. Deborah J.Z.*, 225 Wis.2d 33, 590 N.W.2d 711 (1999), was equally divided in its ruling, and eventually sent the case back to the Court of Appeals, which dismissed the charges. The appellate court held that under state law, attempted first-degree intentional homicide and reckless injury charges may only be brought for actions committed against another "human being" and not against an unborn child.

> ... [O]ur analysis of this case is not about the propriety or morality of Deborah's conduct while pregnant. Nor is it about her constitutional right to reproductive choice guaranteed in *Roe*. On the contrary, this appeal is one of statutory construction....

> ... The legislature clearly intended to exclude an unborn child when it limited the definition of a "human being" to include only "one who has been born alive...."

> ... [W]e decline the State's overture to give the statute such a broad construction. Under such a construction, a woman could risk criminal charges for any perceived self-destructive behavior during her pregnancy that may result in injuries to her unborn child....

The State Takes Custody of a Fetus

In September 1999, a district judge in Oklahoma "took custody" of a fetus which he considered to be in danger. Julie Ann Starks, who was seven months pregnant, was arrested on charges of trying to manufacture methamphetamine. The judge ruled that her illegal activity was harmful to the unborn child's health because the child was being subjected to potentially harmful chemicals.

In early November 1999, Starks gave birth to a son, who showed no traces of illegal drugs in his system. The case has not been resolved. The infant went home with his parents, but remains technically under state custody.

THE FETUS AS A VICTIM OF A CRIME

On September 14, 1999, the House Judiciary Committee approved and passed out of committee the Unborn Victims of Violence Act (H.R. 2436), the first federal bill recognizing the fetus as a victim of a crime. The bill makes it "a separate offense" to injure or cause the death of "a child, who is in utero [in the womb] during the commission of a federal crime of violence against a pregnant woman. The bill does not impose the death penalty in case of fetal death, but the offender may be sentenced to life imprisonment.

Although the bill does not seek the prosecution of "conduct relating to an abortion," abortion advocates claim that this bill sets the stage for dismantling the legal right to abortion. Gloria Feldt, president of the Planned Parenthood Federation of America, claimed that the "[a]nti-choice members of Congress have introduced the Unborn Victims of Violence Act to do what the Human Life Amendment and other anti-abortion bills have failed to do — separate the fetus from the woman and attach rights of personhood on the fetus." Representative John Conyers, Jr. (D-MI) considered the bill "a back-door attack on *Roe v. Wade*. The American Civil Liberties Union (ACLU) pointed out that the bill sponsors failed to address the issue of violence against women.

The National Right to Life Committee, consultant to the primary sponsor of the bill, Lindsey Graham (R-SC), said the new "right-to-life bill" recognizes the unborn child as "a member of the human family" throughout his or her development in the womb. "It seems obvious that when an unborn baby is injured or killed by an act of violence, there are two victims, the mother and the child." On September 30, 1999, Senator Michael DeWine (R-OH) introduced a similar bill (S. 1673) in the Senate. As of this writing, this bill had not been considered in committee.

Some States Recognize Fetuses as Victims

Currently, 11 states have homicide laws that recognize unborn children as victims throughout the entire prenatal period. Another 13 states have homicide laws that recognize unborn children as victims during part of their prenatal development. (See Table 7.2.)

In September 1999, the father of an unborn child and his accomplices were charged with murder in the death of a fetus. The Arkansas man hired three men to beat up his pregnant girlfriend so as to cause the death of his unborn daughter. He did not want any children. This was the first case tried under Arkansas' Fetal Protection Law that was newly enacted in April 1999. The law states that "the killing of an 'unborn child' of 12 weeks or greater gestation is murder, manslaughter, or negligent homicide." In the past, the attackers could have been charged only with the crime against the pregnant woman. Abortions do not fall within this state law.

FETAL RIGHTS VERSUS WOMEN'S RIGHTS

Opponents of fetal rights believe that if a fetus is granted the same legal rights traditionally granted to persons, the law will be forced to embark on the "slippery slope" of what control the state should have over women (and men). If drug use can be prohibited, then everything a woman does that might potentially harm the fetus could be regulated. Her eating and drinking, her work, her health habits could all be scrutinized by the courts. Would a woman who inadvertently harmed a fetus before she knew she was pregnant be held liable? Can a woman be criminally prosecuted for failing to seek prenatal care?

Child Sues Mother for Fetal Injury

In July 1999, Canada's Supreme Court ruled that a child cannot sue his or her mother for permanent disabilities caused by her negligence while pregnant. The woman who allegedly was driving too fast under snowy conditions collided head-on with another automobile. Her baby was born prematurely that day. When the child was six years old, his maternal grandfather sued on his behalf to

TABLE 7.2
States with Homicide Laws That Recognize Unborn Victims Throughout the Entire Prenatal Period (as of 1999)

Arizona	Ohio
Illinois	Pennsylvania
Louisiana	South Dakota
Minnesota	Utah
Missouri	Wisconsin
North Dakota	

States with Homicide Laws That Recognize Unborn Victims During Part of Their Prenatal Development (as of 1999)

Arkansas	Nevada
California	Oklahoma
Florida	Rhode Island
Georgia	South Carolina
Massachusetts	Tennessee
Michigan	Washington
Mississippi	

Source: Compiled by Information Plus from various sources

collect money from the mother's insurance company to help defray medical expenses.

The Court held that the fetus, being one with its mother, has no legal right. Anti-abortion groups argued that the fetus was a distinct person who had the right to sue his or her mother for injuries sustained due to her negligence.

Fathers Are Not Penalized

Today, corporate policies and health warnings alert women of childbearing age concerning hazards to the fetus, although no information is given to men about the reproductive risks they may be incurring. Medical research has found increasing evidence that the woman's behavior is not the only influence on the fetus. Men who smoke, abuse drugs and alcohol, or work with toxic chemicals may be damaging their sperm, thereby causing genetically defective fetuses. Men, however, have not yet been charged with abuse of the unborn.

Previous research has tended to ignore or reject the man's influence on the fetus, assuming that because sperm are constantly renewed, they are not in a man's body long enough to be damaged. In addition, researchers consider the sperm the active partner in fertility. Only the most fit is believed to be the one to impregnate the egg. Studies, however, have proven this assumption wrong and have found that the ovum tends to pick the sperm.

For pro-lifers, the issue is the health and life of both the mother and child. They believe that cases pitting the life of the fetus against that of the mother are red herrings (things that draw attention away from the issue at hand) used by abortion advocates to unnecessarily complicate the issue. Certainly, for most pro-lifers, pragmatic reality will tend to favor the life of the mother over that of the fetus, but that should not take away from the reality of the life of a human fetus and its right to existence.

CHAPTER VIII

ABORTION AROUND THE WORLD

Abortion is regularly used as a method of birth control all over the world. Because women are fertile for almost half of their lives, many have unwanted pregnancies at one time or another. Regardless of whether abortion is legal or not, women in all countries and cultures have always relied on abortion to control fertility. Abortion rates around the world generally reflect the religious and political power in the country, the cultural values, and the availability of contraception.

The Alan Guttmacher Institute (AGI) of New York, an organization that strongly supports a woman's right to choose abortion, and the World Health Organization (WHO) of the United Nations are the major organizations that compile international abortion statistics. In countries where abortion is illegal or severely restricted, it is impossible to know how many women get private abortions and how many of those who turn up at the hospital with a "spontaneous abortion" (miscarriage) have actually induced the abortion through a home method. In addition, many countries where abortion is legal do not keep complete medical records.

The Alan Guttmacher Institute, in "Induced Abortion Worldwide" (*Facts in Brief*, New York, 1999), reported that of the estimated 210 million pregnancies that occur all over the world, more than one-fifth (22 percent, or 46 million) end in abortions (Figure 8.1). A great number of women either do not want any more children or do not want a child at that time.

Each year, in developed countries, about half (49 percent) of the 28 million pregnancies that occur are unwanted. One-third (36 percent) end in abortion. In developing countries, approximately one-third (36 percent) of pregnancies are unwanted. One-fifth (20 percent) end in abortion.

ABORTION LAWS WORLDWIDE

Anika Rahman, Laura Katzive, and Stanley K. Henshaw, in "A Global Review of Laws on Induced Abortion, 1975-1997" (*International Family Planning Perspectives,* vol. 24, no. 2, June 1998), reported on the current abortion laws worldwide and the changes undergone by these laws since 1985. Countries are categorized based on the restrictiveness of abortion laws.

- To save the woman's life — Fifty-four countries, mostly in Latin America and Africa, com-

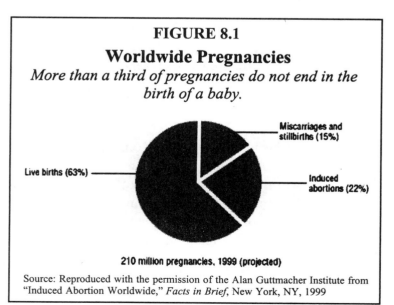

FIGURE 8.1

Worldwide Pregnancies

More than a third of pregnancies do not end in the birth of a baby.

Miscarriages and stillbirths (15%)

Live births (63%)

Induced abortions (22%)

210 million pregnancies, 1999 (projected)

Source: Reproduced with the permission of the Alan Guttmacher Institute from "Induced Abortion Worldwide," *Facts in Brief*, New York, NY, 1999

TABLE 8.1

Countries, by restrictiveness of abortion law, according to region, 1997

Abortion restrictiveness	The Americas and the Caribbean	Central Asia, the Middle East and North Africa	East and South Asia and the Pacific	Europe	Sub-Saharan Africa
To save the woman's life	Brazil–R Chile–ND Colombia Dominican Republic El Salvador–ND Guatemala Haiti Honduras Mexico–R Nicaragua–SA/PA Panama–PA/R/F Paraguay Venezuela	Afghanistan Egypt–SA Iran Lebanon Libya–PA Oman Syria–SA/PA United Arab Emirates–SA/PA Yemen	Bangladesh Indonesia Laos Myanmar Nepal Papua New Guinea Philippines Sri Lanka	Ireland	Angola Benin Central African Rep. Chad Congo (Brazzaville) Côte d'Ivoire Dem. Rep. of Congo–F Gabon Guinea-Bissau–SA/PA Kenya Lesotho Madagascar Mali Mauritania Mauritius Niger Nigeria Senegal Somalia Sudan–R Tanzania Togo Uganda
Physical health	Argentina–R (limited) Bolivia–R/I Costa Rica Ecuador–R/I (limited) Peru Uruguay–R	Kuwait–SA/PA/F Morocco–SA Saudi Arabia–SA/PA	Pakistan Rep. of Korea–SA/R/I/F Thailand–R	Poland–R/I/F	Burkina Faso–R Burundi Cameroon–R Eritrea Ethiopia Guinea Malawi–SA Mozambique Rwanda Zimbabwe–R/I/F
Mental health	Jamaica–PA Trinidad & Tobago	Algeria Iraq–SA/F/R/I Israel–F/R/I Jordan	Australia Hong Kong–F/R/I Malaysia New Zealand–F/I	Northern Ireland Portugal–PA/F/R Spain–F/R Switzerland	Botswana–F/R/I Gambia Ghana–F/R/I Liberia–F/R/I Namibia–F/R/I Sierra Leone
Socioeconomic grounds			India–PA/R/F Japan–SA Taiwan–SA/PA/I/F	Finland–R/F Great Britain–F	Zambia
Without restriction as to reason	Canada–L Cuba*–PA United States–PV Puerto Rico–PV	Armenia* Azerbaijan* Georgia* Kazakstan* Kyrgyz Rep.* Tajikistan* Tunisia* Turkey*–SA/PA Turkmenistan* Uzbekistan*	Cambodia†–PA China–PA/L Mongolia* N. Korea–L Singapore‡ Vietnam–L	Albania* Austria† Belarus* Belgium† Bosnia-Herzegovina*–PA Bulgaria* Croatia*–PA Czech Rep.*–PA Denmark*–PA Estonia* France*–PA Germany† Greece*–PA Hungary† Italy§–PA Latvia* Lithuania* Macedonia*–PA Moldova* Netherlands–PV Norway*–PA Romania† Russian Fed.* Slovak Rep.*–PA Slovenia*–PA Sweden** Ukraine* Yugoslavia*–PA	South Africa*

*Gestational limit of 12 weeks. †Gestational limit of 14 weeks. ‡Gestational limit of 24 weeks. §Gestational limit of 90 days. **Gestational limit of 18 weeks. *Notes:* For gestational limits, duration of pregnancy is calculated from the last menstrual period, which is generally considered to occur two weeks prior to conception. Thus, statutory gestational limits calculated from the date of conception have been extended by two weeks. ND=Existence of defense of necessity is highly doubtful. SA=Spousal authorization required. PA=Parental authorization required. R=Abortion allowed in cases of rape. I=Abortion allowed in cases of incest. F=Abortion allowed in case of fetal impairment. L=Law does not indicate gestational limit. PV=Law does not limit previability abortions.

Source: Reproduced with the permission of the Alan Guttmacher Institute from A. Rahman, L. Katzive, and S. K. Henshaw, "A Global Review of Laws on Induced Abortion, 1985-1997," *International Family Planning Perspectives*, 1998, 24(2): 56-64, Table 1.

pletely prohibit abortion or allow it only to save the woman's life. One in 4 of the world's women live in countries where abortion is a crime. These countries, most of them developing countries, punish the abortion provider and, in many cases, the woman who has obtained an abortion.

- To preserve the woman's physical health — Twenty-three countries, accounting for 10 percent of the women in the world, allow an abortion if it threatens a woman's physical health.

- To safeguard the woman's mental health — Twenty countries, accounting for 4 percent of the world's women, allow the termination of pregnancy if continuing it would jeopardize a woman's mental health. However, what constitutes a threat to mental health varies from country to country, from psychological distress caused by rape to mental anguish because the woman is carrying a fetus that might have abnormalities.

- Socioeconomic grounds — Six countries permit abortion, taking into consideration the woman's inability to support another child, inadequate housing, or being unmarried. One in 5 women lives in these countries, most notably in India.

- Without restriction as to reason — Forty-nine countries, where 41 percent of the world's women live, allow abortion without limiting the reasons for pregnancy termination.

In addition, a woman may obtain a legal abortion based on "juridical grounds" (rape or incest) or "fetal impairment grounds" (probable genetic defects). Countries that recognize these grounds for legal abortion may be classified under any of the five categories of restrictiveness. (See Table 8.1; the additional grounds [identified as R, I, and F; see footnote] are added after the country's name.) The authors further pointed out that some countries allow abortion based on other grounds not found in Table 8.1. In Israel, for example, a woman may have an abortion if she is "unmarried, under 'marriage age,' or older than 40."

Abortion Limitations
Even When Laws Are Liberal

In the 49 countries where abortion is not restricted as to reasons and in the six countries that allow abortion based on socioeconomic grounds, the laws usually mandate certain conditions for allowing the abortion. According to the Alan Guttmacher Institute (*Sharing Responsibility: Women, Society and Abortion Worldwide*, New York, 1999), these countries may impose gestational limits; consent, counseling, and/or waiting-period requirements; and limitations on the place of abortion and the person performing the proce-

dure. For example, a woman in Turkey needs her husband's permission, and in Germany, a woman is required to receive counseling that is intended to discourage her from having the abortion.

Some Countries
Prosecute Women for Abortion

In April 1999, the Legislative Assembly of El Salvador voted to completely ban abortion, allowing for no exceptions. A woman who obtains an abortion faces a prison sentence of 2 to 8 years. A health professional who performs an abortion can be sentenced to 6 to 12 years, and a person causing a woman to have an abortion without her consent is punished with a jail term of 4 to 8 years. Anyone who encourages a woman to have an abortion, pays for the procedure, or otherwise facilitates the abortion faces a sentence of 12 to 15 years.

In Chile, a person can be prosecuted for having, providing, or facilitating an abortion. In Nepal, a woman found to have had an abortion could be convicted of homicide. Those who are prosecuted are usually poor women who cannot afford to have the procedure done by a private physician or in another country where it is legal.

STATISTICS

Stanley K. Henshaw, Susheela Singh, and Taylor Haas, in "The Incidence of Abortion Worldwide" (*International Family Planning Perspectives*, vol. 25, Supplement, January 1999), reported that, in 1995, an estimated 45.5 million abortions were performed around the world. Nearly 26 million were legal and 19.9 million were illegal. The overall abortion rate was 35 abortions per 1,000 women ages 15 to 44. About one-quarter (26 percent) of all pregnancies ended in abortion. (See Table 8.2.)

Regional Estimates

Asia accounted for the biggest number of abortions (26.8 million), followed by Europe (7.7 million), Africa (5 million), Latin America (4.2 million), North America (1.5 million), and Oceania

(0.1 million). Approximately 3 in 5 abortions (59 percent) were performed in Asia. (See Table 8.2.)

Europe, where abortions are generally legal, had the highest abortion rates — 48 abortions per 1,000 women ages 15 to 44. Interestingly, Europe encompassed the two subregions with the highest and lowest rates — Eastern Europe, with 90 abortions, and Western Europe, with 11 abortions per 1,000 women ages 15 to 44. In Europe, nearly half (48 percent) of all pregnancies ended in abortion, compared to 15 percent in Africa. Among the subregions, Eastern Europe accounted for the highest proportion (65 percent) of pregnancies terminated by abortion. (See Table 8.2.)

Country Estimates

Table 8.3 illustrates the abortion numbers, rates, and ratios for countries with populations exceeding one million for which the AGI obtained information using available national statistics and surveys. The authors pointed out that the upper category, "Believed to be complete," includes countries for which the abortion statistics are thought to be within 20 percent of the actual numbers. The lower "Incomplete" category includes countries whose statistics may be inaccurate by at least 20 percent or the data may be of unknown completeness.

Among countries where abortion is legal and data are believed to be complete, Cuba, Belarus, and Estonia had the highest abortion rates — 77.7, 67.5, and 53.8 abortions per 1,000 women ages 15 to 44, respectively. Belgium (6.8 per 1,000 women) and the Netherlands (6.5 per 1,000 women) had the lowest abortion rates, followed by Germany (7.6 per 1,000 women) and Switzerland (8.4 per 1,000 women). (See Table 8.3.)

Among countries where abortion is legal but the data are incomplete, the authors surmised that the actual abortion rates are higher than shown in Table 8.3. Henshaw et al. noted that the actual rates for Vietnam (83.3 per

1,000 women) and Romania (78 per 1,000 women) were probably higher because only public-sector abortion numbers were available in the AGI survey. China's rate of 26 abortions per 1,000 women is more likely to be between 30 and 35 abortions. (See below for more information on China.) Unofficial surveys of women in Japan tend to indicate that the abortion rates probably exceeded 20 abortions per 1,000 women rather than the reported 13 abortions per 1,000 women. Similarly, Bangladesh's and India's reported rates of 3.8 and 2.7 abortions per 1,000 women, respectively, are more likely to be several times these numbers. The highest proportions of pregnancies terminated by

TABLE 8.2

Estimated number of induced abortions, by legal status, percentage of all abortions that are illegal, abortion rate and abortion ratio, all according to region and subregion, 1995

Region and subregion	No. of abortions (millions)			% illegal	Rate*	Ratio†
	Total	Legal	Illegal			
Total	**45.5**	**25.6**	**19.9**	**44**	**35**	**26**
Developed regions	**10.0**	**9.1**	**0.9**	**9**	**39**	**42**
Excluding Eastern Europe	3.8	3.7	0.1	3	20	26
Developing regions	**35.5**	**16.5**	**19.0**	**54**	**34**	**23**
Excluding China	24.9	5.9	19.0	76	33	20
Africa	**5.0**	**‡**	**5.0**	**99**	**33**	**15**
Eastern Africa	1.9	‡	1.9	100	41	16
Middle Africa	0.6	‡	0.6	100	35	14
Northern Africa	0.6	‡	0.6	96	17	12
Southern Africa	0.2	‡	0.2	100	19	12
Western Africa	1.6	‡	1.6	100	37	15
Asia	**26.8**	**16.9**	**9.9**	**37**	**33**	**25**
Eastern Asia	12.5	12.5	‡	§	36	34
South-central Asia	8.4	1.9	6.5	78	28	18
South-eastern Asia	4.7	1.9	2.8	60	40	28
Western Asia	1.2	0.7	0.5	42	32	20
Europe	**7.7**	**6.8**	**0.9**	**12**	**48**	**48**
Eastern Europe	6.2	5.4	0.8	13	90	65
Northern Europe	0.4	0.3	‡	8	18	23
Southern Europe	0.8	0.7	0.1	12	24	34
Western Europe	0.4	0.4	‡	§	11	17
Latin America	**4.2**	**0.2**	**4.0**	**95**	**37**	**27**
Caribbean	0.4	0.2	0.2	47	50	35
Central America	0.9	‡	0.9	100	30	21
South America	3.0	‡	3.0	100	39	30
Northern America	**1.5**	**1.5**	**‡**	**§**	**22**	**26**
Oceania	**0.1**	**0.1**	**‡**	**22**	**21**	**20**

*Abortions per 1,000 women aged 15–44. †Abortions per 100 known pregnancies. (Known pregnancies are defined as abortions plus live births.) ‡Fewer than 50,000. §Less than 0.5%. Notes: Developed regions include Europe, Northern America, Australia, New Zealand and Japan; all others are considered developing. Regions are as defined by the United Nations (UN). Numbers do not add to totals due to rounding. Sources: Populations—UN, The Sex and Age Distribution of the World Population, The 1996 Revision, New York: UN, 1997. Births—UN, World Population Prospects: The 1996 Revision, Annex II & III, Demographic indicators by major area, region and country, New York: UN, 1996. Illegal abortions— WHO, 1998, op. cit.

Source: Reproduced with the permission of The Alan Guttmacher Institute from S. K. Henshaw, S. Singh, and T. Haas, "The Incidence of Abortion Worldwide," *International Family Planning Perspectives*, 1999, 25 (Supplement): S30-S38, Table 1.

TABLE 8.3

Measures of legal abortion, by completeness of data, country and data year

Completeness and country	No.*	Rate†	Ratio‡	Total abortion rate§
Believed to be complete				
Australia, 1995–1996	91,900	22.2	26.4	0.57
Belarus, 1996	155,700	67.5	61.9	2.04
Belgium, 1996**	14,600	6.8	11.2	0.21
Bulgaria,1996	89,000	51.3	55.2	1.55
Canada, 1995††	106,700	15.5	22.0	0.49
Cuba, 1996	209,900	77.7	58.6	**2.33**
Czech Republic,1996	46,500	20.7	34.0	0.63
Denmark, 1995	17,700	16.1	20.3	0.48
England & Wales, 1996‡‡	167,900	15.6	20.5	0.48
Estonia, 1996	16,900	53.8	56.0	1.63
Finland, 1996	10,400	10.0	14.7	0.31
Germany, 1996	130,900	7.6	14.1	**0.23**
Hungary, 1996	76,600	34.7	42.1	1.07
Israel, 1995	17,600	14.3	13.1	0.43
Kazakhstan, 1996	178,000	43.9	41.3	**1.32**
Latvia, 1996	23,100	44.1	53.9	1.33
Netherlands, 1996‡‡	22,400	6.5	10.6	**0.20**
New Zealand, 1995	13,700	16.4	19.1	0.49
Norway, 1996	14,300	15.6	19.1	0.47
Puerto Rico, 1991–1992	19,200	22.7	23.0	**0.68**
Scotland, 1996§§	12,300	11.2	17.2	0.34
Singapore, 1996	14,400	15.9	22.8	**0.48**
Slovak Republic, 1996	24,300	19.7	28.8	**0.59**
Slovenia, 1996	10,400	23.2	35.7	0.70
Sweden, 1996	32,100	18.7	25.2	0.56
Switzerland, 1996*†	12,800	8.4	13.3	**0.25**
Tunisia, 1996	19,000	8.6	7.8	**0.26**
United States, 1996	1,365,700	22.9	25.9	**0.69**
Incomplete or of unknown completeness				
Albania, 1996	21,200	27.2	23.7	**0.82**
Armenia, 1996	31,300	35.4	39.4	**1.06**
Azerbaijan,1996	28,400	16.0	18.0	0.49
Bangladesh, 1995–1996*‡	100,300	3.8	3.1	**0.11**
China, 1995	7,930,000	26.1	27.4	**0.78**
Croatia, 1996	12,300	12.9	18.7	0.38
France, 1995	156,200	12.4	17.7	0.37
Georgia, 1996	26,600	21.9	33.2	0.66
Hong Kong, 1996	25,000	15.1	27.9	0.45
India, 1995–1996	566,500	2.7	2.1	**0.08**
Ireland, 1996*§	4,900	5.9	8.9	**0.18**
Italy, 1996	140,400	11.4	21.1	**0.34**
Japan, 1995	343,000	13.4	22.4	0.40
Korea (South), 1996†*	230,000	19.6	24.6	**0.59**
Kyrgyzstan, 1996	24,600	22.4	17.5	**0.67**
Lithuania, 1996	27,800	34.4	41.5	**1.03**
Macedonia, 1996	14,200	28.5	31.1	**0.86**
Moldova, 1996	38,900	38.8	42.7	0.83
Mongolia, 1996	15,600	25.9	18.2	**0.78**
Romania, 1996	394,400	78.0	63.0	**2.34**
Russian Federation, 1995	2,287,300	68.4	62.6	2.56
South Africa, 1997	26,400	2.7	2.4	**0.08**
Spain, 1996	51,000	5.7	12.6	**0.17**
Tadjikistan, 1990†‡	55,500	49.1	21.2	**1.47**
Turkey, 1993†*	351,300	25.0	20.5	**0.75**
Turkmenistan, 1990†‡	37,200	44.9	22.9	**1.35**
Ukraine, 1996	635,600	57.2	57.6	**1.72**
Uzbekistan, 1996	63,200	11.8	9.5	**0.35**
Vietnam, 1996†§	1,520,000	83.3	43.7	**2.50**
Yugoslavia, 1993	119,300	54.6	45.8	**1.64**
Zambia, 1983	1,200	0.4	0.4	**0.01**

*Rounded to the nearest 100. †Abortions per 1,000 women aged 15–44. ‡Abortions per 100 known pregnancies. §The number of abortions that would be experienced by the average woman during her reproductive lifetime, given present age-specific abortion rates. Numbers in bold were estimated by multiplying the rate by 30 and dividing by 1,000.**Including abortions obtained in the Netherlands. ††Including abortions obtained in the United States. ‡‡Residents only. §§Including abortions obtained in England and Wales. *†Includes estimates for two of the 26 cantons. *‡Menstrual regulations. *§Based on Irish residents who obtained abortions in England. †*Based on surveys of ever-married women aged 20–44(Korea) and 15–49(Turkey). †‡Includes spontaneous abortions. †§Excludes an estimated 500,000 private-sector abortions.

Source: Reproduced with the permission of The Alan Guttmacher Institute from S. K. Henshaw, S. Singh, and T. Haas, "The Incidence of Abortion Worldwide," *International Family Planning Perspectives*, 1999, 25 (Supplement): S30-S38, Table 2.

abortion (63 percent each) occurred in Russia and Romania. (See Table 8.3.)

In countries where abortion is illegal, the AGI estimated the number of induced abortions based on such factors as the proportion of women hospitalized due to complications and surveys of health care professionals. The authors, however, warned that even in cases where women sought hospitalization, many other factors came into play — "the extent to which safe abortion is practiced, the probability of complications arising from procedures provided by nonphysicians, and the ease of access to a hospital." (See below for abortion information about Latin American countries where abortion is illegal.)

ABORTION IN SELECTED COUNTRIES

Poland

The collapse of Communism in Poland in 1989 led to the prohibition of abortion, which had been legal since 1956. As soon as Lech Walesa's Solidarity Party gained control of the Parliament, it amended the existing abortion law. With the strong support of the Roman Catholic Church, the Parliament severely restricted access to abortion, requiring a woman requesting a state-funded abortion to present written approval from three physicians and a psychologist (from a state-approved list of doctors). The state also stopped funding contraceptives for the needy.

The new abortion provision granted physicians and hospital staffs in public hospitals the right to refuse to perform abortions. As a result, the number of abortions in state-funded hospitals fell from 105,300 in 1988 to about 31,000 in 1991. The government further reduced funding for the Polish Affiliate of the International Planned Parenthood Association, resulting in the closing of half of its offices.

Pope John Paul II, the current pope who is from Poland, strongly supported the abolition of the 1956 abortion law, which he considered "the last bas-tion of Communist totalitarianism." Anti-abortion activists pushed for a new bill to ban abortion in nearly all cases, including rape, and to impose a prison term on women and doctors who attempted abortion. Women who had had abortions were publicly denounced, especially during Sunday mass, while pharmacies selling contraceptives were picketed. Priests refused the sacraments to those who did not sign an anti-abortion petition. Nonetheless, nationwide opinion polls showed that the general population did not agree with the pope's or the anti-abortionists' call for a total ban of abortion.

In March 1993, a new anti-abortion law, granting protection to a fetus from the moment of conception, went into effect. The law allowed abortion only if the pregnancy seriously threatened a woman's life or health, in cases of rape or incest, or if the fetus had irreparable abnormalities. Private clinics were forbidden to perform abortions, and physicians performing illegal abortions were liable for up to two years' imprisonment. If the mother died of complications, the physicians could face up to ten years' imprisonment. On the other hand, women who had abortions were not punishable.

The new law also required that reproductive services be funneled through the Catholic Church and that sex education be offered on "family and conceived-life values as well as on methods and means of conscious procreation." The anti-abortion activists considered "conscious procreation" (a euphemism for contraception) as information on how to have a large family.

Henry P. David and Anna Titkow, in "Abortion and Women's Rights in Poland, 1994" (*Studies in Family Planning*, vol. 25, no. 4, July/August 1994), reported on the situation in Poland one year after the passage of the restrictive anti-abortion law. Women with money continued to obtain abortions privately or abroad, while some poor women resorted to infanticide or became involved with illegal adoption rings. In 1993, in Warsaw, the rate of abandoned babies more than doubled from the previous year.

Because the law punished the doctor, not the pregnant woman, some doctors refused to abort even if a woman's serious health condition allowed a legal abortion. And since the conscience clause gave doctors the legal right to refuse to perform an abortion, women found it harder to have an abortion under accepted circumstances.

The Federation for Women and Family Planning claimed to have had increased calls on its hot line regarding marital rape and violence, sexual abuse of teens, and incest. Many calls also came from frustrated husbands whose wives refused sexual relations for fear of getting pregnant.

Officially reported legal abortions performed in hospitals declined from about 31,000 in 1991 to 11,640 in 1992 and just 777 in 1993. On the other hand, miscarriages increased by 1,225 in 1993, a strong indication that women were practicing self-induced abortions. Despite the low number of legal abortions, the total fertility rate (TFR; lifetime births per woman) declined. In 1998, the TFR reached an all-time low of 1.4 births per woman. (See Table 8.4.)

In 1994 (latest data available), only 782 legal abortions were reportedly performed in Poland. Pro-choice organizations, however, estimated that 40,000 to 50,000 women had abortions abroad or at home illegally.

In November 1995, Lech Walesa lost the presidential election to Aleksander Kwasniewski. Many analysts believed that an anti-Catholic Church sentiment resulting from what many considered the Church's intrusion into the people's lives contributed to Walesa's defeat. Although about 90 percent of Poles are Catholic, a number of surveys have found that most favored liberalization of Poland's restrictive abortion law.

A year later, in November 1996, the Polish government again legalized abortion. The new law permitted women to obtain an abortion until the twelfth week of pregnancy if they were financially or emotionally unprepared for childbirth. A woman

TABLE 8.4

Demographic Indicators

Date	Growth rate (percent)	Total fertility rate	Life expectancy at birth		Infant mortality
			Male	Female	
1960	1.3	2.98	64.8	70.5	54.80
1970	0.8	2.20	66.8	73.8	33.40
1980	0.9	2.28	66.9	75.4	21.30
1990	0.4	2.04	66.5	75.5	15.77
1994	0.2	1.83	67.9	76.4	12.57
1998	0.0	1.40	—	—	13.00

Source: *Women in Poland*, International Programs Center, Bureau of the Census, Washington, DC, 1999

seeking an abortion was required to obtain counseling and wait three days before having the procedure. The new law forbade abortion against a woman's will or after the fetus had become viable (potentially capable of surviving outside the womb). The law further addressed the abortion issue by providing for government funding of oral contraceptives and sex education.

In May 1997, Poland's highest court, the Constitutional Tribunal, struck down the 1996 abortion law, declaring the provision allowing abortions "for compelling social and financial reasons" unconstitutional. The Tribunal ruled that "the first article of our Constitution names Poland as [a] democratic state based on the rule of law. The highest value in a democracy is human life, which must be protected from its beginning to the end." In December 1997, the newly elected Parliament, dominated by pro-Church legislators, reinstated the strict 1993 anti-abortion law (see above).

Romania

For more than 20 years, abortion and contraception were rigorously forbidden in Romania. Nicolai Ceausescu, the Communist dictator during those two decades, had hoped to build his country into a powerful nation based on population growth. Beginning in 1966, abortion was allowed only when a woman was over 45 years old and had had at least five children. Modern contraception was also severely restricted. Nonetheless, over time, the birth rates did not increase. Although the 1967-1968 total fertility rate (3.6 lifetime births

TABLE 8.5

Number and percent distribution of abortions, according to period of gestation: Russian Federation and United States, selected years 1985–95

Country and period of gestation	1985	1990	1991	1992	1993	1994	1995
Russian Federation				Number of abortions			
Ministry of Health	4,257,581	3,920,287	3,525,904	3,265,718	2,977,935	2,808,103	2,574,834
Combined reports	4,454,000	4,103,000	3,608,000	3,530,800	3,476,000	3,006,000	2,753,000
Period of gestation:				Percent distribution			
Less than 6 weeks	- - -	24.3	24.0	26.2	26.8	26.1	25.4
6 weeks or more	- - -	75.7	76.0	73.8	73.2	73.9	74.6
United States				Number of abortions			
Centers for Disease Control and Prevention . . .	1,328,570	1,429,577	1,388,937	1,359,145	1,330,414	1,267,415	1,210,883
Alan Guttmacher Institute	1,589,000	1,609,000	1,557,000	1,529,000	- - -	1,400,000	- - -
Period of gestation:				Percent distribution			
Total	100.0	100.0	100.0	100.0	100.0	100.0	100.0
Less than 9 weeks	50.3	51.6	52.3	52.1	52.3	53.7	54.0
Less than 7 weeks	- - -	- - -	- - -	13.7	14.7	15.7	15.7
7 weeks	- - -	- - -	- - -	15.0	16.2	16.5	17.1
8 weeks	- - -	- - -	- - -	21.4	21.6	21.6	21.2
9–10 weeks	26.6	25.3	25.1	24.2	24.4	23.5	23.1
11–12 weeks	12.5	11.7	11.5	12.0	11.6	10.9	10.9
13–15 weeks	5.9	6.4	6.1	6.0	6.3	6.3	6.3
16–20 weeks	3.9	4.0	3.9	4.2	4.1	4.3	4.3
21 weeks or more	0.8	1.0	1.1	1.5	1.3	1.3	1.4

- - - Data not available.

NOTE: Columns may not add to 100.0 because of rounding.

Source: F. C. Notzon et al., "Maternal and Child Health Statistics: Russian Federation and United States, Selected Years, 1985-95," *Vital and Health Statistics*, series 5, no. 10, March 1999

per woman) more than doubled the 1966 level, it declined to 2.9 in 1970, fell to 2.2 during 1980-1984, and remained at 2.3 births per woman from 1985 through the end of Communism in 1989.

It was only after Ceausescu's regime was overthrown that the terrible situation in Romania was revealed to the world. Without contraception, women resorted to abortion to prevent unwanted births. An estimated 10,000 women died from illegal abortions, self-induced or induced by untrained persons. During the 10-year period (1979-1989) prior to Ceausescu's fall from power, Romania had the highest maternal mortality rate in Europe, 10 times higher than any other European country. Many women also suffered permanent disfigurement.

Romania's interim government after the revolution made abortion available on request through the twelfth week of pregnancy. Abortions up to the twenty-fourth week of pregnancy were permitted in cases of rape, incest, and endangerment of the woman's life if she were to carry her pregnancy to term. After abortion was legalized, the total fertility rate declined from 2.3 live births to 1.5 live births per woman (1990 to 1993), while the total induced abortion rates doubled, from 1.7 to 3.4 abortions per woman. With the shift in policy allowing abortion on demand, the Romanians have resorted to abortion as a principal method of birth control.

The attitudes about contraception have not changed. Many couples continue to rely on traditional family planning methods (withdrawal and rhythm methods), and less than 1 in 10 women uses modern contraceptives to prevent unwanted pregnancies. Although the abortion rates have declined, from 182 abortions per 1,000 women ages 15 to 49 (1990) to 93 abortions per 1,000 women (1994) to 78 abortions per 1,000 in 1996, Romania continues to have the highest abortion rate among all European countries. Stanley K. Henshaw (see above) reported that "[t]he highest abortion rate ever documented in official statistics was recorded in Romania in 1965 (252 per 1,000 women)."

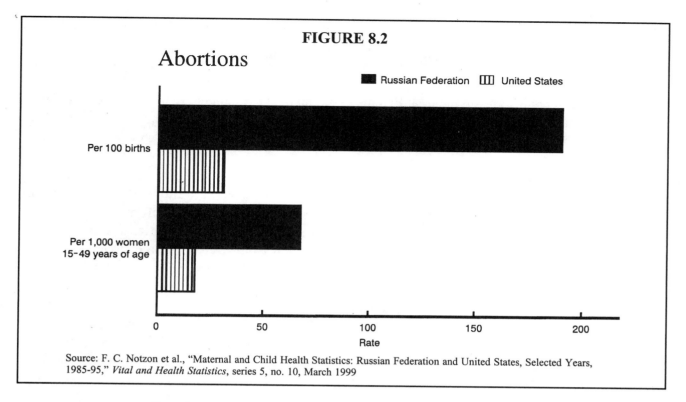

FIGURE 8.2

Abortions

■ Russian Federation ▥ United States

Per 100 births

Per 1,000 women
15–49 years of age

Rate

Source: F. C. Notzon et al., "Maternal and Child Health Statistics: Russian Federation and United States, Selected Years, 1985-95," *Vital and Health Statistics*, series 5, no. 10, March 1999

Russia

Abortion law was liberalized in Russia in 1956. Abortions are allowed on demand through the twelfth week of pregnancy and for medical and social reasons through the twenty-second week. Because modern methods of contraception were unavailable for many years, most women relied on abortion to control childbirth. In 1989, there were generally two abortions for every live birth. A Russian woman who did not want more than two children would likely have as many as four or more abortions in her lifetime.

Between 1990 and 1995, the number of abortions dropped by 33 percent, from 4.1 million to 2.8 million (Table 8.5). Although Russia's abortion rate remained one of the highest in the world, in 1995, the abortion rate continued to decline, with an estimated 68 abortions performed per 1,000 women ages 15 to 49, down from 109 per 1,000 women in 1990. The abortion ratio of 190 abortions per 100 live births and stillbirths was about six times the U.S. ratio of 31 abortions per 100 live births. (See Figure 8.2.)

Contraceptive Use

The first official survey of family planning practice (1990) among Russian women found that only 19 percent were using some form of contraceptive regularly. Nine percent "sometimes" used contraception, while another 9 percent had never heard of the practice. In comparison, in the United States and most European countries, at least 75 percent of fertile women use some form of contraception.

Starting in 1993, the Russian Ministry of Health, the Russian Family Planning Association, and Western pharmaceutical companies joined together to disseminate contraception information to Russian women. Russia's total fertility rate plunged from 2.1 births in 1989 to 1.3 births per woman in 1996, similar to most of the former Communist countries of eastern Europe (Figure 8.3).

Ireland

Ireland is the only European country that still bans abortion, except in cases where the mother's life is threatened (Table 8.1). In 1992, the Supreme

Court ruled that abortion could be legally performed if there was a threat to the mother's life, including the threat of suicide. This landmark case involved a 14-year-old girl who was raped, became pregnant, and sought an abortion in Great Britain. When she was forbidden to do so, she threatened suicide.

In a ballot referendum in late 1992, Irish voters approved a law giving women the right to obtain information regarding abortion services abroad and allowing women to travel abroad to get abortions. (A ballot referendum refers to the submission of a law, proposed or already in effect, to a direct vote of the people.) The voters rejected a proposed constitutional amendment that excluded the threat of suicide as a ground for abortion.

Polls taken in the wake of the court case found changing attitudes against abortions. A 1980 Gallup poll found that 80 percent of respondents approved the total ban on abortion. In 1992, however, *The Irish Times* reported that two-thirds of the Irish people supported amending the constitution to allow limited access to abortion. A *Sunday*

Press poll revealed that 62 percent of adults and 66 percent of women believed abortion should be legal in certain (unspecified) circumstances, while only 31 percent of men and women thought it should be illegal under all circumstances. In 1997, an *Irish Times* poll found that 77 percent of respondents believed abortion should be allowed.

In May 1995, the Irish Supreme Court ruled constitutional a measure allowing doctors and clinics to provide women with information about foreign abortion clinics. The law, however, barred physicians from advising women to have an abortion and from directly helping women make arrangements with clinics abroad.

In November 1997, an incident similar to the 1992 case, this time involving a 13-year-old rape victim, again divided Ireland. Anti-abortion groups offered to adopt the baby, putting pressure on the parents to let the girl give birth. In the end, the girl was allowed to have an abortion in Great Britain.

According to the British government, about 5,000 Irish women travel to Great Britain every

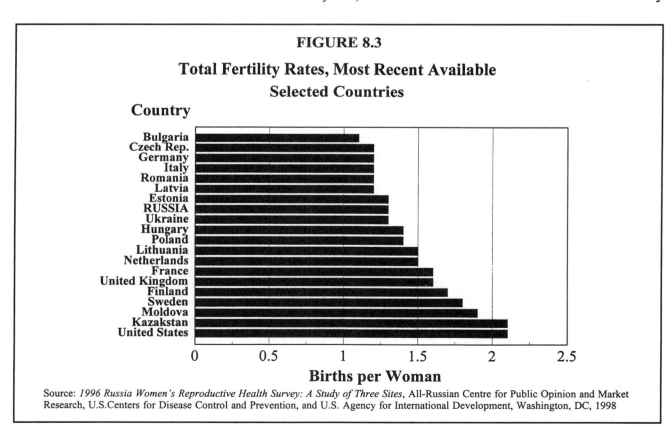

FIGURE 8.3

Total Fertility Rates, Most Recent Available

Selected Countries

Source: *1996 Russia Women's Reproductive Health Survey: A Study of Three Sites*, All-Russian Centre for Public Opinion and Market Research, U.S. Centers for Disease Control and Prevention, and U.S. Agency for International Development, Washington, DC, 1998

TABLE 8.6

Total Fertility Rate (TFR), 1982-92

Year	TFR
1982	2.86
1983	2.42
1984	2.35
1985	2.20
1986	2.42
1987	2.61
1988	2.33
1989	2.29
1990	2.09
1991	1.87
1992	1.72

Source: *1992 National Fertility and Family Planning Survey, China,* The State Family Planning Commission, Beijing, China, The World Health Organization Collaborating Center in Perinatal Care and Health Services Research in Maternal and Child Health, and U.S. Centers for Disease Control and Prevention, Atlanta, GA, 1997

ethnic minorities. The latest survey of fertility and family planning found that, between 1982 and 1992, the total fertility rate declined by about one child, from 2.86 to 1.72 lifetime births per woman (Table 8.6). In 1998, China's total fertility rate has remained low at 1.8 lifetime births per woman (Figure 8.4).

In addition, in 1992, the proportion of couples of childbearing age who were sterilized or used contraception rose to 83.4 percent, up from 71.1 percent in 1988. Because Chinese women are allowed, at most, two children, most are through bearing children at an early age, leaving many years of fertility to regulate. Contraceptives are generally provided free by local family planning services, and the abortion-inducing drug mifepristone (see Chapter IV), approved in 1988, is widely used.

In some circumstances, the government can mandate that an abortion be performed. In 1994, under the provisions of the Maternal Health Care Law, in order to prevent "inferior births," couples planning to marry had to submit to prenatal testing. An abortion would be recommended if the fetus had a severe hereditary disease or was seriously impaired. Critics considered this a "eugenics law," designed to terminate the birth of defective babies.

year for abortions. In 1998, records showed that the number was at least 5,900, with an abortion rate of 5.6 abortions per 1,000 women ages 15 to 44. Currently, the abortion issue in Ireland has not been resolved.

China

In China, abortion is permitted to save the mother's life, to preserve physical health, and to safeguard mental health. Abortion is also permitted in cases of rape, incest, fetal impairment, and for economic or social reasons.

In the 1970s, China initiated a stringent family planning program that has resulted in one of the fastest fertility declines in the world. The program promotes one-child families in urban areas and two-child families in rural areas and for

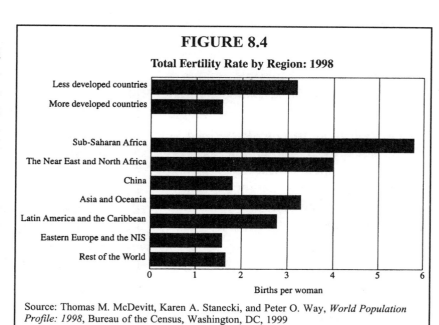

FIGURE 8.4

Total Fertility Rate by Region: 1998

Source: Thomas M. McDevitt, Karen A. Stanecki, and Peter O. Way, *World Population Profile: 1998*, Bureau of the Census, Washington, DC, 1999

China amended the law the following year, deleting the controversial language concerning "inferior births." A couple planning to get married was required to undergo a medical examination to determine the presence of genetic disorders. If such disorders were found, they had to agree to long-term contraception, or they could not get married. Although the law specified that a woman carrying an imperfect fetus could not be coerced to abort, her physician must advise her to do so.

Sex Selection

Critics observe that a pervading cultural preference for boys in China, coupled with the limitation on the number of births per family, endangers females. Every year, countless girls are abandoned, killed, aborted, or hidden from the family planning authorities. The State Family Planning Commission of Beijing, China, in the *1992 National Fertility and Family Survey, China* (Beijing, China, and Atlanta, Georgia, 1997), observed, "The effects of sex preference on fertility behaviors is not only reflected in whether or not [women] will progress to the next birth, but also in the selection of the sex of children they want through medical technologies."

Normally, approximately 105 boys are born worldwide for every 100 girls. The *sex ratio at birth* (SRB) indicates the number of male births for every 100 female births. In China, the SRB rose from 108.5 in 1981 to 111 in 1987 to 117.2 in 1992. Figure 8.5 shows the SRB by parity (number of children borne by one woman) and the number of sons the woman had had before her current childbearing. For example, at second parity, rural women with a daughter had a sex ratio of 184.1, while that for women with a son was 103.4. The State Family Planning Commission suggested that women without a son would continue selecting the sex of their fetus with each pregnancy. The commission also concluded that women with no son or few sons were more likely to underreport female births and practice selective abortion.

India

When the Indian government started providing family planning services in 1951, it became the first developing country to promote population control. Overall, the total fertility rate (TFR) has been declining. In 1971, the TFR was 5.9 lifetime births per woman. By 1999, the TFR was down to 3.2 births. Nonetheless, the population has continued to grow, more than doubling between 1960 (about 446 million) and 1998 (nearly 1 billion). Eventually, India is expected to become more populous than China.

In 1969, India legalized abortion to control its population growth, but government facilities have not been able to keep up with the great number of women seeking abortions. In rural areas, where facilities are lacking or inadequate, women obtain abortions from midwives and untrained practitioners. An estimated 15,000 to 25,000 women die each year from unsafe abortions. In 1995-1996, an estimated 566,500 abortions were reported (Table 8.3); however, the actual number is said to be higher.

In India, as in China, there is a strong preference for sons. This preference is strongly connected

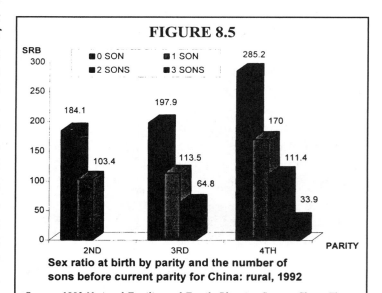

FIGURE 8.5

SRB
- 0 SON
- 1 SON
- 2 SONS
- 3 SONS

285.2
197.9
184.1
170
113.5
111.4
103.4
64.8
33.9

300 / 250 / 200 / 150 / 100 / 50 / 0

2ND / 3RD / 4TH / PARITY

Sex ratio at birth by parity and the number of sons before current parity for China: rural, 1992

Source: *1992 National Fertility and Family Planning Survey, China*, The State Family Planning Commission, Beijing, China, The World Health Organization Collaborating Center in Perinatal Care and Health Services Research in Maternal and Child Health, and U.S. Centers for Disease Control and Prevention, Atlanta, GA, 1997

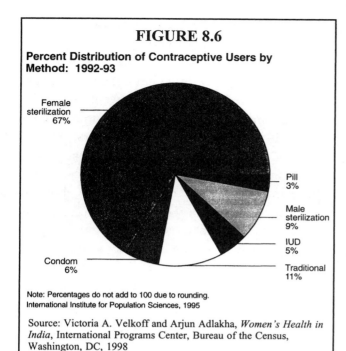

FIGURE 8.6

Percent Distribution of Contraceptive Users by Method: 1992-93

Female sterilization 67%

Pill 3%

Male sterilization 9%

IUD 5%

Condom 6%

Traditional 11%

Note: Percentages do not add to 100 due to rounding.
International Institute for Population Sciences, 1995

Source: Victoria A. Velkoff and Arjun Adlakha, *Women's Health in India*, International Programs Center, Bureau of the Census, Washington, DC, 1998

to the custom of providing a suitable dowry (money or property brought by a bride to her husband at marriage), which puts a great financial burden on the bride's parents. Customarily, sons live with their parents after marriage, providing both financial and emotional support, especially as the parents age.

Medical advances have made sex-selective abortions easier. Prenatal testing has become routine among educated middle- and upper-class women, who often terminate their pregnancies if they are carrying a daughter. Modern technology has also reached some rural areas, where vans with ultrasound machines enable expectant mothers to determine the sex of their fetuses. The enactment of laws forbidding sex selection has not deterred selective abortion practices.

Despite the promotion of family planning, the use of modern contraceptives remains low. Since the mid-1970s, female sterilization has become the main form of contraception recommended by the government. (See Figure 8.6.) In 1997, even after the government launched a program advocating informed

choice regarding women's contraception selection, a woman who indicated that she did not want any more children or already had two or more children was encouraged to undergo sterilization.

Latin America

Except in Cuba, induced abortion is illegal throughout Latin America. Although abortion is generally permitted in cases of endangerment of the woman's life, rape, incest, and fetal abnormality, these exceptions are rarely used. Hence, abortions have become a clandestine (kept secret or hidden) affair in Latin America.

Deirdre Wulf and Susheela Singh, in "An Overview of Clandestine Abortion in Latin America" (*Issues in Brief*, The Alan Guttmacher Institute, New York, 1996), reported that, each year, an estimated four million women in Latin America obtain illegal abortions (Table 8.7). At least 800,000 women are hospitalized for abortion complications (Table 8.8).

The latest available data show that Peru had the highest abortion rate (51.8 per 1,000 women ages 15 to 49), followed by Chile (45.4 per 1,000 women) and the Dominican Republic (43.7 per 1,000 women). Overall, women average one abor-

TABLE 8.7

Abortion Incidence

Country/year	Annual no. of abortions	Rate per 1,000 women	Average per woman
Total	**2,768,150**	**33.9**	**1.2**
Brazil, 1991	1,433,350	36.5	1.3
Chile, 1990	159,650	45.4	1.6
Colombia, 1989	288,400	33.7	1.2
Dom. Republic	82,500	43.7	1.5
Mexico, 1990	533,100	23.2	0.8
Peru, 1989	271,150	51.8	1.8
Latin America*	**4,000,000**	**33.9**	**1.2**

*Estimated on the assumption that these six countries account for 70% of the population of Latin America and that all countries in the region have similar hospitalization levels; rounded to the nearest 100,000.

Source: Reproduced with the permission of The Alan Guttmacher Institute from D. Wulf and S. Singh, "An Overview of Abortion in Latin America," *Issues in Brief*, New York, NY, 1996

TABLE 8.8

Unsafe Abortions

Country/year	Number of hospitalizations
Total	**555,630**
Brazil, 1991	288,670
Colombia, 1989	57,680
Chile, 1990	31,930
Dom. Republic, 1992	16,500
Mexico, 1990	106,620
Peru, 1989	54,230
Latin America*	**800,000**

*Estimated on the assumption that these six countries account for 70% of the population of Latin America and that all countries in the region have similar hospitalization levels; rounded to the nearest 100,000.

Source: Reproduced with the permission of The Alan Guttmacher Institute from D. Wulf and S. Singh, "An Overview of Abortion in Latin America," *Issues in Brief*, New York, NY, 1996

Characteristics of Latin American Women Having Abortions

Most of the women having an abortion in Latin America were in their twenties or older and married. Many also had children. In contrast, in most developed countries, women who obtain an abortion are generally very young, single, and childless (50 percent). For example, a survey of hospitalized abortion patients in Bolivia, Colombia, Peru, and Venezuela found that most of the women (86 percent) were 20 years or older. About 4 in 5 (79 percent) were married and half (51 percent) had two or more children.

Reasons for Abortion

The women had a number of reasons for seeking an abortion. Many married women, especially the poor, already had all the children they could afford to raise. Single women might not have

tion over their lifetime. (See Table 8.7.) In Brazil, Chile, the Dominican Republic, and Peru, about one-third of pregnancies ended in abortion (Figure 8.7).

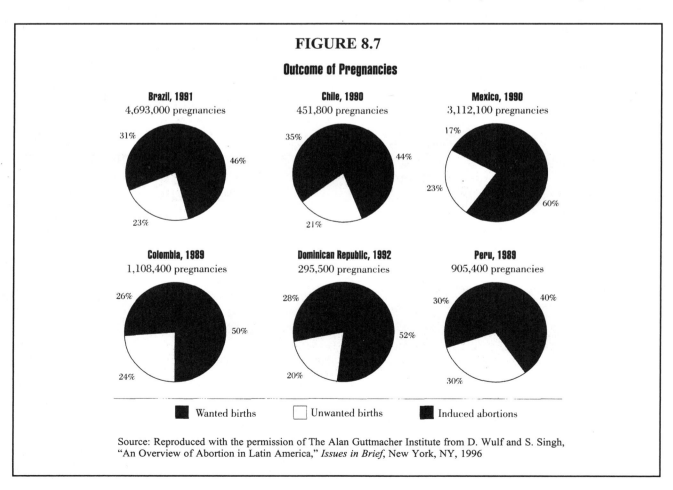

FIGURE 8.7

Outcome of Pregnancies

Brazil, 1991
4,693,000 pregnancies
46% / 31% / 23%

Chile, 1990
451,800 pregnancies
44% / 35% / 21%

Mexico, 1990
3,112,100 pregnancies
60% / 17% / 23%

Colombia, 1989
1,108,400 pregnancies
50% / 26% / 24%

Dominican Republic, 1992
295,500 pregnancies
52% / 28% / 20%

Peru, 1989
905,400 pregnancies
40% / 30% / 30%

■ Wanted births   □ Unwanted births   ■ Induced abortions

Source: Reproduced with the permission of The Alan Guttmacher Institute from D. Wulf and S. Singh, "An Overview of Abortion in Latin America," *Issues in Brief*, New York, NY, 1996

wanted to raise a child alone or could not support a child by themselves. Working women and those with more education did not want additional children.

Some women continued to get pregnant because they were not using any contraception or they were using traditional, unreliable methods, such as withdrawal. These women represented approximately 17 percent of fertile women in Colombia and up to 43 percent in Bolivia. Others had unwanted pregnancies because they did not know about the likely time of conception or were using contraceptives incorrectly or irregularly.

South Africa

Under apartheid (racial segregation to promote White supremacy), abortion was illegal in South Africa except in cases where the pregnancy threatened the woman's mental health. The government, fearing that Blacks would outnumber Whites, used tax credits to encourage White women to have children. Nonetheless, upper- and middle-income women with unwanted pregnancies sought abortions in private physicians' offices or abroad. Poor women, on the other hand, either terminated their own pregnancies or used the services of unqualified abortionists.

In 1975, reacting to pressures from the medical profession and women's groups, the legislature enacted the Abortion and Sterilization Act. Nonetheless, due to the stringent provisions of the law, such as the approval of two physicians and that of a psychiatrist, many women continued seeking illegal abortions. Sally Guttmacher, Farzana Kapadia, Jim Te Water Naude, and Helen de Pinho, in "Abortion Reform in South Africa: A Case Study of the 1996 Choice on Termination of Pregnancy Act" (*International Family Planning Perspectives*, vol. 24, no. 4, December 1998), reported that, between 1975 and 1996, clandestine abortions numbered approximately 120,000 to 250,000 annually.

In November 1996, South Africa's first democratically elected Parliament passed a new abortion law. Under the law, women and adolescents could get state funding for abortions up to the twelfth week of pregnancy. From the thirteenth up to and including the twentieth week of pregnancy, abortion is legal in cases of danger to the mother's physical or mental health, rape, incest, and fetal defect. The law further allows abortion if continuing the pregnancy would affect the woman's social or economic circumstances. Abortion after twenty weeks of pregnancy is also allowed if a physician or trained midwife finds that continuation of the pregnancy would threaten the woman's health or result in fetal abnormality. Although adolescents are counseled to consult their parents, the law allows them to have an abortion without parental knowledge.

CROSS-BORDER ABORTIONS

For most of the 1990s, there has been a pervasive trend of European women crossing borders to get abortions. Each year, about 15,000 European women travel abroad to obtain abortions that are illegal in their own countries. Abortion laws in Europe run the gamut from a total ban in Ireland to the twenty-four-week gestation limit in Great Britain and the Netherlands. Women who wish to terminate an early pregnancy can travel to France, Great Britain, Scotland, and Sweden and have a medical abortion with the help of the abortion-inducing pill, RU-486 (see Chapter IV). As expected, women of means are more able to circumvent their country's abortion laws by going to a country that suits their situation.

DEATHS FROM ABORTION

Stan Bernstein, in *The State of the World Population 1997* (United Nations Population Fund, New York, 1997), estimated that 70,000 women die each year as a result of unsafe abortions, about 13 percent of all maternal deaths. (See Figure 8.8.) An unknown, but much greater, proportion suffer infection, injury, and trauma. Of the estimated 20 million unsafe abortions each year, 90 percent occur in developing countries.

While illegal abortions are more likely to be performed under unsafe conditions, Bernstein pointed out that even legal abortions may prove

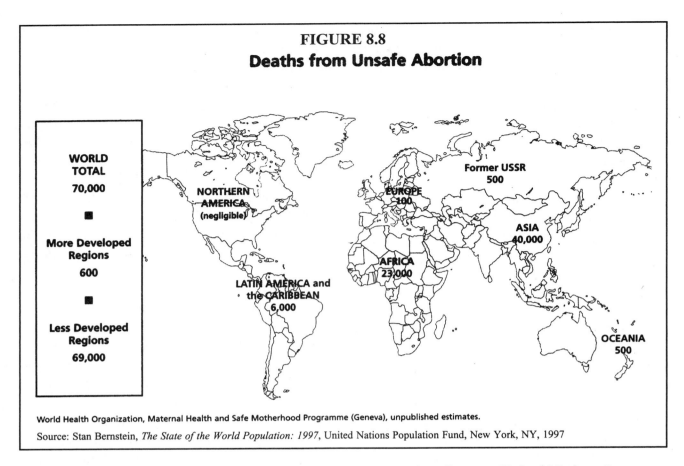

FIGURE 8.8
Deaths from Unsafe Abortion

WORLD TOTAL 70,000

More Developed Regions 600

Less Developed Regions 69,000

NORTHERN AMERICA (negligible)

LATIN AMERICA and the CARIBBEAN 6,000

Former USSR 500

EUROPE 100

ASIA 40,000

AFRICA 23,000

OCEANIA 500

World Health Organization, Maternal Health and Safe Motherhood Programme (Geneva), unpublished estimates.

Source: Stan Bernstein, *The State of the World Population: 1997*, United Nations Population Fund, New York, NY, 1997

unsafe "when access is restricted by bureaucracy (as in the former Soviet Union), where services are poor or not available, or where [the] medical staff refuse to perform the operation." According to the World Health Organization, in *Abortion in the Developing World* (Geneva, Switzerland, 1998), the risk of dying from an unsafe abortion is 1 in 250 procedures in developing countries, compared to 1 in 3,700 procedures in developed countries.

THE CAIRO AND BEIJING CONFERENCES

We must be courageous in speaking out on the issues that concern us: we must not bend under the weight of spurious arguments invoking culture or traditional values. No value worth the name supports the oppression and enslavement of women. The function of culture and tradition is to provide a framework for human well-being. If they are used against us, we will reject them, and move on. We will not allow ourselves to be silenced. — Dr. Nafis Sadik, executive director, United Nations Population Fund, Beijing, September 1995

At the landmark International Conference on Population and Development (ICPD) in Cairo, Egypt (September 1994), 179 nations reached consensus on the role of population in the development of a country and agreed on the *Programme of Action* to implement goals set for 2015. Among the goals, the delegates recognized that improving the status of women and protecting their rights, particularly their reproductive rights, would play a critical role in population policies. The Cairo conference was the first where the pervasiveness of abortions throughout the world was openly discussed.

The Vatican (a nonvoting member of the UN but a permanent observer) was alarmed at the introduction of reproductive issues for inclusion in the *Programme of Action*. Charging that the *Programme* promoted abortion both on demand and as a method of birth control, the Vatican campaigned among conservative Catholic and Muslim countries to object to any abortion language.

110

The Vatican argued that all references to unsafe abortion should be eliminated because all abortions are unsafe for the fetus. It also objected to references to reproductive health, reproductive rights, and sexual health because they implied access to abortion, modern methods of birth control, and otherwise irresponsible sexual behavior.

Despite the Vatican's objections, the international community agreed on a common position regarding abortion, which states,

> In no case should abortion be promoted as a method of family planning. All Governments and relevant intergovernmental and non-governmental organizations are urged to strengthen their commitment to women's health, to deal with the health impact of unsafe abortion* as a major public health concern and to reduce the recourse to abortion through expanded and improved family planning services. Prevention of unwanted pregnancies must always be given the highest priority and all attempts should be made to eliminate the need for abortion. Women who have unwanted pregnancies should have ready access to reliable information and compassionate counseling....

The 1995 Fourth World Conference on Women in Beijing, China, reiterated the Cairo *Programme of Action.* On the issue of abortion, the Vatican attached a "conscience clause" to the draft of the Beijing *Platform for Action*, stating, "Nothing ... in the present *Platform for Action* is intended to require any health professional or health facility to provide [or refer for] services to which they have objections on the basis of religious belief or moral conviction as a violation of conscience." In the end, this clause was deleted and replaced with one that indicated that prevailing codes of medical ethics should guide health professionals.

ICPD+5

In July 1999, as agreed upon during the Cairo conference (see above), 179 countries met to assess the progress of the *Programme of Action.* The five-year review process, known as ICPD+5, or Cairo+5, found that countries implementing the *Programme* recommendations had improved conditions in their countries. For example, over 40 countries had introduced reproductive health services, and nearly half the countries had addressed the issue of adolescent reproductive health needs. Almost all Latin American countries had introduced policies or laws to safeguard women's rights, and more than half the Asian countries and some African countries had protected women's rights in such areas as inheritance, property, and employment.

Nonetheless, the delegates agreed that much work still needs to be done. Despite opposition from the Vatican and conservative Catholic and Muslim countries, the delegates agreed on new proposals, including the instruction of school children regarding sexual and reproductive health issues to protect them from unwanted pregnancies and sexually transmitted diseases. Affirming the Cairo proposal that adolescents should be given "appropriate services and advice" relating to sexual and reproductive matters, ICPD+5 added that, "with due respect for the rights, duties, and responsibilities of parents," adolescents' right to privacy, confidentiality, and informed consent should be respected.

Finally, the delegates stressed that "in circumstances where abortion is not against the law, health systems should train and equip health-service providers and should take measures that ensure that such abortion is safe and accessible."

---

* Unsafe abortion is defined as a procedure for terminating an unwanted pregnancy either by persons lacking necessary skills or in an environment lacking the minimal standards or both (World Health Organization).

CHAPTER IX

PUBLIC ATTITUDES TOWARD ABORTION*

ATTITUDES TOWARD THE 1973 SUPREME COURT RULING

The U.S. Supreme Court, in *Roe v. Wade* (410 U.S. 113), ruled in 1973 that, during the first trimester (three months) of pregnancy, the state had no right to prohibit abortion and that, during the second trimester, the state could prohibit abortion unless the pregnancy endangered the mother's health or life. After the point of fetal viability (when the fetus could potentially survive outside the womb), the state may prohibit abortion except when it is necessary to preserve the life or health of the mother. In the more than 25 years since *Roe*, the Supreme Court has permitted increasing limits by the states on abortion (see Chapter II).

Although the decision in *Roe v. Wade* has been at the center of the abortion issue for many years, only about 30 percent of Americans can recall, unprompted, that the case was about abortion rights. Far fewer remember the details of the decision. Because of this, polling organizations generally include a brief description of the decision in their questions. For the most part, this description refers only to the portion of *Roe* that permits unlimited abortion in the first trimester.

Louis Harris and Associates has regularly polled the American public for their opinions on the abortion issue. The Harris Poll found that in the past 25 years, Americans' attitudes about abortion have not changed significantly. In 1973, a few months after the *Roe* decision, the Harris Poll asked, "In 1973, the Supreme Court decided that state laws which made it illegal for a woman to have an abortion up to three months of pregnancy were unconstitutional, and that the decision on whether a woman should have an abortion up to three months of pregnancy should be left to the woman and her doctor to decide. In general, do you favor or oppose this part of the U.S. Supreme Court decision making abortions up to three months of pregnancy legal?" Half (52 percent) of the respondents favored the decision, while 42 percent opposed it. In 1998, on the twenty-fifth anniversary of *Roe,* when the Harris Poll asked the same question, the proportions for and against the decision were about the same, 57 percent and 41 percent, respectively. (See Table 9.1.)

---

* Like all statistics, public opinion polls should be viewed cautiously. The way a question is phrased influences the respondents' answers. Many other factors may also influence a response in ways that are often difficult to determine. A respondent might never have thought of the issue until asked, or he/she might be giving the pollster the answer he/she thinks the pollster wants to hear. Organizations that survey opinions do not claim absolute accuracy — their findings are approximate snapshots of the attitudes of the nation at a given time. The surveys presented here have been selected from numerous polls taken on abortion. The Gallup Poll, Louis Harris and Associates, and the National Opinion Research Center are well respected in their fields, and their surveys are accepted as representative of public opinions. A typical, well-conducted survey claims accuracy to about plus or minus three points.

In 1999, the Pew Research Center for the People & the Press surveyed the American public about the changes that have taken place over the last century and whether these changes have been for the better or for the worse. Two in 5 (42 percent) respondents thought that, over the past 100 years, legalized abortion has been a change for the worse, while one-third (34 percent) thought it has been a change for the better. Of the same respondents, 72 percent believed the development of the birth control pills has been a change for the better, while just 10 percent felt birth control pills have been a change for the worse.

ON THE TWENTY-FIFTH ANNIVERSARY OF *ROE V. WADE*

On January 10-12, 1998, approximately two weeks before the twenty-fifth anniversary of *Roe v. Wade*, the *New York Times* and CBS News conducted a survey to determine whether or not Americans had changed their attitudes toward abortion. This was the first *New York Times*/CBS News Poll since 1989. Sixty percent approved of the 1973 Supreme Court ruling on *Roe*, which upheld a woman's constitutional right to have an abortion. (However, as with the Harris Poll [see above], the

respondents had to be reminded of what the Court ruling was about.)

Overall, 32 percent supported generally available legal abortion, down from 40 percent in 1989. Those who said abortion should be available but with controls rose from 40 percent to 45 percent. On the other hand, those against legal abortion increased from 18 percent in 1989 to 22 percent in 1998.

Half (50 percent) of the respondents considered abortion murder, while over a third (38 percent) believed abortion is not murder because "the fetus really isn't a child." However, among those who considered abortion murder, one-third (32 percent) thought that "abortion is sometimes the best course in a bad situation."

About one-half were not interested in what politicians thought about abortion, while almost 60 percent indicated politicians had no business being involved with decisions about whether abortions should be legal. Indicative of the public attitude that abortion is a private, moral issue and not a political one, more than three-quarters opposed a constitutional amendment banning abortion.

SHOULD ABORTION BE LEGAL?

In 1999, Gallup Poll researchers asked, "Do you think abortions should be legal under any circumstances, legal only under certain circumstances, or illegal in all circumstances?" About one-quarter (27 percent) of Americans thought abortions should be legal under any circumstances, while one-half (55 percent) thought abortions should be legal only under certain circumstances, and 16 percent thought abortions should never be legal (Figure 9.1).

FIGURE 9.1

Do you think abortions should be legal under any circumstances, legal only under certain circumstances, or illegal in all circumstances?

◆ Legal Under Any Circumstances   ○ Legal Under Some Circumstances   □ Illegal in all circumstances

Source: The Gallup Organization, Princeton, NJ, 1999

The Gallup Poll has asked the above question often since 1975. Despite the continuing debate on abortion, attitudes towards abortion have more or less remained stable. Over the past two and a half decades, 48 to 61 percent of Americans supported a middle position (legal only under certain circumstances). In 1999, the proportion of those believing abortion should always be legal fell about 4 to 7 percentage points from the early to mid-1990s (31 to 34 percent) and that of abortion opponents increased 3 to 4 points (12 to 13 percent). However, those taking the middle ground have remained about the same. (See Figure 9.1.)

In 1999, men and women generally held similar views about the legality of abortion — 41 percent of women and 35 percent of men thought it should be legal under all or most circumstances. A large percentage of both women (57 percent) and men (60 percent) believed abortion should be limited to few circumstances. Overall, women (60 percent) were more likely than men (47 percent) to say they felt very strongly about their views on abortion.

Opinions of College Freshmen

Since 1973, the Higher Education Research Institute of the University of California, Los Angeles (UCLA), has surveyed freshman students nationwide on such current issues as abortion. In 1998, the Institute surveyed over 275,800 freshmen and asked, among other questions, whether or not abortion should be kept legal. For the sixth straight year, the proportion of freshmen in favor

TABLE 9.2

ATTITUDES TO ABORTION IN FIRST, SECOND AND THIRD TRIMESTER OF PREGNANCY

"In general, do you think that abortion should be legal or illegal during the following stages of pregnancy?"

	Legal %	Illegal %	Don't Know/ Refused %
The first three months of pregnancy	63	34	3
The second three months of pregnancy	26	69	4
The third three months of pregnancy	13	81	5

Source: The Harris Poll, Louis Harris and Associates, Inc., New York, NY. 1998

of keeping abortion legal has been dropping, reaching a low of 50.9 percent, down from 53.5 percent in 1997 and 64.9 percent in 1990.

During Which Stage of Pregnancy Should Abortion Be Legal?

In 1998, the Harris Poll surveyed the American people to find out during which stage of pregnancy they thought abortion should be legal. While two-thirds (63 percent) thought abortion should be legal during the first trimester (three months) of pregnancy, just one-quarter (26 percent) thought it should be legal during the second trimester, and only 13 percent felt it should be legal during the last trimester. (See Table 9.2.)

Under What Specific Situations Should Abortion Be Legal?

The National Opinion Research Center periodically surveys social issues. Like most other surveys, it has found that for many people, abortion is a difficult issue, permissible in some situations but not in others. In 1998, most respondents approved of abortion if there was a strong chance of a defect in the baby (75 percent), if the woman's health was seriously endangered by the pregnancy (84 percent), or if she became pregnant as a result of rape (76 percent). (See Table 9.3.)

However, fewer than half thought a woman should be able to obtain a legal abortion if she was married and did not want any more children (40 percent), if the family had a very low income and could not afford any more children (42 percent), or if the woman was not married and did not want to marry the man (40 percent). A similar percentage (39 percent) of the public approved of an abortion if a woman wanted it for any reason at all. (See Table 9.3.)

RESTRICTIONS ON ABORTION

In 1992, the U.S. Supreme Court heard a case that threatened to overturn *Roe v. Wade. Planned Parenthood of Southeastern Pennsylvania v. Casey* (505 U.S. 833) challenged a restrictive abortion law that required a one-parent consent for minors with a judicial bypass, spousal notification, a 24-hour waiting period, and information on abortion and fetal development to be given to women (see Chapter II). The High Court upheld all restrictions except the husband-notification provision.

In 1996, the Gallup Organization asked Americans questions regarding six potential laws, four of which were similar to the 1989 Pennsylvania Abortion Control Act (see *Casey* above). Most Americans favored laws requiring parental consent for minors (74 percent), spousal notification (70

TABLE 9.3

Should a legal abortion be possible under the following circumstances?

	1993	1994	1998
Strong chance of serious defect in the baby			
Yes	78	79	75
No	18	17	20
Married and doesn't want more children			
Yes	45	47	40
No	50	50	55
Woman's health endangered by pregnancy			
Yes	86	88	84
No	10	9	12
Very low income and can't afford more children			
Yes	47	49	42
No	48	48	53
Pregnancy is due to rape			
Yes	79	81	76
No	16	16	19
Not married and does not want to marry			
Yes	45	46	40
No	49	51	55
Abortion on demand			
Yes	43	45	39
No	51	52	56

Source: Data from National Opinion Research Center, University of Chicago, IL, 1998; table constructed by Information Plus

TABLE 9.4

Six Potential Abortion Laws

Next, do you favor or oppose each of the following proposals. First, a law requiring women seeking abortions to wait 24 hours before having the procedure done; a law requiring doctors to inform patients about alternatives to abortion before performing the procedure; a law requiring women under 18 to get parental consent for any abortion; a law requiring that the husband of a married woman be notified if she decides to have an abortion. [following 2 asked last, ROTATED] a law which would make it illegal to perform a specific abortion procedure conducted in the last six months of pregnancy known as a "partial birth abortion," except in cases necessary to save the life of the mother; a constitutional amendment to ban abortion in all circumstances, except when necessary to save the life of the mother.

	Inform about alternatives		24-hour waiting period		Under-18 parental consent		No "partial birth" abortions	
	Favor	Oppose	Favor	Oppose	Favor	Oppose	Favor	Oppose
National	86%	11	74%	22	74%	23	71%	23
Sex								
Male	83%	14	70%	25	73%	23	72%	23
Female	88%	9	77%	19	75%	22	69%	24
Age								
18-29 years	91%	8	75%	23	73%	25	74%	22
30-49 years	87%	11	75%	22	74%	23	71%	24
50-64 years	83%	14	71%	22	67%	29	65%	26
65 & older	82%	11	75%	18	78%	15	72%	21
Region								
East	86%	12	68%	29	73%	27	63%	32
Midwest	90%	8	77%	21	74%	22	72%	22
South	84%	13	74%	19	77%	20	74%	19
West	84%	11	76%	18	71%	23	73%	22
Community								
Urban	82%	13	71%	22	71%	24	66%	27
Suburban	88%	10	74%	24	72%	26	71%	25
Rural	87%	11	77%	18	79%	17	76%	18
Race								
White	87%	10	75%	22	74%	23	70%	24
Non-white	81%	16	70%	22	71%	25	75%	21
Black	82%	15	67%	23	71%	26	72%	25
Education								
College postgraduate	81%	14	66%	30	65%	33	56%	36
Bachelor's degree only	83%	16	73%	23	72%	26	72%	23
Some college	95%	4	80%	17	81%	16	76%	19
High school or less	83%	13	73%	22	72%	24	71%	23
Politics								
Republicans	91%	7	83%	13	80%	15	75%	19
Democrats	83%	14	71%	24	72%	26	71%	25
Independents	84%	13	68%	28	70%	26	66%	26
Ideology								
Liberal	74%	21	66%	31	55%	40	64%	30
Moderate	89%	10	74%	23	76%	22	69%	25
Conservative	90%	8	79%	16	80%	16	76%	20
Clinton approval								
Approve	85%	12	72%	24	72%	26	69%	25
Disapprove	91%	8	78%	19	79%	17	75%	21
2-way Trial Heat								
Clinton	84%	13	71%	24	67%	30	67%	27
Dole	89%	8	81%	15	81%	15	78%	19
Income								
$75,000 & over	89%	9	75%	22	72%	24	66%	28
$50,000 & over	89%	10	74%	23	69%	29	68%	28
$30,000-49,999	89%	9	77%	19	75%	22	78%	21
$20,000-29,999	87%	9	78%	20	78%	19	73%	21
Under $20,000	82%	13	67%	26	75%	21	69%	25
Female: Employment								
Employed	90%	8	80%	18	77%	21	70%	23
Not employed	91%	8	75%	22	71%	28	66%	31
Retired	81%	8	70%	19	71%	22	72%	19

Note: "No opinion" omitted.

(continued)

percent), a 24-hour waiting period (74 percent), and the giving of information about abortion alternatives (86 percent). About 7 in 10 (71 percent) also favored the banning of partial-birth abortion (vetoed twice by President Clinton after passage in Congress; see Chapter III and 1999 poll below), but only 38 percent favored a constitutional amendment banning abortion in all cases, except when necessary to save the mother's life. (See Table 9.4.)

TABLE 9.4 (Continued)

Six Potential Abortion Laws (continued)

| | | Spousal notification | | Constitutional ban | | Number of |
		Favor	Oppose	Favor	Oppose	interviews
National		70%	26	38%	59	1008
Sex						
	Male	74%	23	35%	64	497
	Female	67%	29	41%	54	511
Age						
	18-29 years	75%	24	40%	58	204
	30-49 years	68%	28	32%	65	439
	50-64 years	66%	30	37%	59	194
	65 & older	77%	17	48%	45	161
Region						
	East	61%	36	39%	59	234
	Midwest	76%	21	38%	59	268
	South	74%	22	41%	55	303
	West	69%	26	33%	63	203
Community						
	Urban	65%	30	34%	62	312
	Suburban	70%	27	35%	63	417
	Rural	77%	20	45%	51	279
Race						
	White	71%	26	37%	60	819
	Non-white	70%	25	43%	53	182
	Black	72%	26	46%	51	110
Education						
	College postgraduate	51%	45	18%	82	182
	Bachelor's degree only	62%	30	23%	76	150
	Some college	73%	25	38%	60	276
	High school or less	76%	20	47%	48	396
Politics						
	Republicans	78%	17	40%	57	321
	Democrats	66%	31	40%	57	354
	Independents	68%	28	34%	62	333
Ideology						
	Liberal	60%	38	27%	72	181
	Moderate	68%	30	32%	67	416
	Conservative	78%	17	47%	48	378
Clinton approval						
	Approve	66%	31	35%	63	570
	Disapprove	80%	17	42%	55	372
2-way Trial Heat						
	Clinton	60%	36	32%	66	467
	Dole	81%	15	44%	52	343
Income						
	$75,000 & over	61%	35	29%	70	137
	$50,000 & over	61%	36	23%	75	295
	$30,000-49,999	70%	28	33%	65	228
	$20,000-29,999	77%	21	43%	56	177
	Under $20,000	75%	20	52%	42	236
Female: Employment						
	Employed	60%	36	32%	66	312
	Not employed	77%	20	53%	41	94
	Retired	77%	17	53%	37	103

Source: *The Gallup Poll Monthly*, August 1996, Princeton, NJ

The 1996 Gallup Poll results concerning the offering of information about abortion alternatives, a 24-hour waiting period, parental consent for minors, and spousal notification were very similar to the results of its 1992 poll. However, when asked about a constitutional amendment to ban abortion, more Americans were in favor of the ban (50 percent) in 1984 than in 1996 (38 percent). Within a three-month period, from April to July 1996, those in favor of banning partial-birth abortion rose from 57 to 71 percent. (See Table 9.5.)

Partial-Birth Abortion

On October 21, 1999, for the third time in three years, the Senate approved the Partial-Birth Abortion Ban (S. 1692) by a vote of 63 to 34. The act amends the federal criminal code to prohibit any physician from knowingly performing a partial-birth abortion in or affecting interstate or foreign commerce, unless it is necessary to save the mother's life that is endangered by a physical disorder, illness, or injury. On October 25, 1999, the bill was received in the House of Representatives for consideration. (See Chapter III for more on the bill and Appendix I for the text of the legislation.)

In early 1999, the Gallup researchers asked the American public how they would vote, if it were possible to do so, on a law that would make partial-birth abortion illegal. One-third (34 percent) would oppose such a law, while nearly twice as many (61 percent) would vote to make the procedure illegal, except to save the life of the mother. (See Table 9.6.)

TABLE 9.5

Potential Laws – Trend

	Favor	Oppose	No opinion
Inform about alternatives			
1996 Jul 25-28	86%	11	3
1992 Jan 16-19	86%	12	2
24-hour waiting period			
1996 Jul 25-28	74%	22	4
1992 Jan 16-19	73%	23	4
Under-18 parental consent			
1996 Jul 25-28	74%	23	3
1992 Jan 16-19	70%	23	7
No "partial birth" abortions			
1996 Jul 25-28	71%	23	6
1996 Apr 25-28	57%	39	4
Spousal notification			
1996 Jul 25-28	70%	26	4
1992 Jan 16-19	70%	25	2
Constitutional ban			
1996 Jul 25-28	38%	59	3
1996 Apr 25-28	42%	56	2
1984	50%	46	4

Source: *The Gallup Poll Monthly*, August 1996, Princeton, NJ

TABLE 9.6

If you could vote on this issue directly, would you vote for or against the following: a law which would make it illegal to perform a specific abortion procedure conducted in the last six months of pregnancy known as a "partial birth abortion," except in cases necessary to save the life of the mother?

	Favor making it illegal	Oppose making it illegal	No opinion
	%	%	%
99 Apr 30-May2	61	34	5
98 Jan 16-18	61	36	3
97 Mar	55	40	5
96 Apr	57	39	4

(vol.) volunteered response

Source: The Gallup Organization, Princeton, NJ, 1999

GOVERNMENT'S ROLE IN ABORTION

In June 1999, the NBC News and the *Wall Street Journal* surveyed the American public about the government's role in abortion issues. Approximately one-third (30 percent) of respondents felt the government should pass more laws to limit the availability of abortion. On the other hand, more than twice as many respondents (65 percent) thought the government should not interfere with a woman's access to abortion.

ABORTION AS A VOTING ISSUE

The 1999 Gallup Poll found that a significant proportion of the public would consider abortion a critical election issue. When asked how the abortion issue might affect their vote for major offices, one-fifth (19 percent) of the respondents said the abortion issue would be critical (in that they would vote only for those candidates who shared their views). One-quarter (27 percent) indicated abortion would not be a major voting issue for them, while half (51 percent) would consider abortion as one of many important factors when voting for major offices. (See Table 9.7.) Among pro-life voters, 24 percent reported that abortion was critical in their choosing a major candidate, while among pro-choice voters, 16 percent considered it critical.

PRO-CHOICE OR PRO-LIFE IN THE ABORTION ISSUE

According to the 1999 Gallup Poll, 48 percent of Americans considered themselves pro-choice and 42 percent as pro-life (Figure 9.2). When the respondents from both groups were further asked how strongly they felt about their position on abortion, two-thirds indicated they were very strongly pro-life, while just over half of the pro-choice groups stated they were very strongly pro-choice.

A 1998 *Newsweek* poll found that half (51 percent) of the respondents "sympathized with the pro-choice movement that believes a woman has the right to choose what happens to her body, including the right to have an abortion." About 2 in 5 (39 percent) "sympathized with the right-to-life movement that believes abortion is the taking of human life and should be outlawed."

PARENTS' PERSPECTIVE

For many Americans, abortion involves a blend of social, moral, and legal issues. In 1998, ABC News wanted to know about the public's attitude when abortion becomes a family issue. The researchers asked, "Suppose you had a 15-year-old unmarried daughter who told you she had recently become pregnant and decided to have an abortion. Would you support or oppose her decision?" Half (50 percent) of the respondents indicated they would oppose the daughter's decision, while 44 percent would support it.

Abortion in Sex Education Classes

A 1998 Gallup Organization/Phi Delta Kappa poll found that 70 percent of the American public favored including abortion as a topic in sex education classes for high school students, while 30 percent opposed such inclusion.

MIFEPRISTONE (RU-486)

Mifepristone, popularly known as RU-486, is an abortion-inducing drug currently being reviewed by the Food and Drug Administration (FDA) for possible approval. Mifepristone is an alternative to surgical abortion during the early stages of pregnancy. Methotrexate, an FDA-approved drug for cancer treatment, is currently being used in medical abortions. (See Chapter IV.) In 1997, the Henry J. Kaiser Family Foundation found that an equal proportion of women (24 percent) and men (23 percent) knew there are medications that can be taken to cause an abortion, but more than half (58 and 53 percent, respectively) did not know there are presently medications for inducing an abortion.

TABLE 9.7

Thinking about how the abortion issue might affect your vote for major offices, would you -- [ROTATE 1-3/3-1]: 1) Only vote for a candidate who shares your views on abortion, 2) Consider a candidate's position on abortion as just one of many important factors when voting or would you 3) Not see abortion as a major issue?

	Candidate must share views	One of many important factors	Not a major issue	No opinion
99 Apr 30-May 2	19%	51%	27%	3%
96 Jul 25-28	16	51	30	3
96 Jul 18-21	18	48	30	4
92 Jun 29 (**)	13	46	36	5

(**) based on registered voters
(vol.) volunteered response

Source: The Gallup Organization, Princeton, NJ, 1999

FIGURE 9.2

With respect to the abortion issues, would you consider yourself to be pro-choice or pro-life?

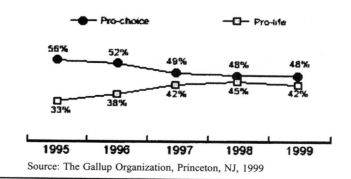

Source: The Gallup Organization, Princeton, NJ, 1999

Surprisingly, despite the wide media coverage of abortion-inducing drugs, just 43 percent of women and 51 percent of men had heard of them (Figure 9.3). Among women who had heard of mifepristone, nearly half (43 percent) were ages 40 to 44, and one-quarter (27 percent) were between the ages of 18 and 24. White (44 percent) and Hispanic (36 percent) women were more likely than Black women (21 percent) to have heard of the drug. The higher the women's income (60 percent of those earning $60,000 or more versus 23 percent of those earning less than $20,000) and education (66 percent of college graduates, compared to 21 percent of high school graduates), the more likely that they had heard of mifepristone.

Among women who had heard of mifepristone or methotrexate, most (72 percent) knew the drugs could induce an abortion (Figure 9.4). However, the women were not sure "when the earliest in a pregnancy RU-486 or methotrexate can be taken to have an abortion." Half (51 percent) did not know, while one-quarter (24 percent) thought the earliest time the drugs would induce abortion is right after unprotected sex. Mifepristone is effective only up to 49 days from a woman's last menstrual period.

When asked if they would obtain an abortion if they got pregnant in the next year, most (74 percent) women indicated they would not do so. The researchers asked the remaining 26 percent if they would choose a medical abortion if they decided to terminate a pregnancy. More than 7 in 10 (72 percent) indicated they would likely have a medical abortion.

Opinions of Women Who Had Medical Abortions

The Population Council, which received the patent rights to RU-486 (see Chapter IV) and conducted clinical trials involving 2,121 women in health centers across the country, interviewed these women about their experience with mifepristone. Virtually all of the women (96 percent) would recommend mifepristone to other women, and 9 in 10 (91 percent) would choose medical abortion again if they decided to end a pregnancy.

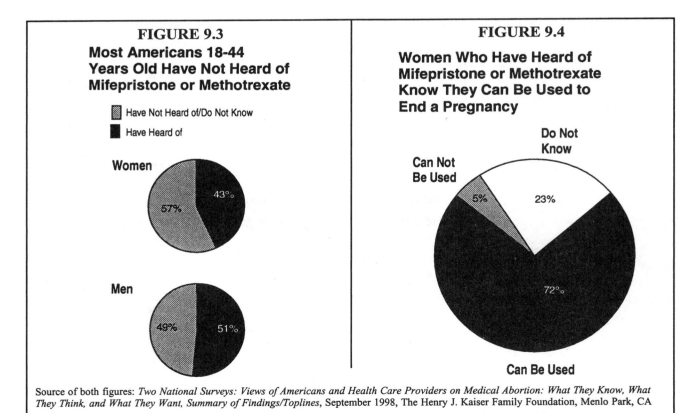

FIGURE 9.3
Most Americans 18-44 Years Old Have Not Heard of Mifepristone or Methotrexate

Have Not Heard of/Do Not Know
Have Heard of

Women
43%
57%

Men
49%
51%

FIGURE 9.4

Women Who Have Heard of Mifepristone or Methotrexate Know They Can Be Used to End a Pregnancy

Do Not Know
Can Not Be Used
5%
23%
72%
Can Be Used

Source of both figures: *Two National Surveys: Views of Americans and Health Care Providers on Medical Abortion: What They Know, What They Think, and What They Want, Summary of Findings/Toplines*, September 1998, The Henry J. Kaiser Family Foundation, Menlo Park, CA

TABLE 9.8

Most pregnant women today undergo prenatal tests that can detect potential health problems in their unborn babies. Please tell me whether you think it would be morally wrong or not morally wrong for a woman to have an abortion if a prenatal test indicated any of the following conditions. First, if a prenatal test indicated the unborn baby had mental retardation such as Downs Syndrome — do you think it would be morally wrong or not morally wrong if the mother had an abortion? How about when it indicated a condition that would cause chronic health problems or death in early adulthood, such as Cystic Fibrosis; a disease that could lead to the child's death within five years, such as Tay Sachs disease? (RANDOM ORDER)

	Morally wrong	Not morally wrong	Depends (vol.)	No opinion
Mental retardation	51%	39	5	5
Condition causing chronic health problems	49%	39	4	8
Disease leading to child's death	38%	52	4	6

TABLE 9.9

What comes closer to your view about prenatal tests: they are a good thing because they help parents identify potential health problems of their unborn babies, or, they are a bad thing, because they could lead to abortions if the parents don't like the sex or potential intelligence of the unborn baby? (ROTATED)

Good thing	76%
Bad thing	18
No opinion	6
	100%

Source of both tables: *The Gallup Poll Monthly*, August 1997, Princeton, NJ

Nearly half of the women had had a surgical abortion in the past. When asked to compare the two methods of abortion, most (77 percent) preferred mifepristone, and 13 percent found both methods satisfactory. The remaining 10 percent thought mifepristone to be less satisfactory.

VIOLENCE BY ABORTION OPPONENTS

Although many Americans do not support abortion on demand, most do not support the actions of radical anti-abortion groups. In October 1998, Dr. Barnett Slepian, an abortion provider in Buffalo, New York, was killed by a sniper (see Chapter VI). That month, a *Newsweek*/Princeton survey found that nearly 9 in 10 (87 percent)

Americans thought "using physical force against abortion clinics and doctors 'hurts' the Right-to-Life or anti-abortion cause." Only 7 percent thought such action "helps" the anti-abortion cause. Most respondents indicated "the government should be doing more than it is doing now to investigate groups who might commit acts of violence against abortion providers" (75 percent of respondents) and "protect abortion providers from physical violence" (63 percent).

PRENATAL TESTING AND ABORTION

Obstetricians generally recommend prenatal testing to detect possible abnormalities in the fetus, especially in cases of older pregnant women.

The use of prenatal testing is often linked to the possibility that a woman may choose to terminate a pregnancy if her fetus has an inherited disease or mental retardation.

In 1997, the Gallup researchers found that half of the American public thought it would be morally wrong for a woman to have an abortion if a prenatal test indicated that the fetus had mental retardation (51 percent of respondents) or a condition causing chronic (long-term) health problems. Nearly 2 in 5 (38 percent) thought it would be morally wrong to terminate a pregnancy if the pre-natal test indicated the fetus had a disease that could lead to death. (See Table 9.8.)

Overall, three-quarters (76 percent) of the Gallup respondents reported that prenatal tests are "a good thing because they help parents identify potential health problems of their unborn babies." Approximately one-fifth (18 percent) felt prenatal tests are "a bad thing because they could lead to abortions if the parents don't like the sex or potential intelligence of the unborn baby." (See Table 9.9.)

CHAPTER X

ABORTION AND THE CATHOLIC CHURCH

CHURCH HISTORY

Theological and moral debates on the proof of prenatal (before birth) life and abortion have been going on since the formation of the Christian Church two thousand years ago. During the first century of Christianity, abortion was condemned primarily because it usually was used to hide the consequences of the sexual sins of fornication and adultery.

St. Augustine (354-430 C.E.), a Doctor of the Church, whose teachings helped establish the theological foundation of the Church, taught that abortion is not infanticide. He wrote, "The law does not provide that the act [abortion] pertains to homicide, for there cannot yet be said to be a live soul in a body that lacks sensation when it is not formed in flesh and so is not endowed with sense." Similarly, in the *Irish Canons* (c. 675 C.E.), the penalty for illicit intercourse was far more severe than the penance for abortion (minimum of seven years on bread and water versus three and one-half years).

St. Thomas Aquinas (1225-1274), generally considered the greatest Catholic theologian, developed the concept of *hylomorphism* that defines a human being as the unity of body and soul. This resulted in the belief that there could be no human being without the presence of both elements. The soul, in other words, can only exist in a fully formed body. In *Summa Theologica* (Part I, Question 90, Article 4), St. Thomas Aquinas reasoned, "... [T]he soul, as part of human nature, has its natural perfection only as united to the body...."

In 1312, at the Council of Vienne, the Catholic Church officially adopted St. Thomas Aquinas' hylomorphic theory of human life and upheld this traditional doctrine through the sixteenth century. As a result, priests would not baptize a premature infant unless it had a human form.

Nonetheless, although the Church endorsed St. Thomas Aquinas' theory, theological discussions on abortion and the fetus continued. Various popes issued differing pronouncements on abortion and the fetal status. (See Chapter I for more on the Catholic position on abortion.)

Papal Infallibility

In 1869, Pope Pius IX, in *Apostolicae sedis*, declared abortion a homicide and, therefore, grounds for excommunication. It was also during his reign that papal infallibility was proposed. Papal infallibility means that the pope, with the authority derived from his office, is incapable of error when he proclaims a doctrine on faith or morals. Although the Catholic Church's teaching on abortion is not considered infallible, *immediate hominization* (the fetus is a human being with a body and soul at conception) has become an accepted teaching.

Moral Questions

The Tribunal of the Holy Office decides moral questions relating to the teachings of the Catholic Church. In 1884, and, again, in 1889, the Tribunal ruled that "it cannot be safely taught in Catholic schools that it is lawful to perform any surgical operation which is directly destructive of the life of the fetus or the mother."

In 1895, the Tribunal condemned abortion by name, ruling that a physician was not allowed to *cause* an abortion to save the mother's life by delivering a nonviable fetus, knowing the fetus would not survive outside the womb. In 1902, the Tribunal decreed that, even in cases of ectopic pregnancies (in which the embryo develops outside the uterus, most commonly in the fallopian tube), "... no acceleration of birth is licit unless it be done at a time, and in ways in which, according to the usual course of things, the life of the mother and the child be provided for."

Exception

The Catholic Church, however, maintains that, if during the course of treating or operating on a pregnant woman in order to save her life, the fetus dies "as a regretted but unavoidable consequence," the action does not constitute an abortion. On the other hand, the Church further stipulates,

> Of course, provision must be made for the child's spiritual as well as for its physical life, and if, by the treatment or operation in question, the child were to be deprived of Baptism, which it could receive if the operation were not performed, then the evil would be greater than the good consequences of the operation. In this case, the operation could not lawfully be performed.

When Does the Fetus Acquire a Soul?

Despite Pope Pius IX's strong pronouncement and the decisions of the Tribunal of the Holy Office, the Church has constantly changed its stance on abortion. Its 1974 "Declaration on Procured Abortion" stated, "... From the time that the ovum is fertilized, a life is begun.... It would never be made human if it were not human already." But then the Church acknowledges that "[t]his declaration expressly leaves aside the question of the moment when the spiritual soul is infused." While the Church admits that its pronouncement is a moral judgment and that there is continuing debate among its theologians, it advises its adherents that since hominization (the point at which a fetus acquires a soul and becomes a human being) cannot be absolutely ascertained, it is better to play it safe and avoid abortion altogether.

THE CATHOLIC BISHOPS

Although the Church, like any organization, can exert an influential role in U.S. politics, it does not ally itself with any one political party. The National Conference of Catholic Bishops (NCCB — the lobbying and publicity arm of the Church) claims, "Our moral framework does not easily fit the categories of right or left, Republican or Democrat."

As an organization with strong moral positions, the NCCB walks a fine line in order to maintain its tax-exempt status (which requires no political activity) in its efforts to affect public policy. The bishops have written to the White House to protest presidential actions, have issued pastorals (letters to their followers) concerning social issues, and have provided specific directives as to how Catholics should react to certain government policies.

No issue has elicited more passionate response from these religious leaders than abortion. A ban on abortion is an ongoing commitment for the bishops. In 1973, following the *Roe v. Wade* decision legalizing abortion on demand in the United States, the Administrative Committee of the NCCB issued a pastoral message, opposing the new law as well as indicating a Catholic course of action (see below). The bishops constantly admonish their followers not to vote for pro-choice candidates. Catholic politicians who do not share the bishops' position can suffer a variety of repercussions — from refusal of sacraments to threat of excommunication.

In 1994, the American cardinals and bishops lobbied President Bill Clinton regarding U.S. policy at the International Conference on Population and Development in Cairo, Egypt. (See Chapter VIII for the Vatican's controversial role at the Cairo and Beijing conferences.) In September 1996, eight of the nation's cardinals and about 80 bishops held a prayer service at Capitol Hill to pressure Congress to override President Clinton's veto of a ban against partial-birth abortion. (See Chapter III for more discussion of the partial-birth abortion controversy and Chapters XV and XVI for arguments for and against partial-birth abortion.)

MAJOR CATHOLIC PRONOUNCEMENTS ON ABORTION

Statements of Pope John Paul II

In 1995, Pope John Paul II delivered the *Evangelium Vitae* (Gospel of Life), an encyclical letter reasserting the Vatican's position on abortion. The document reaffirmed the Church's ban on abortion, contraception, and euthanasia. It further condemned selective abortion for eugenic purposes (to terminate the birth of defective babies), as well as human embryo experimentation.

Excerpts from Evangelium Vitae

… Among all the crimes which can be committed against life, procured [that which is obtained as opposed to natural] abortion has characteristics making it particularly serious and deplorable.…

… The moral gravity of procured abortion is apparent in all its truths if we recognize that we are dealing with murder.… The one eliminated is a human being at the very beginning of life.…

… [W]hat is at stake is so important that, from the standpoint of moral obligation, the mere probability that a human person is involved would suffice to justify an absolutely clear prohibition of any intervention aimed at killing a human embryo. Precisely for this reason, over and above all scientific debates and those philosophical affirmations to which the Magisterium [the

teaching authority of the Roman Catholic Church] has not expressly committed itself, the Church has always taught and continues to teach that the result of human procreation, from the first moment of its existence, must be guaranteed that unconditional respect which is morally due to the human being in his or her totality and unity as body and spirit.…

The texts of the *Sacred Scripture* never address the question of deliberate abortion and so do not directly and specifically condemn it. But they show such great respect for the human being in the mother's womb that they require as a logical consequence that God's commandment "You shall not kill" be extended to the unborn child as well.…

Excerpts from Ecclesia in America

In 1999, in *Ecclesia in America* (Church in America), Pope John Paul II exhorted Americans, among other things, to do away with their "culture of death."

… The Church in America has recently celebrated the fifth centenary [500 years] of the first preaching of the Gospel on its soil.…

Nowadays, in America as elsewhere in the world, a model of society appears to be emerging in which the powerful predominate, setting aside and even eliminating the powerless: I am thinking here of unborn children, helpless victims of abortion … and the many other people relegated to the margins of society by consumerism and materialism.… This model of society bears the stamp of the culture of death, and is therefore in opposition to the Gospel message.…

In this regard, the Synod Fathers, echoing recent documents of the Church's

Magisterium, forcefully restated their unconditional respect for and total dedication to human life from the moment of conception to that of natural death, and their condemnation of evils like abortion.... If the teachings of the divine and natural law are to be upheld, it is essential to promote knowledge of the Church's social doctrine and to work so that the values of life and family are recognized and defended in social customs and in State ordinances. As well as protecting life, greater efforts should be made ... to promote adoptions and to provide continuing assistance to women with problem pregnancies, both before and after the birth of the child. Special pastoral attention must also be given to women who have undergone or actively procured an abortion.

... I appeal to Catholics working in the field of medicine and health care, to those holding public office or engaged in teaching, to make every effort to defend those lives most at risk, and to act with a conscience correctly formed in accordance with Catholic doctrine.... At the same time, it is essential for the Church in America to take appropriate measures to influence the deliberations of legislative assemblies, encouraging citizens, both Catholics and other people of good will, to establish organizations to propose workable legislation and to resist measures which endanger the two inseparable realities of life and the family....

Excerpts from NCCB Statement on the 1973 *Roe v. Wade* Decision

The Supreme Court, in its recent decision striking down the laws of Texas and Georgia regulating abortion, has stated that the unborn child is not a person in the terms of the Fourteenth Amendment. Moreover, the Court held that the right of privacy encompasses a woman's decision to terminate a pregnancy, although the right of privacy is not an absolute right, and is not explicitly mentioned in the Constitution. In effect, the Court is saying that the right of privacy takes precedence over the right to life....

The court has apparently failed to understand the scientific evidence clearly showing that the fetus is an individual human being whose prenatal development is but the first phase of the long and continuous process of human development that begins at conception and terminates at death. Thus, the seven judge majority went on to declare that the life of the unborn child is not to be considered of any compelling value prior to viability, i.e., during the first six or seven months of pregnancy, and of only questionable value during the remaining months....

We find that this majority opinion of the Court is wrong and is entirely contrary to the fundamental principles of morality. Catholic teaching holds that, regardless of the circumstances of its origin, human life is valuable from conception to death because God is the Creator of each human being....

In the light of these reasons, we reject the opinion of the U.S. Supreme Court as erroneous, unjust, and immoral. Because of our responsibility as authentic religious leaders and teachers, we make the following pastoral applications:

- Catholics must oppose abortion as an immoral act. No one is obliged to obey any civil law that may require abortion.

- Those who obtain an abortion, those who persuade others to have an abortion, and those who perform the abortion procedures are guilty of breaking God's law. Moreover, ... those who undergo or perform an abortion place themselves in a state of excommunication.

- We urge the legal profession to articulate and safeguard the rights of the fathers of unborn children....

- We praise the efforts of pro-life groups ... and encourage them to ... combat the general permissiveness legislation can engender [and] ... set in motion the machinery needed to assure legal and constitutional conformity to the basic truth that the unborn child is a "person" in every sense of the term from the time of conception....

Statement of John Cardinal Krol, NCCB President, January 22, 1973

The Supreme Court's decision today is an unspeakable tragedy for this nation. It is hard to think of any decision in the 200 years of our history which has had more disastrous implications for our stability as a civilized society. The ruling drastically diminishes the constitutional guaranty of the right to life and in doing so sets in motion developments which are terrifying to contemplate.

The ruling represents bad logic and bad law. There is no rational justification for allowing unrestricted abortion up to the third month of pregnancy. The development of life before and after birth is a continuous process and in making the three-month point the cutoff for unrestricted abortion, the Court seems more impressed by magic than by scientific evidence regarding fetal development. The child in the womb has the right to life, to the life he already possesses, and this is a right no court has the authority to deny.

Apparently the Court was trying to straddle the fence and give something to everybody — abortion on demand before three months for those who want that, somewhat more restrictive abortion regulations after three months for those who want that. But in its straddling act, the Court has done a monstrous injustice to the thousands of unborn children whose lives may be destroyed as a result of this decision.

No court and no legislature in the land can make something evil become something good. Abortion at any stage of pregnancy is evil. This is not a question of sectarian morality but instead concerns the law of God and the basis of civilized society. One trusts in the decency and good sense of the American people not to let an illogical court decision dictate to them on the subject of morality and human life.

Admonition of the American Bishops to Catholic Politicians (*Living the Gospel of Life: A Challenge to American Catholics,* 1998)

... We urge those Catholic officials who choose to depart from Church teaching on the inviolability of human life in their public life to consider the consequences for their own spiritual well-being, as well as the scandal they risk by leading others into serious sin. We call on them to reflect on the grave contradiction of assuming public roles and presenting themselves as credible Catholics when their actions on fundamental issues of human life are not in agreement with Church teaching. No public official, especially one claiming to be a faithful and serious Catholic, can responsibly advocate for or actively support direct attacks on innocent human life. Certainly there are times when it may be impossible to overturn or prevent passage of a law which allows or promotes a moral evil — such as a law allowing the destruction of nascent [coming into being] human life. In such cases, an elected official, whose position in favor of life is known, could seek legitimately to limit the harm done by the law.... Those who justify their inaction on the grounds that abortion is the law of the land need to recognize that there is a higher law, the law of God. No human law can validly contradict the Commandment: "Thou shalt not kill"....

NOT ALL CATHOLICS AGREE

The Catholic Church's position on abortion, and contraception for that matter, is not held by a significant number of the 62 million American Catholics. In a survey of approximately 10,000 abortion patients, Stanley K. Henshaw and Kathryn Kost, in "Abortion Patients in 1994-1995: Characteristics and Contraceptive Use" (*Family Planning Perspectives*, vol. 28, no. 4, July/August, 1996), reported that Catholic women were as likely as women in the general population to obtain an abortion. This was a surprise to the authors since the Catholic Church is more publicly anti-abortion than most other religions.

A 1997 Roper Center survey, prepared for *Catholic World Report*, found that 3 in 5 (59 percent) Catholics in the United States disagreed with the statement that abortion is never justified. A 1996 survey by the Pew Center for People & the Press found that 73 percent of self-described "progressive" Catholics and 43 percent of self-described "traditional" Catholics thought that abortion should be generally available or available with restrictions. Only 10 percent of Catholic respondents agreed with the bishops' position that abortion should be illegal in all circumstances.

Similarly, many U.S. Catholics disagree with the pope and bishops that using artificial means of birth control is morally wrong. A 1998 survey by the magazine *US Catholic* found that 81 percent of Catholics believed that "a married couple has the right to follow their own conscience on the decision to use birth control."

Many Catholics believe that religious leaders should not try to influence their members to vote for a political candidate based on his or her position on abortion. A 1996 CBS News/*New York Times* poll found that three-quarters (77 percent) of Catholics, and 72 percent of all Americans, felt it was not appropriate for religious leaders to encourage their members to vote for a candidate based on his or her stand on abortion.

Catholics for a Free Choice

The Catholics for a Free Choice (CFFC) disagrees with the bishops' stand that there is only one Catholic position on abortion, and it disputes the long-held belief that the Catholic Church has always banned abortion. (The Church reserves the right to excommunicate any Catholic who supports the right to abortion. This includes not only those who have had an abortion but also those who speak publicly on the issue.) The CFFC further advocates family planning to reduce the incidence of abortions. The CFFC observes,

The church is ... more than the pope and bishops. It includes all the people of God. Clergy, theologians and laity work together to develop church teachings. Many theologians and lay people today believe that abortion can sometimes be a moral decision and that conscience is the final arbiter of any abortion decision.

CATHOLIC POLITICIANS AND ABORTION

Mary C. Segers, a professor of political theory and religion and politics at Rutgers University, in "What Is a Catholic Politician to Do about Abortion?" (*Conscience*, 1996), considers the dilemma Catholic politicians face in shaping abortion policies. Segers believes that the duties of Catholic lawmakers cannot be simplified into "enact[ing] Church teaching into civil law." Segers suggests,

... [Catholic legislators] must remind the Church that, in a pluralistic democracy, lawmakers have obligations to conscience, constituents, the Constitution, and the common good. When these duties conflict, as they do in the abortion controversy, there are no simple automatic solutions to the question of appropriate public policy. Instead, lawmakers have a duty to seek policy outcomes that balance these competing claims.

… The principled position of pro-choice Catholic lawmakers reflects a commitment to exercise prudence in making sound public policy. It also embodies a commitment to protect the religious freedom of constituents who do not share the anti-abortion views of the Roman Catholic hierarchy.…

THE CHURCH
IN THE HEALTH CARE SYSTEM

Catholic hospitals follow the *Ethical and Religious Directives for Catholic Health Care Services*, prepared by the National Conference of Catholic Bishops. The *Directives* forbid abortion, in vitro fertilization, tubal ligation, vasectomy, and contraception (including condoms for safer sex, counseling, and emergency contraception,* even for rape victims, unless fertilization has not occurred). Since the *Directives* have no instructions on how to determine whether fertilization has taken place, each Catholic hospital renders its own interpretation.

Many health care institutions, fighting for survival in the face of corporate mergers and managed care, are affiliating with hospitals owned by the Roman Catholic Church, the largest nonprofit health care provider in the nation. Liz Bucar, in *Caution: Catholic Health Restrictions May Be Hazardous to Your Health* (CFFC, Washington, DC, 1999), reported a total of 127 mergers and affiliations between Catholic and non-Catholic hospitals from 1990 to 1998. In 1998 alone, 43 mergers and affiliations occurred, up from 14 in 1997 and 24 in 1996. The mergers usually involved an agreement on the part of the secular hospitals to abide by Catholic teaching. In most cases, this meant a total cessation of reproductive services.

Family planning proponents and women's rights groups are very concerned about this further dwindling of reproductive service providers, especially when the merger may result in the Catholic hospital being the only hospital in the community. In 1998, 91 Catholic hospitals were the community's sole provider in 27 states, up from 76 hospitals in 1997. Of the 91 sole providers, 75 percent did not provide emergency contraception, even in cases of rape. A 1998 Catholics for a Free Choice (CFFC) survey of virtually all Catholic hospitals (589) in the United States found that 82 percent did not provide emergency contraception, not even to rape victims.

Communities concerned about the growing number of hospital mergers are protesting, often citing the issue of religious freedom. Advocacy groups, such as Merger Watch, monitor merger activities and help mobilize efforts to preserve reproductive health services in the community. Some protests have caused deals to fall apart; others have brought about compromises where reproductive services are excluded from the partnership agreement, while still others have resulted in the establishment of separate centers for reproductive services. As the number of mergers rise, some activists have proposed legislation to empower state attorneys general or health commissioners to prevent any merger that would eliminate reproductive health services.

---

* Emergency contraception refers to taking a high dose of regular contraceptives immediately after unprotected sex to prevent pregnancy.

CHAPTER XI

ADULTS ACCOMPANYING MINORS ACROSS STATE LINES TO OBTAIN AN ABORTION SHOULD BE PROSECUTED

TESTIMONY OF LINO A. GRAGLIA, A. DALTON CROSS PROFESSOR OF LAW, UNIVERSITY OF TEXAS SCHOOL OF LAW, HEARING ON THE CHILD CUSTODY PROTECTION ACT (H.R. 1218)* BEFORE THE SUBCOMMITTEE ON THE CONSTITUTION, HOUSE JUDICIARY COMMITTEE, MAY 27, 1999

... Roe v. Wade was wrongly decided ... because it violates the principles of federalism and representative self-government that are the essence of our constitutional system. Under the federal system of government created by the Constitution, the abortion issue is very clearly an issue to be decided by the people of each state for themselves through the ordinary political process, not by unelected, life-tenured officials of the national government for the nation as a whole. Because *Roe v. Wade* is grossly inconsistent with our constitutional system, anything Congress can do to move control of the issue back into the hands of the states is a move in the right direction.

The primary purpose of the [Child Custody Protection] Act ... is "to protect the right of parents to be involved in the medical decisions of their minor daughters." ... It seems to me that that is, in fact, what the Act does and all it does, and that it is, therefore, constitutionally and legally unobjectionable. What the opponents of the Act really object to is not that the Act protects this parental right, but the fact that there *is* such a right, because such a right can present an impediment to the unrestricted availability of abortion.... [T]he Act does not purport to either increase or diminish the abortion right, whatever its extent; it operates only to protect the parental notification and consent rights that have been established by [the Supreme] Court....

TESTIMONY OF EILEEN ROBERTS, FOUNDER, MOTHERS AGAINST MINORS' ABORTIONS (MAMA), HEARING ON THE CHILD CUSTODY PROTECTION ACT BEFORE THE SUBCOMMITTEE ON THE CONSTITUTION, HOUSE JUDICIARY COMMITTEE, MAY 27, 1999

... I am the mother of a daughter who at age 14 underwent an abortion without my knowledge....

... During my daughter's rebellion towards our parental authority, my daughter was encouraged by her boyfriend, with the assistance of an adult friend, to obtain a secret abortion without my knowledge. This adult friend drove my daughter to the abortion clinic, 45 miles away from our home, and even paid for my daughter's abortion....

... As a result of her depression, my daughter was hospitalized, at which time it was discovered that the abortion had been incompletely performed and required surgery to repair the damage done by the abortionist....

---

* On June 30, 1999, the Child Custody Protection Act passed the House of Representatives by a vote of 270-159. On July 1, 1999, the Senate received the bill. As of November 1999, the Senate had not acted on the bill.

The following year my daughter developed an infection and was diagnosed as having pelvic inflammatory disease, which again required a two-day hospitalization for IV antibiotic therapy....

To add insult to injury, my husband and I were responsible for our daughter's medical costs which amounted to over $27,000.

I am here today to ask this committee to reject the eccentric notion that any adult stranger has the right to abduct our minor-aged daughters and take them to another state for a secret abortion. I speak today for those parents I know around the country, who's [sic] daughters have been taken out of state for their abortions. Many times these attempts to evade parental notification and consent laws are also attempts to conceal criminal activity, such as statutory rape....

Please allow parents the opportunity to put their arms around their daughters and say, "I love you, we can work this through together," which parental notification and consent laws restore and this legislation will protect....

STATEMENT OF REPRESENTATIVE ILEANA ROS-LEHTINEN* (R-FL; BILL SPONSOR), HEARING ON THE CHILD CUSTODY PROTECTION ACT BEFORE THE SUBCOMMITTEE ON THE CONSTITUTION, HOUSE JUDICIARY COMMITTEE, MAY 21, 1998

... The legislation we are discussing today goes beyond the issue of abortion. It goes right to the heart of the right of states to implement and enforce their laws. It allows parents their fundamental right to counsel their daughters on a critical life decision.

Today, 22 states have parental consent or notification laws on their books. The Child Custody Protection Act will help these states enforce their parental consent laws which can be circumvented by strangers who escort young girls across state lines to obtain a life-threatening medical procedure in complete disregard for the law.

How can we explain that in my hometown of Miami, Florida, my alma mater, Southwest High School requires a parent to sign a release form, a permission slip, for a student to leave school grounds to attend even an educational and chaperoned field trip?

This same high school requires any student to obtain parental consent to receive mild medication such as aspirin in order to alleviate them of any discomfort they may experience during school hours.

In most schools, parents are given full notification of their children's educational choices; they are made aware that their children are enrolled in a basic sex education class and are given the option to withdraw them from the course.

These important rules and regulations are aimed at ensuring the safety of our children through parental guidance, yet somehow these same parents can be denied the right to know that their daughter was subjected to a secret and potentially fatal operation.

... [M]any of these same people who are [sic] set out to rescue our children from the dangers of this world have remained silent on ads that entice that [sic] young girls to violate the law and obtain a life-threatening procedure.

... The statements of some organizations claiming their "constitutional right" to procure secret abortions for minors are preposterous. Nowhere in the Constitution does it say that a stranger has more rights to parent and oversee the welfare of my child than I have.

Parents know the medical history of their child; a stranger does not. Parents know a child's reac-

---

* During the 105th Congress, on April 1, 1998, Representative Ileana Ros-Lehtinen first introduced the Child Custody Protection Act (then known as H.R. 3682).

tion to pressure of this nature. Parents are capable of comforting their children in their greatest time of need; a stranger is not.

I am here to protect my rights and the rights of every parent who may fall victim to those looking to violate our laws in the name of *Roe* v. *Wade*.

TESTIMONY OF PROFESSOR TERESA STANTON COLLETT, SOUTH TEXAS COLLEGE OF LAW, HEARING ON THE CHILD CUSTODY PROTECTION ACT BEFORE THE SUBCOMMITTEE ON THE CONSTITUTION, HOUSE JUDICIARY COMMITTEE, MAY 21, 1998

… My testimony represents my professional knowledge and opinion as a law professor, who teaches and writes in the area of medical-legal issues. It is not intended to represent the views of my employer, South Texas College of Law, nor the views of Texas A&M University, with which the College is affiliated.

… At the outset, it is important to establish what this proposed legislation does not do. First, the Act does not establish a national requirement of parental consent or notification prior to the performance of an abortion on young girls who lack sufficient maturity to determine whether abortions are in their best interest. Second, it does not attempt to regulate any purely intrastate activities related to the procurement of abortion services. Finally, this legislation does not seek to reverse or modify any existing case law defining the ability of non-custodians to encourage, counsel, or assist young girls in obtaining secret abortions.

What this legislation does do is build upon two of the few points of agreement in the national debate over abortion: the desirability of parental involvement in a minor's decisions about an unplanned pregnancy and the need to protect the physical health of the pregnant girl.

… While courts have forbidden absolute requirements that all minors seek parental consent for abortions, they allow notification or consent statutes, which contain provisions to judicially bypass parental involvement where it is found to be in the best interest of the pregnant girl.

… Yet for all the good inherent in a system of diverse state regulation, the differing approaches taken by the states permit some unintended evil as well. Differing regulations allow opportunistic behavior by those who seek to avoid parental involvement, not out of concern for the well-being of the pregnant girl, but out of a desire to evade responsibility or avoid discovery of criminal acts. By transporting the pregnant girl from a state that requires parental involvement to one that has no such requirements, it is presently possible to obtain abortion services with no knowledge on the part of the girl's parents. This evasion is troubling on two counts: First, it forecloses any attempts by the parents to assist their daughter in her decision; and second, it deprives the girl of the protection afforded by a judicial assessment of the motivations of those urging her to obtain an abortion. It is these harms that the Child Custody Protection Act attempts to remedy.

… This legislation does not forbid assisting a minor in her decision concerning the continuation or termination of an unplanned pregnancy. It merely requires any person assisting a young pregnant girl to abide by the state law of the girl's residence. Instead of secreting the girl across state lines to obtain an abortion, then returning her to the very home that abortion rights activists would have us imagine as abusive and violent, the friend could either help the girl inform her parents of her condition in order to comply with the state notification or consent law, or help the girl obtain judicial approval to consent to the abortion. Both of these options remain available under the proposed Child Custody Protection Act.…

… In those few cases where it is not in the girl's best interest to disclose her pregnancy to her parents, yet parental notification or consent is required to obtain an abortion, the girl and those who would assist her have the option of seeking a court determination of the girl's maturity to make decisions regarding her pregnancy. This is not altered by the Child Custody Protection Act.

... [I]t is becoming increasingly clear that most underage pregnancies are the result of a lack of sexual restraint by adult men....

By passage of the Child Custody Protection Act, this Congress can foreclose at least one proven strategy by those men, or their accomplices, who would hide the results of the men's misdeeds. Men who engage in acts that many states classify as statutory rape will no longer be able to pressure their young victims into crossing state lines to obtain abortions without the knowledge or consent of the girl's parents, or judicial approval, when that knowledge or consent or approval is required by the state where the girl resides.

In those few cases where the girl's parents are unable or unwilling to guide and support her during her time of decision, judicial bypass proceedings provide a quick, effective way to insure that those who would cast themselves as guardians of the girl's reproductive freedom are not in reality perpetrators of yet another type of violence against their young victims. I urge the members of this committee to vote in favor of the Child Custody Protection Act.

TESTIMONY OF ROBERT A. GRACI, ASSISTANT DEPUTY ATTORNEY GENERAL OF PENNSYLVANIA, HEARING ON THE CHILD CUSTODY PROTECTION ACT BEFORE THE SUBCOMMITTEE ON THE CONSTITUTION, HOUSE JUDICIARY COMMITTEE, MAY 21, 1998

... I appear before you today on behalf of Pennsylvania Attorney General Mike Fisher.... Imagine that you are a divorced mother working hard to raise your children — to ensure they stay in school, stay away from drugs and alcohol and learn the difference between right and wrong. You awake early one morning to find a note left by your barely teenage daughter. You know something is wrong.

You check with the neighbors. You call her friends' parents. You call her school only to learn that she is not there. Finally, you call the police. No one knows where your daughter is or what happened to her.

That evening she returns home and informs you that she was driven to an abortion clinic, earlier that day, where her child was aborted. She is only 13. You didn't even know she was pregnant. She tells the story of how a few months ago, when she was 12 years old, the then 18-year-old man she had been seeing — the man you tried to keep her from — had given her alcohol, gotten her drunk, and impregnated her.

The man's stepmother [Rosa Marie Hartford], upon learning her stepson had impregnated the girl, helped to arrange a plan to take your daughter, to drive her to another state, and to abort her unborn child — without informing you. Parents might think this was some sort of bad dream. But this nightmare happened in Pennsylvania — to Mrs. Joyce Farley [see below] and her daughter [Crystal] — and it has happened to other parents across the country.

How could this happen? In Pennsylvania, it is against the law to provide an abortion to a minor child without the consent of her parent, legal guardian, or a judge. But, in neighboring states like New York, it is not....

It is my understanding that this tragic case — *Commonwealth v. Rosa Marie Hartford* — was part of the impetus for the introduction of the Child Custody Protection Act.... In many respects, that case underscores the necessity of this legislation.

... Hartford was convicted of violating Pennsylvania's interference with custody of children statute.... This statute, like H.R. 3682 [the name under which H.R. 1218 was known during the 105th Congress], "is intended to protect parental custody from unlawful interruption, even when the child is a willing participant in the interference with custody." ... This is perhaps the first reason why we need the Child Custody Protection Act. It would clearly proscribe (prohibit) the conduct at issue in Hartford's case.

... The Abortion Control Act [Pennsylvania law] vested in Crystal's mother the ability to "discuss the consequences of [Crystal's] decision [to have an abortion] in the context of the values and moral or religious principles of their family." That ability could be taken from her only under the circumstances described in the judicial bypass provisions of the Act, neither of which were followed. Crystal was 13 years old. Under the constitutionally permissible scheme adopted by the Pennsylvania legislature, her mother's consent was required before she could obtain an abortion. Hartford's taking Crystal to an out-of-state abortion clinic so she could have an abortion while Hartford posed as Crystal's stepmother interfered with her mother's custody of Crystal.

STATEMENT OF JOYCE FARLEY OF DUSHORE, PENNSYLVANIA, HEARING ON THE CHILD CUSTODY PROTECTION ACT BEFORE THE SUBCOMMITTEE ON THE CONSTITUTION, HOUSE JUDICIARY COMMITTEE, MAY 21, 1998

I am here today to tell you why I support the Child Custody Protection Act. My daughter was a victim of several horrible crimes between the ages of 12 and 13. My child was provided alcohol, raped, and then taken out of state by a stranger to have an abortion. This stranger turned out to be the mother of the adult male who provided the alcohol and then raped my 12-year-old daughter while she was unconscious. The rapist's mother arranged and paid for an abortion to be performed on my child. This woman lied and falsified records at the abortion clinic to make sure this abortion would be completed without my knowledge. The abortion had been arranged to destroy evidence — evidence that my 12-year-old daughter had been raped....

Following the abortion, the mother of the rapist dropped off my physically and emotionally battered child in another town 30 miles away from our home. The plan was to keep the rape and abortion a secret. If I had not contacted the state police ... when I found my child missing, she might not be alive today. Severe pain and bleeding revealed complications from an incomplete abortion. This required further medical care and a second abortion to be performed....

The bill you are considering today may help prevent this from happening to my neighbor's child, my future grandchildren, or any child in the United States. It has been three years since these crimes were committed, but my daughter still suffers physically and emotionally....

CHAPTER XII

ADULTS ACCOMPANYING MINORS ACROSS STATE LINES TO OBTAIN AN ABORTION SHOULD NOT BE PROSECUTED

TESTIMONY OF DR. JONATHAN D. KLEIN ON BEHALF OF THE AMERICAN ACADEMY OF PEDIATRICS, THE SOCIETY FOR ADOLESCENT MEDICINE, AND ADVOCATES FOR YOUTH, HEARING ON THE CHILD CUSTODY PROTECTION ACT (H.R. 1218)* BEFORE THE SUBCOMMITTEE ON THE CONSTITUTION, HOUSE JUDICIARY COMMITTEE, MAY 27, 1999

... The stated intent by those who support mandatory parental consent laws is that it enhances family communication as well as parental involvement and responsibility. However, the evidence does not support that these laws have that desired effect. To the contrary, there is evidence that these laws may have an adverse impact on some families and that it increases the risk of medical and psychological harm to adolescents. According to the American Academy of Pediatrics, "Involuntary parental notification can precipitate a family crisis characterized by severe parental anger and rejection of the minor and her partner. One third of minors who do not inform parents already have experienced family violence and fear it will recur. Research on abusive and dysfunctional families shows that violence is at its worse during a family member's pregnancy and during the adolescence of the family's children."

... Concern about confidentiality is one of the primary reasons young people delay seeking health services for sensitive issues, whether for an unintended pregnancy or for other reasons. While parental involvement is very desirable and should be encouraged, it may not always be feasible and it should <u>not</u> be legislated. Young people must be able to receive health care expeditiously and confidentially.

... In a regional survey of suburban adolescents, only 45 percent said they would seek medical care for sexually transmitted diseases, drug abuse, or birth control if they were forced to notify their parents.

Of course, it is important for young people who are facing a health-related crisis to be able to turn to someone dependable, someone they trust, to help them decide what is best. Many, many times that person is a parent. Teenagers facing a crisis pregnancy should be encouraged to involve a parent, and many do so. In fact, over 75 percent of teens under age 16 involve at least one parent in their decision, even in states that do not mandate them to do so. In some populations, as many as 91 percent of teenagers younger than 18 years voluntarily consulted a parent or "parent surrogate" about a pregnancy decision.

---

* On June 30, 1999, the Child Custody Protection Act passed the House of Representatives by a vote of 270-159. On July 1, 1999, the Senate received the bill. As of November 1999, the Senate had not acted on the bill.

135

All too often, however, young women know that their parents would be overwhelmed, angry, distraught, or disappointed if they knew about the crisis pregnancy. Fear of emotional or physical abuse, including being thrown out of the house, [is] among the major reasons teenagers say they are afraid to tell their parents about a pregnancy. Young women who are afraid to involve their parents very often turn to another adult in times of difficulty. One study shows that, of young women who did not involve a parent in their abortion decision, over half turned to another adult; 15 percent of these young women involved a stepparent or other adult relative. In my own practice, I have had the situation arise in which an adult female sibling or cousin has been the person the adolescent wanted me to call into the consultation based on the fear of anger and rejection from her mother.

H.R. 1218 would harm young women who are most afraid to involve their parents in an abortion decision and who most need the support of other adults in their lives…. The bill would have the unintentional outcome of placing a chilling effect on teenagers' ability to talk openly with adults — including family members and medical providers — because it sends a message that adults who help young people grapple with difficult decisions are criminals….

This legislation is not only troublesome with regard to its effect on confidential medical care for teens; it is also a harmful and potentially dangerous bill from the perspective of its intent and its potential effect on states and individual rights.

As currently written, H.R. 1218 would apply one state's laws to another state. Young women would be required to abide by the "original" state's (the state where the young woman resides) law regardless of where they seek medical care…. An adult who accompanies a young woman to a legal, accessible, and affordable abortion provider would be placed in the position of risky criminal sanctions.

Applying the laws from one state on women who seek medical care in another state raises important questions about state's rights. As a physician, I have the responsibility to refer patients to the best care possible. In my experience, physicians in any other medical procedure are not subject to guidelines that prohibit proceeding with medical care in one state based on guidelines from the referring state….

This law would be extraordinarily difficult to enforce. Does the law only apply to women who travel to another state in order to exercise their constitutional right to health care? I am afraid that there may be eventual implications for young women who are temporarily living outside their home state because of travel, education, or employment.

… I am very concerned that Congress may put health care providers in the position where they must violate their state's confidentiality statutes in order to meet the obligations of a neighboring state.

In conclusion, I reiterate a statement previously made by the immediate past president of the Society for Adolescent Medicine: "[C]learly the proposed bill is designed to eliminate this [abortion] option for many adolescents. Adolescents who cannot rely on one or both parents to help them through the trauma of a pregnancy and who, for legal or geographical reasons, may need to go to an adjoining state for termination, are effectively precluded from receiving help from those (such as other relative, health professional, or even the clergy) who would be there to help them. In essence, this law would put adolescents in the position of having to take care of themselves (possibly traveling long distances in the process), without supportive care during a traumatic time in their lives."

As physician, a teacher, and most of all, as a parent, who is concerned about the quality and safety of health care for my daughter as well as for the quality and safety of health care for all adolescents in this country, I urge you to reject H.R. 1218.

TESTIMONY OF BILLIE LOMINICK, HEARING ON THE CHILD CUSTODY PROTECTION ACT BEFORE THE SUBCOMMITTEE ON THE CONSTITUTION, HOUSE JUDICIARY COMMITTEE, MAY 27, 1999

… [M]y name is Billie Lominick, and I live in Newbury, South Carolina. In 1990, after 33 years of marriage, I lost my husband Bennie to leukemia. Together, Bennie and I were blessed to see our child grow into a devoted wife and loving mother to our only grandson, "Tom."

… About a year ago, Tom started dating his high school sweetheart, "Mary.…" She is a sweet girl, and it has broken our hearts to hear about all that she and her younger brother have been through. With a great deal of courage, they have managed to survive living with an abusive mother and stepfather.…

… Mary and Tom discovered this past January that Mary was pregnant.… Within a few days, Tom's mother and I also knew. Together, we all went with Mary when she had her ultrasound.

After taking a few days to think things over, Tom and Mary decided that they just weren't ready to become parents. They both wanted to finish school and felt that they didn't yet have the resources to raise a child.

When Tom and Mary told us about their decision to have an abortion, we supported their choice. His parents and I felt that this was their decision to make. We also thought they were too young to bring a child into the world. Mary's parents, however, had a very different reaction to the news. Mary's stepfather hit her in the face, and both parents violently opposed the abortion. Scared to death by this latest abuse, Mary decided to move out of her parents' house. I knew that I could provide a

stable, loving home for her, so I asked her to move in with me.…

Tom and his mother began contacting clinics in South Carolina, who stated that Mary needed her parents' consent in order to have an abortion. We knew that her parents would not give their permission, so we began calling clinics in North Carolina.… [A] clinic staff … in North Carolina … told us … Mary could go before a judge and explain the situation, and that he could grant her request for an abortion.

We … were only able to find two courts in our whole state that would take judicial bypass cases. The closest judge … was over an hour from our home.… Our hopes were dashed, however, when we learned that the judge had announced only a month earlier that the court would only take cases from minors residing within that county.

… Finally, we were able to locate a clinic in Georgia that could help Mary. While Georgia does have a parental notification requirement, we were able to find a judge who was willing to hear judicial bypass cases. We worked with the clinic to arrange the bypass hearing.…

… I decided to take time off from work and go with [Mary and Tom]. We made the trip together.

Mary went before a judge in Atlanta, and was given permission for her abortion. However, she did not meet the requirements of South Carolina's parental consent law before we went to Georgia. Under the law you are considering, I would have been sent to jail for helping Mary go to Georgia for her abortion. I would have been punished for helping her when she had nowhere else to turn. I would have been punished for seeing to it that my grandson and Mary got to Atlanta and home again safely.

Mary is still living with me. She had no complications from the abortion, and feels better now than she has ever felt in her whole life. She has just finished her sophomore year of high school and is looking forward to finishing school in two years and getting a job. I think about this law, and wonder, if I was sent to jail for taking Mary to Georgia, who would be taking care of her now? …

I hope that you will see how wrong this law is, and how much it would hurt families like ours. I hope that you will not make our lives any more difficult than they already are. Please, think of the other girls like Mary who are out there and vote against this bill not for me, but for them.

STATEMENT OF REPRESENTATIVE NITA LOWEY (R-NY), HEARING ON THE CHILD CUSTODY PROTECTION ACT BEFORE THE SUBCOMMITTEE ON THE CONSTITUTION, HOUSE JUDICIARY COMMITTEE, MAY 21, 1998

… I am concerned about this bill because of its impact on the lives, health, and safety of adolescent girls and their families.

… This bill is unnecessary, and it is dangerous. Already, most young women — more than 75 percent, in fact — involve one or both parents in the decision to seek an abortion. As a mother of three, I can only hope and pray that every young person in crisis would seek the assistance and the counsel of loving parents in deciding how to cope with an unwanted pregnancy. Pregnant teens should receive counseling about the full range of options before them, including adoption.

Unfortunately, not every child has loving parents to counsel them…. In an ideal world, every child has parents [he or she] can turn to. But we do not live in an ideal world, and the truth is, family communication and open and honest parent-child relationships cannot be legislated.

So what about the minority of girls who find themselves pregnant and feel they cannot turn to their parents for help? This bill sends them a clear message: Go it alone. You are on your own.

… What will become of these girls who choose to have an abortion, the girls who don't have loving parents to turn to? Some will seek dangerous back-alley abortions close to home. Some will commit suicide. And others will travel to unfamiliar places for abortions by themselves. And how will they get there? Bus? Hitchhiking? Imagine them making their way home alone after the procedure….

… And so what will become of the grandparents or the friends who try to help these young women? They will be thrown in jail. This bill will make criminals of loving grandparents and caring friends.

Currently, more than half of all young women who do not involve a parent in this difficult decision do seek the advice and counsel of another adult, including 15 percent who turn to an adult relative. We should encourage the involvement of responsible adults in this decision — stepparents, aunts or uncles, religious minister, or counselor — not criminalize that involvement.

[Y]oung women leave a state with a parental involvement law to seek an abortion for many reasons. In some cases, it is for reasons of access. Eighty-four percent of counties in this nation have no abortion providers, and in some cases, the nearest abortion provider is across state lines. In other cases, young women cross state lines to escape abusive and dangerous parents. Think of Spring Adams, a 13-year-old sixth-grade student who was shot to death by her father after he learned she was to terminate a pregnancy caused by his acts of incest.

… I firmly believe that we should make abortion less necessary for teenagers, not more dangerous and difficult. We need to teach teenagers to be abstinent and responsible…. We do not need a bill that isolates teenagers and puts them at risk. It simply should not be against the law to cross state lines to access a legal medical procedure.

STATEMENT OF REVEREND KATHERINE HANCOCK RAGSDALE, EPISCOPALIAN PRIEST, HEARING ON THE CHILD CUSTODY PROTECTION ACT BEFORE THE SUBCOMMITTEE ON THE CONSTITUTION, HOUSE JUDICIARY COMMITTEE, MAY 21, 1998

... I am ... a parish priest in a small country parish in Massachusetts, and I suppose I am also one of the strangers about whom we have been hearing today, because it is not so long ago that I went to pick up a 15-year-old girl and drive her to Boston for an abortion. I didn't know the girl yet. I knew her school nurse. The nurse had called me a few days earlier to see if I knew where she might find bus and cab fare for the girl. I was stunned. A 15-year-old girl was going to have to take multiple buses to the hospital all alone.

The nurse shared my concern, but explained that the girl had no one to turn to. She feared for her safety if her father found out, and there were no other relatives close enough to help.... So I went, and during our hour-long drive, we talked. She told me about her dreams for the future, all the things she thought she might like to do and be. I talked to her about the kind of hard work and personal responsibility it would take to get there. She told me about the guilt she felt for being pregnant even though the pregnancy was the result of date rape....

So I talked to her about the limits of personal responsibility, about how not everything that happens to us is our own fault or God's will, and about how very much God loves her. And I took her inside, and I went downstairs to get a couple of prescriptions filled for her. And I paid for them after I was informed that otherwise her father would be billed.

... I despaired that any young woman should ever find herself in such a position, but frankly, it never occurred to me that anyone would ever try to criminalize those who were able and willing to help.

In fact, New Hampshire was closer to that girl's home than Boston, but, as it happened, she was going to Boston, so I didn't take her across state lines. Nor did I, to my knowledge, break any laws. But I am here to tell you that if either of those things had been necessary, I would have done them. And if helping young women like her should be made illegal, I will, nonetheless, continue to do it. I have no choice. I took vows. And if you tell me that it is a crime to exercise my ministry, I will have no choice but to do it anyway. And I am not alone.

I find it troubling that those of us in this room should find ourselves at odds over this issue. Presumably, we all want the same things. We want fewer unplanned pregnancies, and we want young people who face problems, particularly problems that have to do with their health and their futures, to receive love and support and counsel from responsible adults, preferably their parents.

This bill, however, doesn't achieve those goals.... It doesn't resolve the problems with which we are faced. It doesn't even address those problems. This isn't a bill about solutions, it is a bill about punishment....

We should be talking instead about reality-based, age-appropriate sex education and about safe and affordable contraception. We should be talking about education and economics, about child care and welfare, about violence at home, on the streets, and in the schools. We should be looking for new ways to solve our problems, not new ways to punish victims and those who care for them.

... [S]everal years ago, the Episcopal Church passed a resolution opposing any parental consent or notification requirements that did not include a provision for nonjudicial bypass. In our view, any morally responsible requirement had to allow young women to turn for help to some responsible adult other than a parent or a judge, to go instead to a grandparent or an aunt, a teacher or a neighbor, a counselor, or a minister.

... Even if we were to find ourselves drained of the last vestiges of our compassion, there would still be a self-interested reason to fear and oppose this legislation. It imperils all young women, even those in our own happy families. Let's not kid ourselves. Even in the healthiest of families, teens sometimes cannot bring themselves to confide in their parents…. But, sisters and brothers, I am here to tell you that teenagers will, from time to time, exercise poor judgment. It is a fact of nature, and there is no law you can pass that will change that. And the penalty for poor judgment should not be death.

Oppose this bill. Oppose it because, no matter how good the intentions of its authors and supporters, it is in essence punitive and mean-spirited. Oppose it out of compassion for those young people who cannot for reasons of safety comply with its provisions. If all else fails, oppose it for purely selfish reasons. Oppose it because you don't want your daughter or granddaughter or niece to die just because she couldn't face her parents and you had outlawed all her other options.

STATEMENT OF REPRESENTATIVE JERROLD NADLER (D-NY), HEARING ON THE CHILD CUSTODY PROTECTION ACT BEFORE THE SUBCOMMITTEE ON THE CONSTITUTION, HOUSE JUDICIARY COMMITTEE, MAY 21, 1998

… As you know, some states require parental consent from both the father and the mother of the child. What if one of the parents cannot be located or has fled, or has been abusive, or hasn't seen the child since she was born, and then the other parent drives the daughter to another state for an abortion? This bill would make that parent a criminal. This is absurd.

Furthermore, the judicial bypass option in many parental consent laws has proven to be ineffective. Problems have been reported in Indiana and Ohio where a 17-year-old who testified that her father beat her was still not allowed to bypass the parental consent of that parent by the Ohio Supreme Court. Many local judges refuse to hold hearings on this subject or are widely known to be

anti-choice and refuse to grant bypasses despite rulings of the Supreme Court that they cannot withhold the bypass under certain conditions.

Since the bill criminalizes any adult who drives a young woman across state lines for the purposes of obtaining an abortion, it leads to yet another problem. This bill may force a young woman to drive by herself for long distances both before and after her abortion, greatly increasing her own health risks, rather than to allow a responsible adult to accompany the woman to and from the clinic. This is dangerous and unnecessary.

The American Medical Association [AMA] has noted that women who feel they can't involve a parent often take drastic steps to maintain the confidentiality of their pregnancies, including running away from home, obtaining unsafe back-alley abortions, or resorting to risky self-induced abortions. The AMA has reported that, quote, the desire to maintain secrecy has been one of the leading reasons for illegal abortion deaths since 1973.

… This bill is a death sentence for some young women…. This bill, like all parental consent laws and required waiting-period laws, further risks women's health because it delays abortions. As we all know, the further along a pregnancy is, the more dangerous any termination procedure becomes.

Let me remind … everyone … that abortions are legal in the United States despite what some people may wish, and they should be as safe as possible. This bill is a giant step in the wrong direction….

STATEMENT OF REPRESENTATIVE SHEILA JACKSON LEE (D-TX), HEARING ON CHILD CUSTODY PROTECTION ACT BEFORE THE SUBCOMMITTEE ON THE CONSTITUTION, HOUSE JUDICIARY COMMITTEE, MAY 21, 1998

… I don't know where we are going with this legislation primarily because we want to stop it at the prevention end, and then we want to create

dangerous situations at the time when a young person is confused and devastated. This is not about the question of parental consent or having children disobey their parents or the dangers, possibly, of a child going to another state. It is about access to confidential reproductive health services, and this bill raises troubling concerns.

... I ... believe in helping young women find ways of developing their self-esteem and preventing teenage pregnancy. However, as we move toward this legislation, this does not prevent teenage pregnancy. This, in fact, ... jeopardizes the lives of our young women.

... These laws are dangerous, very dangerous, and I would like to cite again the story of 17-year-old Becky Bell's senseless death as an example of this danger. She died from a back-alley abortion as a result of Indiana's parental consent law. Rather than tell her parents about an unwanted pregnancy, she sought an abortion in a back alley. She suffered a fatal lung infection as a result. This is a tragedy that could be avoided and which will be replayed again and again if we do not oppose this law....

A mother taking her daughter across state lines to the closest abortion provider could be prosecuted if the girl's father did not consent to the abortion, even if the parents were divorced and the girl's father could not be located. Or what if this girl, as I said earlier, was a victim of incest? Should the parental consent of the person who harmed her be required?

... [M]any young people fear being recognized at an abortion provider in their hometown. Fifty-eight percent of high school students surveyed in three public schools in central Massachusetts reported having health concerns they wished to keep from their parents, and 25 percent of the students said they would forego seeking certain types of medical treatment if there was a possibility of parental disclosure by physicians.

CHAPTER XIII

ABORTION SHOULD BE OUTLAWED

TESTIMONY OF PROFESSOR RONALD D. ROTUNDA OF THE UNIVERSITY OF ILLINOIS LAW SCHOOL, CHAMPAIGN, IL, BEFORE THE SUBCOMMITTEE ON THE CONSTITUTION, FEDERALISM, AND PROPERTY RIGHTS, SENATE JUDICIARY COMMITTEE, HEARING ON *"THE 25TH ANNIVERSARY OF <u>ROE V. WADE</u>: HAS IT STOOD THE TEST OF TIME?"* JANUARY 21, 1998

The Supreme Court issued its first abortion opinion on January 22, 1973. That opinion, *Roe v. Wade* ... has ushered in a quarter century of criticism by many academic commentators. In so doing, the Supreme Court created a right to abortion (essentially abortion on demand) that was broader than the abortion rights granted by almost any other western nation. It also federalized the abortion issue, an issue that had been left in the custody of the states for nearly two centuries.

Though a fragmented Court itself later backtracked on *Roe* in *Planned Parenthood of Southeastern Pennsylvania v. Casey*..., it did not overrule all of *Roe* because, as the O'Connor-Kennedy-Souter plurality candidly stated, it was important to respect precedent....

Our Constitution respects and protects privacy in many ways, but the Court normally derives this right to privacy from various clauses in the text, such as the privacy rights that derive from the First and Fourth Amendments. The Court has also been protective of activity that occurs in the home, but abortions, which occur in the hospital or in medical clinics, are not private in that sense.

Indeed, the analysis of *Roe* specifically does not rely on any interpretation of the text of the Constitution.... Instead, the *Roe* Court announced that it simply "agree[d]" with the proposition that "the right of privacy, however based, is broad enough to cover the abortion decision," although this right is "not absolute."

... What is the true rationale of *Roe*? It is often described as a women's rights case. Supporters have argued that a woman should have the right to control her own body. However, Justice Blackmun's majority opinion specifically rejected that contention.... The opinion states quite emphatically: "In fact, it is not clear to us that the claim ... that one has an unlimited right to do with one's body as one pleases bears a close relationship to the right of privacy previously articulated in the Court's decisions...."

... It is popularly understood that Justice Harry Blackmun's majority opinion in *Roe* stated that the state has no right to regulate abortion prior to the end of approximately the first trimester. That is when the state's interest reaches, in Blackmun's words, "a compelling point." During the second and third trimesters, the state has more power.

But this is not what Blackmun actually held. He wrote the opinion as if it were a doctor's rights case, not a women's rights case. Consider this strange sentence in his opinion: "[F]or the period of pregnancy prior to this 'compelling' point, the attending physician, in consultation with his patient, is free to determine, without regulation by the state, that, in his medical judgment, the patient's pregnancy should be terminated...."

Under *Roe* and similar abortion decisions that rely on it, the woman does not have the right to choose; she does not have a right to abortion. It is the doctor (whom the *Roe* opinion assumed to be a man) who has that right. In a small bow to women's rights, Justice Blackmun noted that the doctor should consult with his patient, the woman on whom the abortion is to be performed. And when the patient consults with the doctor, the doctor has a constitutional right to be free of "regulation by the state."

Two years after *Roe*, *Connecticut v. Menillo* upheld a Connecticut law making it a crime for "any person" to attempt an abortion. The Court ruled that this criminal statute — although it seemed to go far beyond what *Roe* allowed — was constitutional as applied to an attempted abortion performed by someone other than a licensed physician.... A woman has no right to choose a non-doctor to perform an abortion, even though a non-doctor might be just as safe and even though a woman can choose a non-doctor, such as a midwife, to deliver a full-term baby.

Later cases have confirmed that *Roe* was primarily drafted to protect doctors, not their patients. Thus, the Court has said, in *Colautti v. Franklin*, ... that "neither the legislature nor the courts" can define viability objectively, "be it weeks of gestation, or fetal weight, or any other single factor," because the judgment of the doctor must control.

Planned Parenthood of Central Missouri v. Danforth struck down a section of a law that forbade the use of saline amniocentesis as a method of abortion after the first trimester because the Court ruled that the law was not necessary to protect maternal health. However, the state specifically found that this technique "is deleterious (harmful) to maternal health," and the lower court findings supported this conclusion....

Even though the Court majority admitted that other techniques were safer for women, it simply concluded that saline abortions were "an accepted medical procedure" in the view of doctors ... and

thus were constitutionally protected from state regulation. Women are the victims of this decision.

... Those people who insist that no statute should limit *Roe* in any way, those who believe that we must follow *Roe* without change ... those advocates should read that decision and the others that follow in its wake. The decision is not about protecting women; it is about protecting doctors.

TESTIMONY OF STEVE CALVIN, M.D., SPECIALIST IN MATERNAL-FETAL MEDICINE, BEFORE THE SUBCOMMITTEE ON THE CONSTITUTION, FEDERALISM, AND PROPERTY RIGHTS, SENATE JUDICIARY COMMITTEE, HEARING ON "*THE 25TH ANNIVERSARY OF ROE V. WADE: HAS IT STOOD THE TEST OF TIME?*" JANUARY 21, 1998

... The subspecialty of maternal-fetal medicine is only two decades old and is unique in that we care for two patients in the mother and her unborn child.... Only on very rare occasions are the medical interests of the mother and unborn baby in conflict.

During the last 25 years, progress in the area of obstetrics and maternal-fetal medicine has been astonishing. By 1973, obstetrics had made great strides in making pregnancy and birth a relatively safe experience for women. Since the beginning of this century, developments in antibiotics, transfusion, and anesthesia caused the risk of maternal death to decrease by 50- to 100-fold. Attention was then turned to improving the outcome for the baby....

... The new focus on the baby was achieved by development of fetal ultrasound imaging technology. Prior to 1973, the anatomic development and activities of the fetus were invisible.

... At the time of the *Roe v. Wade* decision, ultrasound during pregnancy was largely experimental. During the '70s and '80s, the beneficial uses of ultrasound in pregnancy multiplied....

Current ultrasound imaging techniques reveal the marvelous complexity of prenatal growth and development…. However, the use of this wonderful window on the womb has become increasingly disconcerting for some who would rather view the fetus as pregnancy tissue or the product of conception.

… In the last two and one-half decades, our ability to obtain clear images of the fetus has expanded the concept of the fetus as a patient….

Unborn babies can be treated with medications for dangerously irregular heart rhythms and can receive blood transfusions if they are anemic. On rare occasions, surgical procedures can be performed before birth….

We are clearly in a new era of obstetrics because of ultrasound and the expanding concept of treatment of the fetus as a patient. Yet there is an inescapable schizophrenia when modern medicine works under ethical rules which say that a fetus is a patient only when the mother has conferred this status. The trouble is that this status can be withheld or withdrawn. The combination of current unrestricted legal abortion and our increasing abilities to diagnose fetal abnormalities and diseases prenatally is a very dangerous two-edged sword.

In many ways, modern obstetrics is becoming an impersonal techno specialty dedicated to the concept of the perfect baby. Prenatal diagnosis can benefit the mother and baby when treatment options are available, but much of prenatal diagnosis is designed to detect fetal abnormalities so that the choice of abortion is available. The majority of these abnormalities, such as Down syndrome, are not usually fatal. Even abortion supporters are horrified by the possibility of abortions based only on the sex of the unborn child. But why is abortion for the most sexist of reasons any worse that abortion for any other reason?

So far we do not have an overtly eugenic social policy but we are certainly encouraging family-based eugenics [selective breeding]. This use of abortion will gradually weaken society's commitment to the inclusion and care of the disabled in our human community.

In 1973, *Roe v. Wade* shattered the issue of abortion into sharp fragments. We are still dealing with the medical, social, and political fallout of the Supreme Court's willingness to go far beyond the traditional boundaries of medical ethics and practice. The tenets of Hippocratic medicine have served us well for more than 2,000 years. But our 25-year experiment with unrestricted abortion has caused the practice of medicine to become increasingly inconsistent. The tension between valuable ethical traditions and currently legal medical practice is untenable (cannot be maintained).

STATEMENT OF JEAN A. WRIGHT, M.D., M.B.A, BEFORE THE SUBCOMMITTEE ON THE CONSTITUTION, FEDERALISM, AND PROPERTY RIGHTS, SENATE JUDICIARY COMMITTEE, ON *"THE 25TH ANNIVERSARY OF ROE V. WADE: HAS IT STOOD THE TEST OF TIME?"* JANUARY 21, 1998

… I would like to focus my remarks on the changes we have seen in the field of pediatrics, particularly the areas of neonatology, surgery, anesthesia, and intensive care. Medical knowledge in those areas provide a new standard of science, upon which a very different conclusion might be reached if *Roe v. Wade* were decided in 1998, rather than the limited information that was available in 1973.

… In 1973, the scientific discussion heavily focused on the issues of fetal viability. At that time, the common understanding was that infants born before 28 weeks could not survive. Today, that age of viability has been pushed back from 28 weeks to 23 and 24 weeks. And some investigators are working on an artificial placenta to support those even younger.

In fact, while the number of children that are born and survive at 23-28 weeks gestation [is] still a minority of the infants in a NICU [Neonatal Intensive Care Unit], they are common enough that the colloquial term "micro-premie" has been coined to describe them, and an additional body of neonatal science has grown to support the care of the very premature infant. So in 25 years, we have gone from a practice in which those infants, once thought to be non-viable, are now beneficiaries of medical advances in order to provide them with every opportunity to survive.

… [V]ery pre-term neonates [newborns] have the neuroanatomic substrate and functional physiologic and chemical processes in the brain responsible for mediating pain or noxious stimuli (known as nociception)….

Anatomic studies have shown that the density of cutaneous nociceptive nerve endings in the late fetus and newborn infant equal or exceed that of adult skin….

… [A] controlled study of intrauterine blood sampling and blood transfusions in fetuses between 20 and 34 weeks of gestation showed hormonal responses that were consistent with fetal perception of pain….

Pre-term neonates born at 23 weeks gestation show highly specific and well-coordinated physiologic and behavioral responses to pain, similar to those seen in full-term neonates, older infants, and small children….

All of the scientific references I have just made are from research breakthroughs in the last 10 years. This information was not available in 1973. As a result of this newly emerging understanding of fetal pain development, Anand and Craig, in a 1996 editorial in the journal PAIN, called for a new definition of pain, a definition that is not subjective and that is not dependent on the patient's ability to provide a self-report.

… Today, we are the beneficiaries of an enormous fund of new medical knowledge, and I believe we should incorporate that into our approach to protecting the life of the unborn.

… [P]laces such as the University of California, with its Fetal Surgery Center, are doing just that. Exciting surgical advances, which allow for the surgeon to partially remove the fetus through an incision in the womb, fix the congenital defect, and then slip the "pre-viable" infant back into the womb, should make us reconsider the outcome and viability of many pre-term infants, particularly those with challenging congenital defects.

… Today we are hearing evidence, both medical and legal, that was not available to our counterparts in 1973. We cannot change the ramifications of their decision, but we can make better and more informed decisions today. Just as the incoming tide raises the level of the water in the harbor, and in doing so, all the boats rise to the same new level, so should we allow the tide of new medical and legal information serve as a tide to raise both our medical and legal understanding of the unborn. And in doing so, lead us to making better decisions for this vulnerable population.

STATEMENT OF REPRESENTATIVE HENRY J. HYDE (R-IL), CHAIRMAN OF HOUSE JUDICIARY COMMITTEE, DECEMBER 10, 1997

My feeling about abortion is based not on whether people should have the right to choose, but rather on when human life actually begins and the respect I have for the civil rights of all human beings. I feel that abortion is an act which violates the constitutional rights of an unborn child, who is helpless and unable to defend or speak for itself. I do not think that the murder of an unborn innocent is ever justified, and the instances in which abortion is considered absolutely necessary in order to save the life of the mother are very rare indeed.

… [T]he Supreme Court decision, *Roe v. Wade*, held that women have the legal right to choose abortion over life for their baby. However, I do not feel the federal government should be responsible for funding these procedures, and I have been successful in placing restrictions on the use of taxpayer dollars to pay for abortions. I have also worked to make partial-birth abortions illegal. These procedures add a gruesome dimension to the debate about abortion, in that they rise to the level of infanticide.

STATEMENT OF REPRESENTATIVE HELEN CHENOWETH (R-ID), NOVEMBER 21, 1997

Twenty-four years ago, the Supreme Court removed a God-given, unalienable right from unborn babies, a right it has the duty to secure and protect. In doing so, it elevated a "judge-made" right, the right of a person's privacy, above the God-given right to life.

It has always been my belief that unborn children should be cherished, and abortion for the convenience of the mother is contrary to the convictions that mean a great deal. I believe the life of an unborn child is to be respected as truly as the life of a newborn.

It grieves my heart that each day more and more lives are lost because of abortion. I think it is unfortunate that the courts have decided to abandon basic principles of the Constitution and of science by legalizing the senseless taking of human life by abortion. What is even more tragic is that many groups, which have termed themselves as "advocates for women," have promoted abortion rights as the premiere principle of women's rights. I find it further appalling that the federal government is forcing states to fund abortions with taxpayer funds by justifying abortion as a necessary function for the reproductive health of women.

I believe that if the Supreme Court continues to uphold the wrong decision made in *Roe v. Wade*, Congress should enact laws that would disallow abortion, except in very extreme circumstances. At the very least, Congress should prohibit the government from funding abortion. However, before we can pass laws forbidding abortion, we must change the dynamic of the debate by educating the American public to favor the protection of life at

its natural beginning — the point of conception. I think that when all Americans, including many women who are confused about the issue, begin to realize the serious ramifications of abortion, they will strongly support the need to protect the sanctity of life.

My position in representing the people of Idaho has always been, and will continue to be, guided by the conviction that abortion is wrong and should only be considered in cases of criminal rape, incest, or when the mother's life is in imminent danger.

STATEMENT OF GIANNA JESSEN, FRANKLIN, TENNESSEE, BEFORE THE SUBCOMMITTEE ON THE CONSTITUTION, HOUSE JUDICIARY COMMITTEE, APRIL 22, 1996

I am Gianna Jessen. I am 19 years of age....

I am adopted. I have cerebral palsy. My biological mother was seventeen years old and seven and one-half months pregnant when she made the decision to have a saline abortion. I am the person she aborted. I lived instead of died.... Some have said that I am a "botched abortion." A result of a job not well done.

I remained in the hospital for almost three months. There was not much hope for me in the beginning. I weighed only two pounds. Today babies smaller than I was have survived.

... I eventually was able to leave the hospital and be placed in foster care. I was diagnosed with cerebral palsy as a result of the abortion.

I have continued in physical therapy for my disability, and after a total of four surgeries, I can now walk without assistance....

I am happy to be alive. I almost died. Every day I thank God for my life. I do not consider myself a by-product of conception, a clump of tissue, or any other of the titles given to a child in the womb....

Abortion is not the solution people say it is. It is no solution. It is murder. Abortion violates the right to life. I was just as much a person when I was aborted as I am today. You will have a hard time convincing me otherwise. You will have a hard time convincing me that abortion helps women when I meet women after women, every day, who tell me of their grief and heartache caused by abortion. They tell me "no one really told me it was a baby." None of these women talk of tissue. They speak of the children they lost at the hand of the abortionist and with the blessings of our legislators.

STATEMENT OF SENATOR JOHN P. EAST (R-NC), JANUARY 16, 1986

Regarding abortion, the source of the current controversy over abortion, of course, is the 1973 *Roe v. Wade* decision of the United States Supreme Court. The *Roe* ruling made two principal determinations. First, *Roe* recognized a federal constitutional right to an abortion throughout pregnancy for virtually any reason. Second, *Roe* determined that the unborn child is not a "person" under the Fourteenth Amendment to the U.S. Constitution, which guarantees a right to life. I disagree with both of these aspects of the *Roe* decision.

The Constitution does not make any explicit or implicit reference to abortion, much less guarantee a right to it. Hence, the *Roe* decision, which invalidated the duly enacted abortion laws of all 50 states, was an unconstitutional act on the part of the Court. It is incumbent upon the Court to recognize its error and overrule the *Roe* recognition of a right to abortion....

Legislative history reveals that the framers of the Fourteenth Amendment clearly intended for its provisions to protect all human beings. Since unborn children are human beings, I believe that the Fourteenth Amendment protects their right to live. The Court ought to overrule *Roe* in this regard as well. Until it does so, I will continue to support congressional initiatives to provide unborn children with a constitutionally guaranteed right to life.

STATEMENT OF SENATOR STROM THURMOND (R-SC), BEFORE THE SUBCOMMITTEE ON THE CONSTITUTION, SENATE JUDICIARY COMMITTEE, FEBRUARY 28, 1983

... First, whatever one's personal views about abortion, the plain fact is that *Roe v. Wade* represented one of the most blatant exercises in judicial activism in the history of this country. In one fell swoop, seven men on the Court reinterpreted what had been the law of the land for nearly two centuries and overturned the laws adopted by the legislatures in every one of the 50 states.

Second, in *Roe v. Wade*, seven men on the Court established as a new law of the land in the area of abortion a policy significantly more permissive of abortion than the policy that had been freely adopted by the legislatures in every one of the 50 states.

Third, in *Roe v. Wade*, seven men on the Court established as a new law of the land a policy on abortion as liberal and permissive of abortion as any law in the entire world. There are absolutely no serious legal or constitutional barriers to a person obtaining an abortion for any reason, at any stage of her pregnancy.

Fourth, since *Roe v. Wade,* we have had a national policy on abortion bitterly opposed by large numbers of individuals in this country who are totally without any recourse to their elected representatives. This is not how public policy is developed in a free society on issues of this bitterness and divisiveness.

Fifth, *Roe v. Wade*, itself, amended the Constitution of the United States in reading in a policy of abortion at odds with its language, at odds with its legislative history, and at odds with the long-standing practices of the states in this country.

STATEMENT OF PROFESSOR LYNN WARDLE, BRIGHAM YOUNG UNIVERSITY SCHOOL OF LAW, BEFORE THE SUBCOMMITTEE ON THE CONSTITUTION, SENATE JUDICIARY COMMITTEE, FEBRUARY 28, 1983

I appear before the subcommittee today to recommend that it propose and the Senate pass an amendment to the Constitution that would reverse *Roe v. Wade*....

I would like to rephrase the issue. I think the question is whether the right of the people to protect human life is to be abridged. A decade has passed since *Roe v. Wade* was decided, a decade in which federal courts have faced a flood of abortion litigation, in which Congress has faced a deluge of abortion proposals, and in which the number of abortions performed annually has reached in excess of 1.5 million, a total approaching 15 million since *Roe v. Wade*.

Moreover, as many commentators had predicted, since *Roe*, there has been a profound and appalling increase in the kinds of inhumane acts that manifest a disregard for and involve even the destruction of other forms of unwanted, defenseless human life. Not only are human beings who bear the stigma of being labeled defective because of some potential physical or mental condition being ruthlessly destroyed before birth, but since *Roe*, they have increasingly become the victims of infanticide and selective nontreatment, to use the euphemism.

... While these practical and doctrinal excesses are approaching shocking extremes, the Supreme Court has refused to reconsider *Roe v. Wade*. Thus, at this time, 10 years after that disaster, I feel the sentiments of the English statesman and orator, Edmund Burke, who is reported to have said, "An event is happening about which it is difficult to speak, but about which it is impossible to remain silent." I believe the time has come for Congress to restore the right of the people to protect all human life.

It is now painfully apparent that the constitutionalization of abortion is a slippery slope, leading ever downward into increasingly more detailed technical questions. As the courts have become increasingly more involved in supervising the enactment and enforcement of abortion regulations, the fundamental question keeps reappearing — why should the courts, rather than state legislatures, be deciding these issues? The answer, of course, is that they should not.

The exercise of judicial power to invalidate legislation affects the relationship between the coequal branches of government. The assumption by the judiciary of a major role in supervising abortion regulation represents a substantial shift in the delicate balance of power.

I believe that the issue of abortion is the type of issue that should appropriately be left to legislative resolution. When employed unwisely or unnecessarily, the Supreme Court's power to declare legislative acts unconstitutional constitutes a threat to the continued effectiveness of the federal courts as well as to the stability of our democratic system. After all, there is some irony that a people who are self-governing cannot establish the laws dealing with such a fundamental question as the regulation and legality of abortion....

STATEMENT OF SENATOR THOMAS F. EAGLETON (D-MO) BEFORE THE SUBCOMMITTEE ON CONSTITUTIONAL AMENDMENTS, SENATE JUDICIARY COMMITTEE, MARCH 6, 1974

The majority opinion blandly sidestepped the key question — the humanity of the unborn. Since they found no clear medical, theological, or philosophical consensus on the subject, the majority concluded that the judiciary was in no position to "resolve the difficult question of when life begins." And therefore, Judge Blackmun wrote, the Court saw no need to resolve the question.

I cannot comprehend how our nation's highest court could find that it was unnecessary to consider the humanity of the unborn. Their humanity is the entire question....

It is my profound moral conviction ... that life is a continuum from first beginnings in the womb to the final gasp of the dying; and the first function of society, the primary responsibility of government, is to protect life and to create conditions which permit each person to flourish and to reach his or her fullest potential.

Therefore, ... I propose that this subcommittee consider amending the Constitution in the broadest possible terms to protect the sanctity of life throughout its full spectrum from womb to tomb. I would provide substantive constitutional guarantees against abortion, infanticide, euthanasia, and the imposition of death as punishment.

STATEMENT OF SENATOR JESSE HELMS (R-NC) BEFORE THE SUBCOMMITTEE ON CONSTITUTIONAL AMENDMENTS, SENATE JUDICIARY COMMITTEE, MARCH 6, 1974

... [T]hose who agree that the life of the unborn must be protected under our Constitution should agree first on these basic principles.

1) There is no moment, biologically speaking, when the fetus is not a human being. This has been the instinctive view of Western civilization for centuries. I do not mean to exclude other cultures; the point is that this has been the view of our culture. It is now confirmed by biological science and by genetics that the fertilized ovum contains everything within it which will be developed in the individual human being. The genetic code has already established that individual's total physical makeup....

2) The beginning, as I have already indicated, is when the egg is fertilized by the sperm. There is a considerable amount of pressure from pro-abortion groups to attempt to redefine the beginning of life at implantation, rather than fertilization. Any constitutional amendment that allows abortion previous to implantation will fail to protect the whole biological life-span of human beings. That is why my amendment protects "from the moment of conception."

3) The fetus is a person from the moment of conception and entitled to equal protection and due process. The fetus is not part of the mother.... [A]n unborn baby is not a private affair between the mother and the abortionist. It is a three-way affair with the life of an individual person in the balance. The mother who seeks to kill her child for pleasure or convenience or whatever and the doctor who is willing to perform the deed for a fee are not the most objective judges to protect the unborn child's interest.

4) Finally, if the fetus is a legal person and a human being, then that person's right to life must be considered equally with that of the mother.... [I]f the lives of two persons are at stake, then one life cannot be favored over the other. Each case must be considered on the individual circumstances. Until the Supreme Court established a rigid curtailment of state laws on abortion, several states had developed individual complex systems to accommodate the specific rights of the two persons involved with the general proposition that the life of any person must be protected. These systems were not perfect. But just as homicide laws distinguish between the kinds of intention and whether criminal or not, juries can decide whether the defendants are guilty of criminal intentions or not.

CHAPTER XIV

ABORTION SHOULD NOT BE OUTLAWED

STATEMENT OF REPRESENTATIVE PETE STARK (D-CA) REGARDING THE TWENTY-SIXTH ANNIVERSARY OF *ROE V. WADE*, FEBRUARY 9, 1999

Friday, January 22nd, 1999, marked the twenty-sixth anniversary of the Supreme Court decision in *Roe v. Wade,* which ensured the right of all women to make decisions concerning their reproductive health. For millions of women, *Roe v. Wade* has secured the constitutional right to seek access to safe and legal family planning and abortion services. Its impact on the health and safety of the lives of women cannot be overstated.

It is an outrage that, despite the Supreme Court's ruling, women still face barriers to seeking abortion without danger. States continue to find ways to restrict access by law, and even more troubling is the recent trend of clinic violence and the harassment of doctors and workers by anti-choice activists. I would like to highlight some cases from this past year of violence and threatening behavior in my home state of California.

In February, a bombing attempt was made on a family planning clinic in Vallejo. The briefcase that contained the alleged bomb was later discovered to be empty.

In April, a firebomb was thrown at a Planned Parenthood family planning clinic in San Diego, causing $5,000 in damages....

In July, a San Mateo family planning clinic worker was accused of physical assault by three anti-choice protestors. The protestors' injuries were not found by the police to warrant charges.

In San Diego, a clinic was vandalized, the buildings covered with the words "baby killer." In September, the new Planned Parenthood headquarters in Orange County faced over thirty chanting anti-choice protestors.

In Fairfield, a physician was harassed by anti-choice protestors as he arrived for work one morning.

These events are mirrored by others across the country and show that the fight for reproductive choice did not end with the *Roe v. Wade* decision. Twenty-six years ago, the Supreme Court held up the right to reproductive choice for women, yet it is still debated on the floor of the House of Representatives on a near daily basis. We must keep up the fight for a woman's right to choose. I remain committed to do all I can to preserve that choice.

STATEMENT OF RONALD M. GREEN, JOHN PHILIPS PROFESSOR OF RELIGION, DARTMOUTH COLLEGE, AND DIRECTOR OF DARTMOUTH'S ETHICS INSTITUTE, BEFORE THE SUBCOMMITTEE ON THE CONSTITUTION, HOUSE JUDICIARY COMMITTEE, APRIL 22, 1996

In considering the question of abortion more than twenty-three years ago, the Supreme Court had to face an extremely difficult set of questions. Among these were the question[s] of how we are to assess the legal and moral claims of prenatal life, and how we are to balance the claims of the embryo or fetus against a woman's rights of autonomy and privacy in reproductive decision-making.

The issue of the moral or legal status of prenatal human life is particularly difficult. In approaching this issue, the court noted the wide diversity of philosophical and religious views on when life begins.

... Obviously the Court could not privilege any one position ... and chose instead to look at the discernible interests of women and society in the matter of state involvement in regulating abortion and protecting prenatal life.

... [T]he Court also acted in the best positive American traditions of separation of church and state by allowing individuals and religious groups the freedom to determine how they themselves view and will decide to treat prenatal human life.

... [T]he justices ... made the decision ... that questions affecting the basic rights of women and involving a determination of the moral and legal status of prenatal life could not be left to the jurisdiction of local communities or the state. It is unthinkable that one state could come to a ruling on this matter, for example, not to protect the fetus, while another could rule differently.

The Court ruled properly, I believe, when it concluded that during the early phases of a pregnancy, maternal privacy and autonomy should take priority over any state interests in prenatal life.

Illegal

... [Some people] argue that even if the early embryo or fetus lacks many of the qualities we normally associate with full humanness, it possesses a unique genetic identity and potential and should be respected for this. However, ... [i]t is now known that, following conception, the embryo can spontaneously fission into two distinct persons, each having an identical genome or genetic blueprint. This is the way that identical twins develop in nature. More surprisingly, during the early phases of development, two distinct embryos can fuse together to create a single individual, with each

genetic cell line integrating itself successfully in the resulting bodily structure.... So it is not true that a unique human genetic identity is forged at conception or that we can unambiguously speak of individual persons as beginning at this time.

After the time of viability, when a fetus can live on its own in the world as a distinct and recognizable human being, the justices believed that it is reasonable to place greater restrictions on a woman's autonomy and privacy in the name of this growing human potential. [But] in cases of conflicts between the life and health of the mother and the life of the fetus, her well-being, as determined by competent medical authority, must come first.

... [A]fter more than two decades the basic framework of *Roe* still makes sense.

As a society we will continue to argue about the specifics of abortion law and policy within this reasonable framework. My own personal view is that we should continue to adhere to the lines drawn by the Court in *Roe*, including the specific application of the trimester approach adopted there. I hold this view because I believe that nothing has happened since 1973 that compels us to change this approach. The age of viability has not changed dramatically during this period and medical technology has not advanced to the point that we can avoid the occasional need for tragic later-term decisions about the woman's health or the health of her child.

STATEMENT OF WALTER DELLINGER, PROFESSOR OF LAW, DUKE UNIVERSITY SCHOOL OF LAW, DURHAM, NORTH CAROLINA, BEFORE THE SUBCOMMITTEE ON CIVIL AND CONSTITUTIONAL RIGHTS, HOUSE JUDICIARY COMMITTEE, OCTOBER 2, 1990

There is no doubt that a woman's right to decide whether or not to terminate a pregnancy is, at a minimum, a liberty interest protected by the due process clause. Any other conclusion would require the Court to overrule *Griswold v. Connecticut* protecting the right of married couples to use birth control…. Restrictive abortion laws give the state control over a woman's basic choices about reproduction and family planning, an intrusion utterly incompatible with any meaningful concept of individual liberty.

It is no exaggeration to say … that mandatory childbearing is a totalitarian intervention into a woman's life.

Congress could, moreover, conclude that restrictive abortion regulations have a clearly disproportionate impact on the equality and liberty interest of poor women, young women, and women of color. The kinds of restrictions that states are enacting even now, while *Roe* still hangs by a thread, are restrictions that have devastating consequences for women who are hostage to youth, poverty, and geography.

… The fact is that in a federal system of open borders and freedom of interstate travel, no state can, in fact, enforce its restrictive abortion policy against its affluent and well-educated residents. What states may do is to enforce restrictive policy against those many of its residents who are vulnerable.

The notion of returning the abortion issue to the states would not actually result in different rules for residents of different states, as much as it would functionally produce different abortion policies for different economic and social classes.

The Congress can clearly take into account the fact that separate state policies would produce a national double standard for rich and poor, wholly incompatible with basic principles of justice. A woman's right to choose would be determined by the fortuitous happenstance of where she lived and whether she had the information and money to travel elsewhere, sometimes to a distant location, to obtain an abortion.

STATEMENT OF SENATOR BOB PACKWOOD (R-OR) BEFORE THE SUBCOMMITTEE ON THE CONSTITUTION, SENATE JUDICIARY COMMITTEE, FEBRUARY 28, 1983

I would urge this committee to recall that, by and large, constitutional amendments are designed to confirm consensus, not create it…. I know those who share my view on abortion cite the polls indicating that by a margin of 2-to-1, people in this country think that a woman ought to have the right to choose whether or not she wants to have an abortion….

There is no … consensus in this country for a constitutional amendment to reverse *Roe v. Wade*….

I am hard-pressed to understand how those who are very strongly opposed to the right to choose, who are convinced that abortion is murder … how they can vote for a states' rights amendment, which says in essence that murder is OK in some states and not in others.

… I think we are all aware that a constitutional amendment would not actually prohibit abortion. Abortion was illegal in most places in this country — and in a few states — prior to *Roe v. Wade*. The difference is that many more women died, because the abortions were … done under the most unsanitary conditions.

Any constitutional amendment we pass may make abortion illegal, but it will not make it impossible, and it will be a sorry day for women in this country if we force them back into the situation that we forced them into prior to *Roe v. Wade*.

STATEMENT OF RHONDA COPELON, CENTER FOR CONSTITUTIONAL RIGHTS, BEFORE THE SUBCOMMITTEE ON THE CONSTITUTION, SENATE JUDICIARY COMMITTEE, MARCH 7, 1983

No decision of the Supreme Court of the United States has meant more to the lives, the health, the well-being, the freedom and the dignity of women in this country than the decisions in *Roe v. Wade*.

Roe v. Wade ranks with other landmark decisions that have moved this nation on the path toward liberty and equality....

Roe v. Wade is not ... a departure from constitutional tradition, rather it applied to women some of the basic concepts upon which this nation was founded, and that is one of the reasons it is so difficult to undo.

It repudiated the historic disregard for the dignity and full personhood of women and the relegation of women to a separate sphere and second class citizenship. It brought legal theory, developed by and for men, closer to encompassing the existence of women.

Consider for a moment the relation of some of our most fundamental constitutional principles to the issue of compulsory pregnancy and childbearing.

We all hold as sacred the physical privacy of our homes. If we guard so jealously our physical environment and possession from intrusion by the state, how can we accord lesser status to the dominion and control over the physical self?

The First Amendment protects our thoughts, our beliefs, our verbal as well as symbolic expression. We can neither be restrained from speech nor forced to break silence. The Constitution protects these rights not only because of a utilitarian view that a marketplace of ideas served the public good but also because of the place of expression in the development of individual identity and the fulfillment of human aspirations.

Is not the commitment to bring a child into the world and to raise it through daily love, nurture and teaching an awesome form of expression, a reflection of each individual's beliefs, thoughts, identity, and the notion of what is meaningful? Men and women speak with their bodies on picket lines and in demonstrations. Women likewise speak in childbearing.

The First Amendment also demands that the state respect diverse beliefs and practices that involve worship, ritual, and decisions about everyday life. We recognize as religious, matters of life and death and of ultimate concern. The decision whether or not to bear a child — like objection to military service — is a matter of conscientious dimension.

The religions and the people of this country are deeply divided over the propriety and, indeed, the necessity of abortion. While for some, any consideration of abortion is a grave evil, others hold that a pregnant woman has a religious and moral obligation to make a decision and to consider abortion rather than sacrifice her well-being, that of her family, or that of the incipient life. The right to abortion is thus rooted in the recognition that women, too, make conscientious decisions.

We deem fundamental also the principle enshrined in the Thirteenth Amendment that no person should be forced into involuntary servitude as a result either of private conspiracy or public law. Does this right not extend to women entitling her to say "no" to the unparalleled labor demanded by pregnancy, childbirth, and childbearing — to say "no" to the expropriation of her body and service for the sake of another? If we strip away the sentimentalism that has rendered invisible the work of childbearing and childrearing, forced pregnancy must surely be recognized as a form of involuntary servitude.

What of the equality of women? Not to apply the foregoing fundamental constitutional principles to the question of the liberty to choose abortion is to deny women equal personhood and dignity in the most fundamental sense.

At the same time, to deny the right to abortion ensures that women will be excluded from full participation in society. Unexpected pregnancy and involuntary motherhood can preclude education, shatter work patterns and aspirations, and make organizational and political involvement impossible. A woman is no more biologically required to remain pregnant than a cardiac patient is to die of a treatable condition.

In sum, the criticism of *Roe v. Wade* has less to do with judicial excess than it does with a view of woman as less than a whole person under the Constitution, as someone whose self and aspirations can and should be legally subordinated to the service of others. The criticism reflects a failure to understand the gravity with which women view the responsibility of childbearing and the violence of forced pregnancy to human dignity.

STATEMENT OF A. JAMES ARMSTRONG, BISHOP OF THE DAKOTAS AREAS, NORTH CENTRAL JURISDICTION, PRESIDENT OF THE BOARD OF CHURCH AND SOCIETY, UNITED METHODIST CHURCH, BEFORE THE SUBCOMMITTEE ON CONSTITUTIONAL AMENDMENTS, SENATE JUDICIARY COMMITTEE, MARCH 7, 1974

The Social Principles of my denomination say: our belief in the sanctity of unborn human life makes us reluctant to approve abortion. But we are equally bound to respect the sacredness of the life and well-being of the mother, for whom devastating damage may result from an unacceptable pregnancy. In continuity with past Christian teaching, we recognize tragic conflicts of life with life that may justify abortion. We call all Christians into a searching and prayerful inquiry into the sorts of conditions that may warrant abortion. We support the removal of abortion from the criminal code, placing it instead under laws relating to other procedures of standard medical practice. A decision concerning abortion should be made after thorough and thoughtful consideration by the parties involved, with medical and pastoral counsel.

It has been assumed by many that the religious community agrees that a fetus becomes a human being at the moment of impregnation. Nothing can be further from the truth. In early centuries, the Roman Catholic Church did not presume to know when life became personal within the womb. St.

Augustine confessed he didn't understand when the soul entered the embryo. St. Thomas Aquinas, the most influential theologian of the Catholic Church, taught that the soul was given to the male in the fortieth day after conception, but to the female not until the eightieth day. That ought to say something about the feminist issue — or about St. Thomas!

The question, when does the fertilized ovum receive a soul, is unanswerable. It deals with the metaphysical speculation, with philosophic abstraction, and is, therefore, virtually irrelevant to the present debate. It was not until 1869 that the Catholic Church decided that the embryo is ensouled at the moment of conception and that abortion, at any time, is the equivalent of murder.

[S]hould a male-dominated religious hierarchy determine the moral posture and legal status of the opposite sex when the woman in question is caught up in a dilemma no man can fully understand? I, for one, rejoice in the post-Vatican II ecumenical mood. New forms of interreligious cooperation dare not blind us, however, to the broader issues of human welfare. A church that proclaims celibacy to reflect the highest level of excellence and that takes the dimmest possible view of scientific methods of birth control is not in a logical position to impose its views on abortion on the remainder of the citizenry.

… No one here is calling for indiscriminate irresponsible abortions. However, the note sadly missing in so much of this debate is a pastoral concern for the woman who suffers the so-called unacceptable pregnancy. Her age and station, the circumstances surrounding her impregnation and her mental health, the size and attitudes of her family, and her economic condition are disregarded. She is viewed, not as a fragile person in crisis, but as a thing — kind of a baby factory — through which a human fetus is passing. Dogmatic speculation is seen as more conclusive, more binding, than an informed medical and pastoral response to human tragedy.

In the summer of 1970, the *Lutheran Church in America* adopted the following statement:

- Since the fetus is the organic beginning of human life, the termination of its development is always a serious matter. Nevertheless, a qualitative distinction must be made between its claims and the rights of a responsible person made in God's image who is in living relationships with God and other human beings. This understanding of responsible personhood is congruent with the historical Lutheran teaching and practice whereby only living persons are baptized.

- On the basis of the evangelical ethic, a woman or couple may decide responsibly to seek an abortion. Earnest consideration should be given to the life and total health of the mother, her responsibilities to others in her family, the stage of development of the fetus, the economic and psychological stability of the home, the laws of the land, and the consequences for society as a whole.

This statement, it seems to me, summarizes an essential Christian position in a pluralistic nation.

CHAPTER XV

PARTIAL-BIRTH ABORTION SHOULD BE BANNED

STATEMENT OF REPRESENTATIVE BARBARA CUBIN (R-WY) DURING HOUSE VOTE TO OVERRIDE PRESIDENT BILL CLINTON'S VETO OF THE PARTIAL-BIRTH ABORTION ACT OF 1997 (H.R. 1122), JULY 23, 1998

In many States, the sanctity of unborn life is already regarded as a lawful right. Criminally, if a woman is assaulted and she, while surviving, loses her unborn child, the person who assaulted her can be charged with manslaughter or murder. If someone negligently kills the father of an unborn child, the mother or a guardian can sue on behalf of the unborn child for negligence. So, the civil courts have already recognized that unborn children have a right to live, yet unborn lives are taken through abortion procedures daily, and no one is held accountable.

While I oppose abortion in general and believe life begins at the time of conception, the partial-birth abortion procedure is especially repugnant and gruesome. Delivering a child up to its head and then removing the brain from that child when he or she can live outside the womb is revolting and against everything we stand for in this country. There is a home somewhere in America where that child could be loved and wanted.

... This bill is Congress' best effort yet to rid this nation of this appalling form of infanticide and I am proud that the U.S. House came together in a bipartisan fashion to override the President's ill-advised veto of the Partial-Birth Abortion Act.

TEXT OF A MAY 19, 1997, LETTER FROM P. JOHN SEWARD, M.D., EXECUTIVE VICE PRESIDENT, THE AMERICAN MEDICAL ASSOCIATION (AMA), TO SENATOR RICK SANTORUM (R-PA), EXPRESSING SUPPORT FOR THE PARTIAL-BIRTH ABORTION BAN ACT OF 1997 AFTER THE SENATE AMENDED THE BILL

The American Medical Association (AMA) is writing to support H.R. 1122, "The Partial-Birth Abortion Ban Act of 1997," as amended. Although our general policy is to oppose legislation criminalizing medical practice or procedure, the AMA has supported such legislation where the procedure was narrowly defined and not medically indicated. H.R. 1122 now meets both those tests.

Our support of this legislation is based on three specific principles. First, the bill would allow a legitimate exception where the life of the mother was endangered, thereby preserving the physician's judgment to take any medically necessary steps to save the life of the mother. Second, the bill would clearly define the prohibited procedure so that it is clear on the face of the legislation what act is to be banned. Finally, the bill would give any accused physician the right to have his or her conduct reviewed by the State Medical Board before a criminal trial commenced. In this manner, the bill would provide a formal role for valuable medical peer determination in any enforcement proceeding.

The AMA believes that with these changes, physicians will be on notice as to the exact nature of the prohibited conduct.

Thank you for the opportunity to work with you towards restricting a procedure we all agree is not good medicine.

OPENING STATEMENT OF DOUGLAS JOHNSON, LEGISLATIVE DIRECTOR OF THE NATIONAL RIGHT TO LIFE COMMITTEE, AT THE JOINT HEARING BEFORE THE SENATE JUDICIARY COMMITTEE AND THE SUBCOMMITTEE ON THE CONSTITUTION OF THE HOUSE JUDICIARY COMMITTEE, MARCH 11, 1997

… President Clinton told the American people that he would sign this bill [Partial-Birth Abortion Act of 1997] — the bill that he vetoed — if an exception were added to cover cases in which he asserts, contrary to medical authorities, that this procedure is necessary to prevent serious injury to the mother….

President Clinton's agents have clearly communicated through other channels that Mr. Clinton will *not* sign this bill, even if a "health exception" is added (which we oppose), unless it is also radically altered in a second way — specifically, unless it is limited to the third trimester.

As we have long emphasized, the vast majority of partial-birth abortions — surely over 90 percent — are *not* performed in the third trimester, but rather, in the fifth and sixth months, on healthy babies of healthy mothers — as Ron Fitzsimmons of the National Coalition of Abortion Providers acknowledged just two weeks ago. This means that under the Clinton-Daschle phony ban, the 4,000 or more partial-birth abortions performed on healthy babies of healthy mothers, in the fifth and sixth months of pregnancy, will continue *with no limitation at all*.

Moreover, the Clinton-Daschle proposal would allow partial-birth abortions to continue *even in the final three months of pregnancy* whenever an abortionist unilaterally asserts that this would enhance the mother's chance of future childbearing, or whenever he asserts that the baby does not meet his idiosyncratic definition of "viability."

The term "partial birth" is legally perfectly accurate. As a matter of law, in every state, if a baby emerges completely from the uterus, and shows even the briefest signs of life, legally a *live birth* has occurred. That is true *regardless* of whether or not the baby has yet reached the stage where she can survive independently of the mother, which is as early as 23 weeks with current neonatal care.

Moreover, even under the doctrine of the Supreme Court, that living just-delivered baby, no matter how premature, is a person under the Constitution….

Obstetricians and perinatologists confirm that even during the 20- to 23-week range, if a baby is expelled or removed completely from the uterus, she will usually gasp for breath for some time, even though her lung development is still insufficient to permit successful sustained respiration before 23 weeks. So the victim of a partial-birth abortion is indeed only "inches from her first breath" when the surgical scissors penetrates her skull — just as we have said.

… Even at 23 weeks, the baby now has between a one-in-four and a one-in-three chance of survival, and the survival rate curves sharply upward week by week after that.

Thus, each individual member of the human family killed in a partial-birth abortion is *at most* a few weeks short of the point at which she could survive to live a full lifespan of experiences as wondrous and varied as those of anyone here today, or anyone who views this hearing. *Many* of the victims of partial-birth abortion are actually past the point at which they could survive in our nation's neonatal units.

A partial-birth abortion is really a lethal adaptation of a long-known procedure for delivering babies, feet first, in certain unusual circumstances. But when used as an abortion method, the abortionist must take care that he does not dilate the cervix a little too much, because if he did so, the head could slip across the Supreme Court's constitutional "line of personhood." That must not happen until after the surgical scissors and the suction machine have done their deadly work.

But if we step back for a moment from the Supreme Court's doctrine, we all really know — don't we? — that it is *the same* little girl or boy *whether or not* she or he has traveled that extra three inches.

… [T]o each person, his or her *own* intrinsic uniqueness, his or her own unrepeatable "personhood," and its great value, are really self-evident. Those of us who hold the right-to-life position simply recognize that the same applies to the individual unborn or partly born human beings whom we seek to protect.

Regardless of how many of these abortions actually occur, not one of the victims is disposable, and not one is interchangeable with anyone else who ever came before or who will ever come after.

We need to remember that "birth" and "full-term" are two very different things. My own youngest son Thomas, who is here with my wife Carolyn today, was born *13 weeks* before full term. He weighed only one pound, 12 ounces.

After his delivery — by emergency Caesarian section — as he lay fighting for his life in the intensive care neonatal nursery, he looked as small and hairless as "a skinned squirrel," as my father, a Wisconsin outdoorsman, said later.

But that same "fetus," born so terribly prematurely, now runs to hug me when I return home from work. He likes to engage in all manner of wordplay. He embraces every aspect of life with insatiable curiosity and relentless enthusiasm.

He is one of a kind.

But so are they all.

CHAPTER XVI

PARTIAL-BIRTH ABORTION SHOULD NOT BE BANNED

STATEMENT OF REPRESENTATIVE NANCY PELOSI (D-CA) DURING HOUSE VOTE TO OVERRIDE PRESIDENT BILL CLINTON'S VETO OF THE PARTIAL-BIRTH ABORTION ACT OF 1997 (H.R. 1122), JULY 23, 1998

... I rise today in strong opposition to the override of H.R. 1122, the "late-term" abortion ban, and I ask my colleagues to sustain the President's veto.

... [T]his bill has been vetoed twice by the President because it fails to protect a woman's health and fertility. Once again, conservative members of this body are encroaching on a very private, personal matter by infringing on a woman's constitutionally protected right to make a personal decision regarding her personal health.

... [T]he issue isn't about how many women undergo this procedure, but how many women have no other alternative but this procedure to save their life and reproductive health. This bill challenges the *Roe v. Wade* decision to protect a woman's right to choose. It supersedes safeguards in the Constitution which protect a woman's right to terminate a pregnancy of a viable fetus if an abortion is necessary to protect the life or health of the mother. The *Roe* decision says that a state may "regulate, and even proscribe (prohibit), abortion" except when a woman's life or health is threatened.... [T]he authors of this legislation failed to incorporate the need to protect a mother's health into this legislation.

The terms of this bill are so loose that 18 courts have struck down or severely limited enforcement of the "late-term" abortion ban. Respected judges from around the county have ruled that the definition in the ban is both vague and overly broad, which has resulted in the ban of some of the most safe and common abortion procedures used throughout pregnancy. An undue burden is placed on a woman's right to choose and on a doctor's ability to practice safe medicine.

All of these restrictions on abortion will only make abortions more dangerous. Let us protect not only the privacy and personal choice between a woman and her doctor, but also the rights outlined in the Supreme Court's decision, *Roe v. Wade.*

I ask my colleagues to support and maintain the right of a doctor to determine which is the safest and most appropriate medical procedure based on a woman's individual circumstance within the protection of *Roe v. Wade.*

... Congress has no business coming between a woman and her doctor. When making a medical decision, doctors should not be faced with the threat of imprisonment for having to perform a procedure to save a mother's life or protect her reproductive health. The tragedy behind this unfortunate situation is that most women who undergo this difficult procedure desperately want a successful pregnancy. Listen to the women who have been faced with this tragic situation....

STATEMENT OF THE DEMOCRATIC MEMBERS* OF THE HOUSE JUDICIARY COMMITTEE, MARCH 14, 1997

We dissent from H.R. 929 [a version of the Partial-Birth Abortion Act of 1997, or H.R. 1122]. In our view, the legislation represents an effort to politicize a sensitive and personal issue that is best left to a woman and her doctor, rather than the politicians.

The legislation is disastrous for women. Not only does H.R. 929 fail to provide any protection for womens' health, it does not even fully protect their lives.

Failing to include a "health" exception in the legislation is more than an academic constitutional concern; it will prevent some women from being able to terminate their pregnancies in the manner determined to be safest and most appropriate by their physician, using the intact dilation and evacuation (intact D&E) or dilation and extraction (D&X) method.

At the Committee markup [when subcommittee members make amendments and changes before turning a bill back to the full committee for approval], the majority repeatedly failed to recognize a woman's health interests. Ms. [Sheila] Jackson Lee offered an amendment exempting abortion procedures necessary to preserve the "health of the mother," and Mr. [Barney] Frank offered an even more narrowly drafted amendment, which would have allowed partial-birth abortions where necessary to "avert serious adverse physical health consequences to the mother." Both were rejected on party-line votes.

The majority claims that any health exception, no matter how narrowly written, would be unacceptable because they do not believe any situation exists where the health exception could apply. Yet, the American College of Obstetricians and Gynecologists has written, the intact D&E procedure "may be the best or most appropriate procedure in a particular circumstance to save the life or preserve the health of a woman, and only the doctor, in consultation with the patient, based upon the woman's particular circumstances can make this decision."

... [T]he real reason the majority won't allow a health exception is their belief that under no possible condition is a mother's health problem — no matter how serious — to be equated with the potential life of a fetus. Chairman [Henry] Hyde acknowledged this at the markup.

It is also important to note that even the bill's exception for the mother's life is written in the narrowest possible fashion.... [T]he bill only exempts such procedures "if no other medical procedure would suffice for that purpose." This means that even where the use of an alternative procedure would cause a woman to lose her fertility or face serious injury, the physician would be compelled to forego use of the intact D&E procedure....

... The majority's contention that H.R. 929 falls outside of the restriction of *Roe* because the fetus is "almost" born is fallacious on its face. The intact D&E procedure targeted by the bill falls within the general understanding of abortion. The definitions used in the bill and even the title of the bill repeatedly utilize the term "abortion"....

By banning a particular procedure during the pre-viability phase of a pregnancy, the legislation also places an "undue burden" on the woman's right to choose.... In *Casey*, the Supreme Court allowed the State to require a waiting period based on its interest in protecting potential human life and maternal health. But neither of these factors are present in H.R. 929, which simply forces a woman to choose a more risky procedure over a

---

* John Conyers, Jr. (MI), Barney Frank (MA), Charles Schumer (NY), Howard L. Berman (CA), Jerrold Nadler (NY), Robert C. Scott (VA), Melvin L. Watt (NC), Zoe Lofgren (CA), Sheila Jackson Lee (TX), Maxine Waters (CA), Martin Meehan (MA), William Delahunt (MA), Robert Wexler (FL), and Steven R. Rothman (NJ)

less risky one. Instead of a reasonable measure to protect the woman's health, H.R. 929 deliberately endangers her health....

H.R. 929 is likely to be declared unconstitutionally vague.... Although the legislation appears to target the intact D&E abortion technique, it is not clear the term "partial-birth abortion" would be limited to one particular or identifiable practice. For example, the American College of Obstetrics and Gynecologists has stated that the definitions in the bill "are vague and do not delineate a specified procedure recognized in the medical literature. Moreover, the definitions could be interpreted to include elements of many recognized abortion and operative obstetric techniques."

... H.R. 929 is not a serious effort to deal with the problems of unintended pregnancies in this country or the majority's professed concerns relating to post-viability abortions....

And if the majority were serious about limiting late-term abortions, they would have considered proposals ... banning all post-viability abortions, except those necessary to preserve the woman's life or avert serious health consequences.

The reality is, of course, that the majority has little interest in developing a credible and constitutional proposal that could be signed into law. The majority knows the President cannot sign any bill that fails to protect a woman's health and is inconsistent with *Roe*. Bills such as H.R. 929 are being considered by the House for the very reason that they will not become law.

The stark reality of the movement behind the partial-birth abortion legislation is that it is part of a broader strategy to ban virtually all abortions. The majority itself makes no secret of this fact — their long-standing party platform contains a promise to pass a Constitutional amendment banning all abortions. During the markup, Chairman Hyde frankly acknowledged that his views favored the rights of the unborn and unviable fetus over all of the woman's rights, other than her life. And Sub-

committee Chairman Canady admitted his view that these legal rights go all the way to the very point of conception.

... At the same time, ... H.R. 929 [p]roponents frequently depict fully developed fetuses as being subject to elective partial-birth abortions. For example, they claim that many partial-birth abortions are performed late in pregnancy by high school girls who complain they "won't fit into a prom dress, hate being fat, [and] can't afford a baby and a new car." These characterizations completely ignore the fact that 40 states and the District of Columbia have already passed bans on late-term abortions, except where life or health is involved....

[T]hose who support this legislation appear to be even less interested in responding to the real causes of late-term abortions which may necessitate use of the intact D&E procedure. The reality is that such abortions are often delayed because there is a dearth of physicians in many poor and rural areas; because Medicaid funding for abortions is restricted; because funding has been cut for contraceptive research and development; because many pregnant woman fear violence at local clinics; because teenagers are fearful of notifying their parents and women are subject to delays caused by mandatory notice and biased counseling requirements; and because many women only learn of severe anomalies as a result of late-term ultrasound and amniocentesis tests.

TESTIMONY OF RENEE CHELIAN, PRESIDENT, NATIONAL COALITION OF ABORTION PROVIDERS, AT THE JOINT HEARING BEFORE THE SENATE JUDICIARY COMMITTEE AND THE SUBCOMMITTEE ON THE CONSTITUTION OF THE HOUSE JUDICIARY COMMITTEE, MARCH 11, 1997

... I come here today because I want to put a face on who we are — the several hundred abortion providers in this country and their employees.

Many of us who work in clinics are not political…. Despite physical threats, fear, harassment, and constant worry from our families, we work in clinics because we care deeply about each woman who becomes a patient. We only have to reach out and touch the woman to know why we are abortion providers….

Abortion providers have spent the last 24 years developing methods of abortion without the benefit of medical schools, teaching institutions, or government agencies. We have made abortion the safest surgical procedure done in this country today, and we have also managed to keep it affordable for most women.

It is our quest to continue to develop safe methods of abortion so that we can provide the best medical care. Abortion surgery has been an evolution of physician-developed techniques. Each is a step in advancing the health and safety of our patients. The intact D&E and D&X were developed for precisely that reason. It is a continuum of good health care.

The National Coalition of Abortion Providers is adamantly opposed to banning the intact D&E and D&X procedures. Doing so would set two dangerous precedents.

First, lawmakers should not be practicing medicine. Physicians — not politicians — must be allowed to decide which medical procedure is in the best interest of the patient. This is not just applicable with second-trimester abortion, but is true of many surgeries.

Secondly, until 24 weeks, abortion is a constitutionally protected medical procedure. If you ban this, doctors could use a different procedure. My concern is that you will then try to ban that one, and the next and the next, and suddenly, abortion is no longer available.

… The whole problem with this debate is that by focusing on a particular method of abortion, we as a society continue to avoid the reasons why women have second-trimester abortions. Why, in this age of contraception, public education, and awareness, are there still so many unwanted pregnancies? All of us share the responsibility for the problem of unwanted, unplanned pregnancies. The focus should not be abortion or those who provide abortion services, but rather what can we as a country do to solve the problem.

… When I look at my young daughters and their friends, it is absolutely clear to me that just as the future belongs to them, they must continue to have healthy reproductive options and choices made by them in consultation with their doctors. It must be left to women and physicians, not politicians, religious groups or radical extremist groups, to decide which methods and medical procedures are safest for a particular patient. My daughters' and your daughters' lives depend on this.

STATEMENT OF VIKI WILSON AT THE JOINT HEARING BEFORE THE SENATE JUDICIARY COMMITTEE AND THE SUBCOMMITTEE ON THE CONSTITUTION OF THE HOUSE JUDICIARY COMMITTEE, MARCH 11, 1997

Since June of 1995, I have spoken out against the so-called "Partial-Birth Abortion" ban, and I even testified before the Senate Judiciary Committee in November of 1995. Sharing my story has been extremely difficult, but I will continue to do so until Congress understands that this legislation is ill-conceived and would hurt families like mine.

I am a registered nurse, with nineteen years experience; eleven of those in pediatrics. My husband Bill is an emergency room physician….

In the spring of 1994, I was pregnant and expecting Abigail, my third child, on Mother's Day….

At 36 weeks of pregnancy all of our dreams and happy expectations came crashing down around us. My doctor ordered an ultrasound that detected what all of my previous prenatal testing … had failed to detect, an encephalocoele. Approximately [two-thirds] of my daughter's brain had formed on the outside of her skull.... What I had thought were big, healthy, strong baby movements were in fact seizures. The seizures were being caused by the compression of the encephalocoele that continued to increase as she grew inside my womb.

My doctor sent me to several specialists ... in a desperate attempt to find a way to save her. My husband and I were praying that there would be some new surgical technique to fix her anomalies. But all the experts concurred. Abigail would not survive outside my womb.

Our doctors explained our options, including labor and delivery, C-section, or terminating the pregnancy. Because of the size of her anomaly, the doctors feared that my uterus might rupture in the birthing process, possibly rendering me sterile.... [B]ecause there was no hope of saving Abigail, they could not justify the risks to my health of a major surgery like a C-section.

Losing Abigail was the hardest thing that's ever happened to us in our lives, but I am grateful that Bill and I were able to make this difficult decision ourselves and that we were given all of our medical options. I am grateful too that ... I had access to the intact D&E.

As a practicing Catholic, I couldn't help believing that God had to have some reason for giving my family this suffering. Then I found out about this legislation....

The legislation you are considering ... would affect families like mine. It would limit our medical options. Please do not deny our experience. There will be families in the future faced with this tragedy. Please allow us to have access to the medical procedures we need. Do not complicate the tragedies we already face.

IMPORTANT NAMES AND ADDRESSES

Alan Guttmacher Institute
120 Wall St.
New York, NY 10005
(212) 248-1111
FAX (212) 248-1951
www.agi-usa.org
info@agi-usa.org

American Civil Liberties Union (ACLU)
125 Broad St., 18th Floor
New York, NY 10004-2400
(212) 549-2500
www.aclu.org
aclu@aclu.org

Catholics for a Free Choice
1436 U St. NW, Suite 301
Washington, DC 20009-3997
(202) 986-6093
FAX (202) 332-7995
www.cath4choice.org
cffc@catholicsforchoice.org

Division of Reproductive Health
National Center for Chronic Disease
Prevention and Health Promotion
Centers for Disease Control and Prevention
4770 Buford Hwy. NE, Mail Stop K20
Atlanta, GA 30341-3717
(770) 488-5200
FAX (770) 488-5374
www.cdc.gov/nccdphp/drh
ccdinfo@cdc.gov

Feminist Majority Foundation
1600 Wilson Blvd., Suite 801
Arlington, VA 22209
(703) 522-2214
FAX (703) 522-2219
www.feminist.org
femmaj@feminist.org

Human Life International
4 Family Life Lane
Front Royal, VA 22630
(540) 635-7884
FAX (540) 636-7363
www.hli.org
hli@hli.org

Medical Students for Choice
2401 Bancroft Way, Suite 201
Berkeley, CA 94704
(510) 540-1195
www.ms4c.org
msfc@ms4c.org

National Abortion and Reproductive
Rights Action League (NARAL)
1156 15th St. NW, Suite 700
Washington, DC 20005
(202) 973-3000
FAX (202) 973-3096
www.naral.org
naral@naral.org

National Abortion Federation
1755 Massachusetts Ave. NW
Suite 600
Washington, DC 20036
(202) 667-5881
Hotline: (800) 772-9100
FAX (202) 667-5890
www.prochoice.org

National Campaign to Prevent Teen
Pregnancy
2100 M St. NW, Suite 300
Washington, DC 20037
(202) 261-5655
FAX (202) 331-7735
www.teenpregnancy.org
campaign@teenpregnancy.org

National Center for Health Statistics
U.S. Department of Health and Human
Services
6525 Belcrest Rd.
Hyattsville, MD 20782-2003
(301) 436-8951
FAX (301) 436-4258
www.cdc.gov/nchs
nchsquery@cdc.gov

National Conference of Catholic Bishops
Committee for Pro-Life Activities
3211 4th St. NE
Washington, DC 20017-1194
(202) 541-3070
FAX (202) 541-3054
www.nccbuscc.org/prolife

National Organization for Women (NOW)
733 15th St. NW, 2nd Floor
Washington, DC 20005
(202) 628-8669
FAX (202) 785-8576
www.now.org
now@now.org

National Right to Life Committee
419 7th St. NW, Suite 500
Washington, DC 20004
(202) 626-8800
FAX (202) 737-9189
www.nrlc.org
nrlc@nrlc.org

National Women's Health Network
514 10th St. NW, Suite 400
Washington, DC 20004
(202) 347-1140
FAX (202) 347-1168
www.womenshealthnetwork.org

National Women's Political Caucus
1630 Connecticut Ave. NW, Suite 201
Washington, DC 20009
(202) 785-1100
FAX (202) 785-3605
www.nwpc.org

Network for Life and Choice
Search for Common Ground
1601 Connecticut Ave. NW, Suite 200
Washington, DC 20009
(202) 265-4300
FAX (202) 232-6718
www.sfcg.org/networkm
search@sfcg.org

Operation Save America
P.O. Box 740066
Dallas, TX 75374
(972) 494-5316
FAX (972) 276-9316
www.operationsaveamerica.org
orn@airmail.net

Planned Parenthood Federation of
America
810 Seventh Ave.
New York, NY 10019
(212) 541-7800
FAX (212) 245-1845
www.plannedparenthood.org

Population Action International
1120 19th St. NW, Suite 550
Washington, DC 20036
(202) 659-1833
FAX (202) 293-1795
www.populationaction.org
pai@popact.org

Population Council
1 Dag Hammarskjold Plaza
New York, NY 10017
(212) 339-0500
FAX (212) 755-6052
www.popcouncil.org
pubinfo@popcouncil.org

Religious Coalition for Reproductive
Choice
1025 Vermont Ave. NW, Suite 1130
Washington, DC 20005
(202) 628-7700
FAX (202) 628-7716
www.rcrc.org
info@rcrc.org

United Nations Population Fund
220 E. 42nd St.
New York, NY 10017
(212) 297-5026
FAX (212) 557-6416
www.unfpa.org

World Health Organization
(Regional Office)
No. 2 UN Plaza, DC-2 Bldg.
New York, NY 10017
(212) 963-4388
FAX (212) 223-2920
www.who.org
reproductivehealth@who.ch

RESOURCES

There are two major sources for abortion statistics in the United States — the Centers for Disease Control and Prevention (CDC) in Atlanta, Georgia, and the Alan Guttmacher Institute in New York. The CDC annually publishes its "Abortion Surveillance." The most current information used in the preparation of this book was "Abortion Surveillance — United States, 1996 (*Morbidity and Mortality Weekly Report*, vol. 48, No. SS-4, July 30, 1999).

The CDC also published "Declines in Teenage Birth Rates, 1991-1998: Update of National and State Trends" (*National Vital Statistics Report*, vol. 47, no. 26, October 25, 1999), "Achievements in Public Health, 1900-1999: Healthier Mothers and Babies" (*Morbidity and Mortality Weekly Report*, vol. 48, no. 31, October 1, 1999), "Adoption, Adoption Seeking, and Relinquishment for Adoption in the United States" (*Advance Data*, no. 306, May 11, 1999), and "Trends in Sexual Risk Behaviors Among High School Students — United States, 1991-1997" (*Morbidity and Mortality Weekly Report*, vol. 47, no. 36, September 18, 1998).

Other government publications used in this book include *Stem Cells: A Primer* (1999), prepared by the National Institutes of Health; *Women's Health in India* (1998) and *Women in Poland* (1995), published by the International Programs Center of the U.S. Department of Commerce; and *Teen Pregnancy: State and Federal Efforts to Implement Prevention Programs and Measure Their Effectiveness* (1998) and *Abortion Clinics: Information on the Effectiveness of the Freedom of Access to Clinic Entrances Act* (1998), prepared by the U.S. General Accounting Office.

U.S. government agencies also published abortion information in joint efforts with foreign governments and private U.S. organizations. Those that were helpful in the preparation of this book include the *Maternal and Child Health Statistics: Russian Federation and United States, Selected Years 1985-95* (Ministry of Health of the Russian Federation and the CDC, 1999), the *1992 National Fertility and Family Planning Survey, China* (The State Family Planning Commission of China, World Health Or-

ganization, and CDC, 1997), and the *1997 Assisted Reproductive Technology Success Rates: National Summary and Fertility Clinic Reports* (CDC, American Society for Reproductive Medicine, and RESOLVE, 1999).

The Alan Guttmacher Institute (AGI), which strongly supports abortion as an option, is the major non-government source of abortion statistics in the world. The AGI publishes the results of its abortion surveys in its bimonthly journal, *Family Planning Perspectives*, a primary resource for any study of abortion, family planning, and pregnancy. *Family Planning Perspectives* articles used in this publication include "Pregnancies Averted Among U.S. Teenagers by the Use of Contraceptives" (January/February 1999) by James G. Kahn et al., "Abortion Incidence and Services in the United States, 1995-1996" (November/December 1998) by Stanley K. Henshaw, "Training Family Practice Residents in Abortion and Reproductive Health Care: A Nationwide Survey" (September/October 1997) by Jody E. Steinauer et al., and "Abortion Patients in 1994-1995: Characteristics and Contraceptive Use" (July/August 1996) by Stanley K. Henshaw and Kathryn Kost.

Other *Family Planning Perspectives* articles include "Public Funding for Contraceptive, Sterilization, and Abortion Services, 1994" (July/August 1996) by Terry Sollom et al., "Abortion Training in Obstetrics and Gynecology Residency Programs in the United States, 1991-1992" (May/June 1995) by H. Trent MacKay and Andrea Phillips MacKay, "Parental Involvement in Minor's Abortion Decisions" (September/October 1992) by Stanley K. Henshaw and Kathryn Kost, and "Adolescent Knowledge and Attitudes About Abortion" (March/April 1992) by Rebecca Stone and Cynthia Waszak.

The Alan Guttmacher Institute publishes monographs on family planning issues. *Sharing Responsibility: Women, Society and Abortion Worldwide* (1999), *The Politics of Blame: Family Planning, Abortion, and the Poor* (Patricia Donovan, 1995), *Sex and America's Teenagers* (1994), and *Abortion and Women's Health: A Turning Point for America?* (Rachel Benson Gold, 1990) provided helpful information. In addition, *The Guttmacher Report on Public Policy*, a bimonthly review by AGI's policy analysts, furnished current information on the political aspects of abortion. *Teenage Pregnancy: Overall Trends and State-by-State Information* (www.agi-usa.org, April 1999) provided comprehensive data on teen pregnancy and abortion in the United States.

The Alan Guttmacher Institute also publishes a quarterly journal, *International Family Planning Perspectives*, with articles on family planning, contraception, and abortion around the world. Articles used in this publication include "The Incidence of Abortion Worldwide" (January 1999) by Stanley K. Henshaw et al., "Abortion Reform in South Africa: A Case Study of the 1996 Choice on Termination of Pregnancy Act" (December 1998) by Sally Guttmacher et al., and "A Global Review of Laws on Induced Abortion, 1975-1997" (June 1998) by Anika Rahman et al. An *Issues in Brief* article, "An Overview of Clandestine Abortion in Latin America" (1996) by Susheela Singh and Deirdre Wulf, was also used for this publication. Information Plus would like to express its sincere appreciation to the Alan Guttmacher Institute and its staff for permission to use information from these materials.

Additional information on international abortion statistics was provided by the World Health Organization (WHO) in *Abortion in the Developing World* (Geneva, Switzerland, 1998) and the United Nations Population Fund in *The State of the World Population, 1997* (Stan Bernstein, New York, 1997). The Population Council (New York) furnished abortion data on Poland in "Abortion and Women's Rights in Poland, 1994" (*Studies in Family Planning*, vol. 25, no. 4, July/August 1994) by Henry P. David and Anna Titkow.

Journal articles that provided useful information on abortion include "Early Pregnancy Termination with Mifepristone and Misoprostol in the United States" (*New England Journal of Medicine*, vol. 338, no. 18, April 30, 1998) and "The Relationship of Abortion to Well-Being: Do Race and Religion Make

a Difference?" (*Professional Psychology*, vol. 28, no. 1, 1997).

The National Abortion Federation (NAF, Washington, DC), a national association of abortion providers and a strong abortion advocate, tabulates statistics on incidents of violence against abortion providers. NAF publishes a wide range of consumer education materials on abortion and operates a nationwide toll-free consumer hotline to answer questions and make referrals to qualified abortion providers throughout the United States and Canada. Information Plus thanks the NAF for permission to use its data and graphics.

The National Abortion and Reproductive Rights Action League (NARAL, Washington, DC), also an abortion advocate, gave permission to use information on the status of abortion in the states as published in *Who Decides? A State-by-State Review of Abortion and Reproductive Rights* (2000) and information from its factsheet *State Sexuality and STD/HIV Education Regulations* (1999). Information Plus also thanks the National Campaign to Prevent Teen Pregnancy for the use of data and charts from *No Easy Answers: Research Findings on Programs to Reduce Teen Pregnancy* (1997) and *Whatever Happened to Childhood? The Problem of Teen Pregnancy* (1997).

The National Opinion Research Center (Illinois), Louis Harris and Associates, Inc. (New York), and the Gallup Organization, Inc. (New Jersey) most kindly granted permission to publish their surveys on American attitudes toward abortion. The Henry J. Kaiser Family Foundation (California) graciously granted permission to publish its graphics from *Two National Surveys: Views of Americans and Health Care Providers on Medical Abortion — What They Know, What They Think, and What They Want, Summary of Findings/Toplines* (1998) and *From the Patient's Perspective: The Quality of Abortion Care* (reports prepared for the Kaiser Family Foundation by the Picker Institute [1999]).

INDEX